DO YOU KNOW WHO THESE MEN AND WOMEN WERE—AND WHAT THEY DID?

Lucy Terry Prince, William Still, Sally Hemings, Richard Allen, Denmark Vesey, Sojourner Truth, Frederick Douglass, Harriet Tubman, Dred Scott, John Brown, Harriet Beecher Stowe, The Healys, "Ma" Rainey, "Jelly Roll" Morton, Henry Tanner, Father Divine, Marcus Garvey, W. E. B. Du Bois, George Washington Carver, Josephine Baker, Arthur Ashe, Martin Luther King, Jr., Malcolm X, Toni Morrison

These are but a few of the remarkable people you will meet on these pages. Some are famed, others nearly forgotten. Their lives and deeds are all part of—

EVERYBODY SAY FREEDOM

Everything You Need to Know About African-American History

RICHARD NEWMAN is Fellows Officer at the W. E. B. Du Bois Institute for Afro-American Research at Harvard University. The former Managing Editor of the *Encyclopedia of African-American Culture and History,* he is a member of the Schomburg Commission for the Preservation of Black Culture, and is on the advisory committee for the National African-American Museum project at the Smithsonian Institution. **MARCIA R. SAWYER** is Assistant Professor of Liberal Studies at the California State University at San Marcos. She received her Ph.D. from Michigan State University and has taught at the University of Washington and been a Fellow at the Du Bois Institute.

EVERYBODY SAY FREEDOM

Everything You Need to Know About African-American History

RICHARD NEWMAN

AND

MARCIA SAWYER, Ph.D.

Foreword by Henry Louis Gates, Jr.

A PLUME BOOK

PLUME
Published by the Penguin Group
Penguin Books USA Inc., 375 Hudson Street,
New York, New York 10014, U.S.A.
Penguin Books Ltd, 27 Wrights Lane,
London W8 5TZ, England
Penguin Books Australia Ltd, Ringwood,
Victoria, Australia
Penguin Books Canada Ltd, 10 Alcorn Avenue,
Toronto, Ontario, Canada M4V 3B2
Penguin Books (N.Z.) Ltd, 182-190 Wairau Road,
Auckland 10, New Zealand

Penguin Books Ltd, Registered Offices:
Harmondsworth, Middlesex, England

First published by Plume, an imprint of Dutton Signet,
a division of Penguin Books USA Inc.

First Printing, February, 1996
10 9 8 7 6 5 4 3 2 1

Library of Congress Cataloging-in-Publication Data available upon request.

Printed in the United States of America
Set in New Baskerville

BOOKS ARE AVAILABLE AT QUANTITY DISCOUNTS WHEN USED TO PROMOTE PRODUCTS OR
SERVICES. FOR INFORMATION PLEASE WRITE TO PREMIUM MARKETING DIVISION, PENGUIN BOOKS
USA INC., 375 HUDSON STREET, NEW YORK, NY 10014.

To
Friends and Colleagues
at the
W. E. B. Du Bois Institute

Contents

Everybody knew what she was called, but nobody anywhere knew her name.

—Toni Morrison, *Beloved*

That I the better may attention draw,
be pleased to know I am America.

—a line of a Tawny woman in a 1672 London pageant entitled *West India*. The word *tawny* described a brown skin color with orange and yellow tones. It survives in our word *tan*.

Foreword

"The first thing to do is to get into every school, private, public, or otherwise, Negro literature and history. We aren't trying to displace other literature but trying to acquaint all children with Negro history and literature."

—Booker T. Washington

"History must restore what slavery took away."

—Arthur A. Schomburg

The desire to bring the histories of the African-American people into the classroom, perhaps more than any other single factor, generated black student demands in the late 1960s for the creation of Black Studies. Arthur A. Schomburg, the great black bibliophile and antiquarian, wrote in 1925, in the middle of the Harlem Renaissance, that "the American Negro must remake his past in order to make his future." That could just as well have been our creed in the sixties, as we did battle with reluctant faculties and administrations about creating and instituting this brave new field. For so many colleges and universities, "Black Studies" circa 1970 meant black history.

The number of stellar academic studies in the field of history attests to its dominant, pioneering role in a still emerging field. Among these John Blassingame's *The Slave Community* and Nathan Huggins's *Harlem Renaissance* have withstood the rigors of scholarly reevaluation since the early 1970s. John Hope Franklin's majestical textbook, *From Slavery to Freedom,* assigned to my first survey course in Afro-American history in 1969, remains the most popular text of its kind, and recently was published in its sixth edition. Dozens of works by scholars have firmly established African-American history both as a field of historiography itself and as an integral aspect of any truly *American* historical inquiry.

What the field lacks, on the other hand, is easily accessible introductions to the African-American past, compiled by scholars yet aimed at a broader audience than the college classroom. It is this void that *Everybody Say Freedom* so creatively fills.

Written by Richard Newman, a highly respected scholar and bibliophile, and Marcia Sawyer, one of the central figures in a younger generation of scholars of African-American history, *Everybody Say Freedom* is one of the freshest, most surprising, and delightful introductions to the history of black Americans that I have ever read. It is chock full of remarkable facts that, taken together, reinforce the centrality of African Americans to the larger American experience. These same facts and anecdotes also underscore the sheer richness and depth of the history and culture that black women and men, acting together, have created by and for themselves, seeking—as Arthur Schomburg put it—to "restore what slavery took away."

Superbly researched and beautifully written, *Everybody Say Freedom* is an indispensable introduction to students in high school or college and to any intelligent person seeking a compelling encounter with the veiled past that persons of African descent created in the New World. *Everybody Say Freedom* is a superb contribution to American history, and to all who wish to gain a fuller understanding of race and racism in American society today.

—Henry Louis Gates, Jr.

Introduction

The title of this book, *Everybody Say Freedom*, is taken from an African-American protest song of the same name, a song that came out of southern jails during the Civil Rights movement of the 1960s. That song, in turn, was adapted from a traditional spiritual called "Amen." The struggle for freedom is the persistent thread and theme that runs through all African-American history, so it is an entirely appropriate title—and concept—to call this survey of the black American experience.

The book's subtitle, *Everything You Need to Know About African-American History*, is admittedly a bit overstated. In fact, there are enough other major persons and events in black history to fill many books. Those selected here are central and key, however, and their stories are told in narrative form because anecdotes often can and do reveal larger truths, and because African-American history is finally a series of dramatic and deeply personal encounters and human experiences. In other words, it is about people.

Everybody Say Freedom surveys African-American history from the arrival of the first Africans in British North America in 1619 to the awarding of the Nobel Prize for literature to Toni Morrison in 1993. It is organized in a question-and-answer format because that is a convenient way to focus on some essential personalities and issues. At the end of each question and response is a bibliographic citation for those who want to find out more. In each section, too, relevant quotations in sidebars make it possible to expand and comment on the text by reporting what some people thought about that particular topic.

African-American history is, of course, American history, and the primary rationale for considering it separately is that it has often been unknown or ignored or even distorted by standard and mainstream accounts of our past, an omission that women and other minorities have discovered applies to them as well. The real purpose of separate treatment, though, is to give this neglected information the emphasis it deserves so it can be recognized as important and thus find its way to its rightful place within the canon and textbooks.

It is also true that American history is African-American history. That is, Africans have been on the North American continent since the Spanish explorers. There were wide cultural exchanges over the centuries between Africa and America, exchanges of plants and foods, agricultural techniques, language, and religion, as well as the physical blending of the races. The New World that most Europeans came to was already highly Africanized, a major and perhaps startling fact that we are just beginning to recognize.

This book is meant to be a contribution to black and white people alike by providing information on some people and events often ignored, information that can lead to better understanding. Harold Cruse has written, "The black man's one great and present hope is to know and understand his Afro-American history." And John O. Killens tells us, "Western man wrote 'his' history as if it were the history of the entire human race."

It would be impossible to acknowledge all the people whose books and articles I have read over the years, whose lectures I've heard, and with whom I've been privileged to engage in conversation and discussion. I have learned from them all, and their work is reflected here, although I take full responsibility for what has been written. I must single out Henry Louis Gates, Jr., for his kindness in writing the foreword to this book, and for his invitation to me to join the staff of the W. E. B. Du Bois Institute at Harvard, where he is director. Relationships there with staff and fellows have been so important that this book is dedicated to them.

I must also thank Susan Herner, friend as well as agent; Jill Watts and Betty Gubert, who always had good information as well as good advice; Alisa Bierria, who came through when the going got rough; Marguerite Harrison and Pamela Petro, friends through it all; and there is always Belynda Bady.

—Richard Newman
Boston, Massachusetts
Fall 1995

CHAPTER 1

~

From Jamestown to the American Revolution, 1619–1776

When did the first Africans come to North America?

Where did the slaves come from?

What was the Middle Passage?

What are the three secrets of African-American history?

How did American slavery originate?

What were the effects of slavery?

Did the slaves resist?

What was the first protest against slavery?

Did the spirituals have secret meanings?

What was a slave catechism?

What was the first published protest against slavery?

What is the black church?

What happened in Stono, South Carolina, in 1739?

Who was the first African-American poet?

Who was the first African American to write a book?

Who was the first to die for American independence?

~

When did the first Africans come to North America?

No one knows for sure just when the first Africans or people of African descent came to the New World. One theory is that Africans sailed to the continents of the Western Hemisphere before Columbus and left evidence of their visit, especially in Mexico, in language, plants, and their images on pottery. **Pedro Alonso Niño,** who sailed with Columbus in 1492, was reportedly a man of color. There certainly were Africans in the parties of explorers and adventurers who roamed both South and North America: with Balboa when he crossed the Isthmus of Panama to the Pacific Ocean, with the Jesuits in Canada, with Pizarro in Peru. Estervanico, the first non–Native American to travel in what is now Arizona and New Mexico, was black, as were numerous other sailors, mariners, and pirates along the Atlantic coast.

In what is now the continental United States, the first settlement of Africans (as opposed to traveling explorers) was probably a group of servants in a Spanish colony in the area of South Carolina in 1526. They escaped from the Spaniards and found refuge with Native Americans, the first of many such instances of flight and an early case of African-Indian mixing. Also, an African woman named **Angela** reportedly was brought to Point Comfort, Virginia, sometime before 1619 on the ship *Treasurer*.

The usual date and place given for the arrival of the first permanent blacks in British North America, however, is Jamestown, Virginia, at the end of August or beginning of September in the year 1619. An unnamed, British-manned Dutch man-of-war, a privateer with a captured Spanish cargo, sailed into the harbor at Point Comfort (now Hampton). The ship's captain traded more than twenty Africans with George Yeardley, governor of the twelve-year-old English settlement, for food.

It may be that no more than this is publicly known about the ship because the white settlers at Jamestown were themselves secretly involved in illegal privateering, and information on all ships is scant. The Africans who disembarked are sometimes referred to as slaves, but the kind of slavery that was to develop in North America had not yet begun to emerge, so they were really indentured servants who could—and did—after ten years or so of work, move out of servitude and become fully free. The Africans, about equally divided between men and women, had been given Spanish names—Pedro, Anthony, Isabella—which probably meant they had received an unceremonious and wholesale Roman Catholic baptism as they were forcibly shipped out from Africa. This baptism was an empty gesture, part of the rationalization that slavery benefited the slaves because it made them Christians.

This little group of Africans settled in and their names began to appear in various records and documents. In March 1620, thirty-two Africans were reported living in the Jamestown colony. According to Church of England baptismal records, Anthony and Isabella married and became parents of a son, William, born around 1623, presumably the first child of African parents born in Virginia.

In 1619 there were at least a million Africans in the Spanish and Portuguese colonies of Central and South America, but the men and women in Jamestown are generally considered the first African Americans. The most important fact about them apart from their arrival in 1619 is that in time they did become free, owning property, for example, and there was, so far as we know, no distinction between them and the white indentured servants, who were mostly English convicts. The shift from temporary to permanent servitude that evolved in Virginia over the next few years, however, was to create a unique kind of slavery, such that the apparently innocent Jamestown landing was an event full of unknown and unforeseen consequences. In the words of the African-American historian George Washington Williams, "No event in the history of North America has carried with it to its last analysis such terrible forces."

If you want to know more:

Wesley F. Craven. "Twenty Negroes to Jamestown in 1619?" *White, Red and Black: The Seventeenth-Century Virginian.* Charlottesville, Va.: University Press of Virginia, 1971.

"But like the dead body of the Roman murderer's victim, slavery was a curse that pursued the colonists evermore."

—George Washington Williams

"The ship that sailed up the James on a day we will never know was the beginning of America, and, if we are not careful, the end."

—Lerone Bennett, Jr.

"Travelled he back his proud ancestry
To the rock on Plymouth's shore,
Traced I mine to Dutch ship landing
At Jamestown, one year before."

—James Edwin Campbell

"I am not a ward of America, I am one of the first Americans to arrive on these shores."

—James Baldwin

Where did the slaves come from?

Africa, from which the slaves were forcibly brought, is a huge continent of nearly twelve million square miles, well over three times the size of the United States, and it is the home of a myriad of nations, peoples, languages, religions, and cultures. The existing evidence indicates that the East African savannah was the place some four to five million years ago where human life itself first emerged. And the whole human family developed there as these earliest people, the common ancestors of us all, evolved from food gatherers to food producers, and invented stone and then iron tools, the early defining characteristics of civilization.

Over time, one of the African kingdoms that developed became probably the most sophisticated civilization the world has ever seen. Ancient Egypt flowered into a high culture whose achievements are still dazzling. We are only now beginning to learn just how much of Egypt's genius came from the darker peoples to the south, in Egypt's vital interaction with sub-Saharan cultures. Later, Africa was a center of early Christianity, particularly in Ethiopia, the longest-lasting Christian empire, where a literate, artistic Orthodoxy persists to the present. In fact, Ethiopia was a full-scale rival to Rome and Athens in every measurable sense.

Islam overshadowed Christianity after the Arab invasion of the continent in the seventh century, and warriors for the new religion converted the people of much of North and sub-Saharan Africa. Islam spawned citadels of advanced learning in both the sciences and the humanities, and was the impetus for the growth of great urban centers like the city of Timbuktu. North-south trade routes made much of Africa prosperous in the exchange of gold and salt and fostered an economy which produced and sustained rich medieval West African kingdoms like Mali, Songhay, Ghana, and Karem.

At the very time of Europe's Dark Ages, these stable imperial states, based on control of the gold trade, were enlightened with sacred kingships, strong military establishments providing security and stability, courts of law administering impartial justice, and advanced medicine, metallurgy, and architecture. The trade economy created enriching cultural interchanges as well as financial wealth.

Despite its strengths, West Africa's governments began to

weaken, however, when the commerce in slaves began to compete with the commerce in gold. Outsiders introduced attractive merchandise—especially Europeans, who brought in guns, which touched off an arms race among the kingdoms. In the resulting wars, captives became slaves. The Arabs began the slave trade with their market for imported women and girls to the East. The Portuguese traded male slaves in Europe with minimal success in the fifteenth century, but they sold more in the sixteenth century as laborers in the sugar cane plantations in the islands off the West African coast.

Several West African countries deeply involved in slave trading began to suffer internal dissent as the European powers, which were colonizing more and more of North and South America, demanded more slave labor to work the money-making plantations and mines of the New World. By 1700 slavery was taking some 50,000 people a year from Africa. By 1800 the number was at least 100,000 annually. The African kingdoms fractured, divided by internal wars and weakened by the population drain. When Europeans visited the continent in the eighteenth century, they saw the last stages of collapsed civilizations. These travelers reported what they saw, and Africa was perceived in Europe and North America as a desolate, destitute, and benighted place, its glorious history forgotten and unknown.

If you want to know more:

Oliver Roland and J. D. Fage. *A Short History of Africa.* New York: Penguin Books, 1990.

"Out of Africa, always something new."
                                —Pliny the Elder

"Africa my Africa . . .
I have never known you
But my face is full of your blood."
                                —David Diop

"There are no other savages in Africa than some whites acting crazily."

—Felix von Luschen

What Was the Middle Passage?

Of all the horrors of slavery, the slave trade, and the slave system, probably no aspect was worse than the Middle Passage, the transport of Africans by ship across the Atlantic from Africa to the New World. Slaves were brought, usually by forced march, from the interior of the continent to the western coast. This march itself was brutal, and the explorer **David Livingstone** claimed (although the number is hard to believe) that only 10 percent survived the grueling trek to various ports where they were penned like cattle awaiting shipment.

Captured, stolen, separated from their families, homes and customs, thrown in with strangers, the Africans' first reaction was anger at their plight, and fear for their future. Many knew that those taken and sold to white people never returned, unlike Africans captured in warfare by other Africans. With only limited information of a land beyond the sea, Africans reported they could only assume that they would be eaten by whites, who must be insatiable cannibals.

Stripped naked and branded like animals to identify ownership, the Africans were stowed as cargo in ships bound for America. Slavery was a business, so the higher the ratio of slaves to cubic foot of hold space, the greater the income, and the less they were fed, the greater the profits. Slaves were chained together, usually by shackles on the ankles, and arranged in cramped ships' holds, unable to move, turn, or stand, often lying against each other like spoons on shelves only eighteen inches high. Women and children were usually allowed more mobility, but this was so that the white sailors could have sexual access to them. Continual rape was the norm: the crew had "unlimited license," according to **John Newton,** the slave ship captain who later became an abolitionist.

Slaves were allowed on deck once or twice a day, where they were forced under the lash to dance for exercise in the hope that more would survive the brutal trip. Dancing, for many Africans, was part of their religious ritual, and to profane sacred acts took away even the consolation of religion. Food and water were minimal. Slaves on deck sometimes were kept under canvas at night, especially in bad weather. The transatlantic crossing took no fewer than five weeks and could stretch to three months, depending on the weather. A becalmed ship in summer heat was a virtual hell on earth.

How did the Africans respond? There were mutinies and the occasional killing of crews, but these uprisings were usually put down quickly by armed whites. Some slaves committed suicide in their desperation, jumping overboard or either cutting their own throats or asking fellow slaves to do it for them. Others went mad in the terrible horror of it all, and were thrown overboard. A number tried to starve themselves to death, having no other means of suicide, but their mouths were burned with hot coals as punishment, their jaws forced open with iron clamps, and food shoved down their throats.

Sickness took many lives, especially epidemic diarrhea and dysentery. The flow of blood and flux turned ships' holds into slaughterhouses, and the stench could be so foul a slave ship could be smelled as far as five miles away. Sick slaves were often simply dumped overboard, since legal jettison was covered by insurance. The death rate has been estimated at something around 15 percent. If one considers the hundreds of thousands of men, women, and children shipped every year for hundreds of years, the total of those who did not survive is formidable.

The term *Middle Passage* has come to mean a transition, perhaps even a rite of passage. But its use as metaphor can hardly mean very much in the light of the terrible reality of the cruel and barbarous voyages that brought Africans to America. As novelist Toni Morrison points out, the passage was so horrible, no song, tale, legend, or conscious memory of it was retained by the survivors.

If you want to know more:

Pascoe G. Hill. *Fifty Days on Board a Slave Vessel.* Reprint of the 1848 edition. Baltimore: Black Classic Press, 1993.

"They had not so much room as a man in his coffin."
—A slave ship's captain

"The acts of barbarity proved upon the slave captains are so extravagant that they have been attributed to insanity."
—Charles W. Elliott

"Every circumstance I met with [during the Middle Passage] served only to render my state more painful, and heightened my apprehensions and my opinion of the cruelty of whites."
—Olaudah Equiano

"Fri., May 12, 1843. I have today witnessed a spectacle such as I had frequently heard to have occurred in slave-vessels, but hardly knew how to describe. In a tub, placed on the slave deck, for necessary purposes, a boy was found, who had fallen backwards, and, too weak to extricate himself, was smothered in it."
—Pascoe G. Hill

"Middle Passage:
Voyage through death
To life upon these shores."
—Robert Hayden

What are the three secrets of African-American history?

Arthur A. Schomburg, the African-American bibliophile and historian, had a purpose in mind when he collected books by and about Africans and people of African descent. He, and others like him, knew that in the standard history books, black history was largely forgotten or ignored or even deliberately falsified, leaving blacks and whites alike ignorant of the black past or with seriously damaged misconceptions about it. Schomburg gathered a library of books because he found in them the documentation of the lost history he wanted to regain, as well as the false history he wanted to correct.

As a result of his studies, Schomburg said that there were three major facts for which his library provided evidence, and that the suppression of these facts has caused misconceptions in the way black people and their history have been thought of.

The first was that blacks have been and continue to be participants, and often pioneers, in the struggle for their freedom and advancement. This means that abolitionism and the antislavery movement, for example, which Eurocentric histories describe as essentially the work of beneficent whites, was in fact just as much if not more a black enterprise. Also, the campaign for civil rights and enlightened legislation following the Civil War was as much the work of black people as it was the work of white Radical Republicans in the Congress. And although Schomburg did not live to comment on the Freedom Movement of the 1960s, the same point can be made: the real movement was the work, time, genius, energy, money, and risk of African Americans.

Schomburg's second conclusion was that African Americans "of attainment and genius have been unfairly disassociated from the group, and group credit lost accordingly." This means that any outstanding black person has been perceived and understood as an "exception" to the rule of black inferiority and inability. As a result, the race has suffered for having been seen as a community unable to produce genius, and as a continually benighted group to which there are merely occasional exceptions.

Schomburg's third discovery was that "the remote racial origins of the Negro, far from being what the race and the world have been given to understand, offer a record of credible group achievement when scientifically viewed." In other words, Africa, far from being a jungle of barbarism, in fact produced in its day a high culture of grandeur and sophistication. This is particularly important, Schomburg thought, because it bears on the very origins of civilization as we know it.

It has taken history and historians, from specialized scholars

to amateurs, a long time to face these three facts, and to un-
learn the misconceptions. Not all have yet done so. Arthur
Schomburg and his bibliophile colleagues collected as they did
so they could present books and other documents that would
clearly and honestly speak for themselves by saying simply,
"Here is the evidence."

If you want to know more:

Arthur A. Schomburg. "The Negro Digs Up His Past," in *The
   Negro: An Interpretation,* edited by Alain Locke. New York: Albert and Charles Boni, 1925, pp. 231–237.
See "Who collected books by and about African Americans,"
   p. 219.

"Already the Negro sees himself against a reclaimed
background, in a perspective that will give pride and
self-respect ample score, and make history yield for him
the same values that the treasured past of any people
affords."

—Arthur A. Schomburg

"We seem lately to have come at least to realize what
the truly scientific attitude requires, and to see that the
race issue has been a plague on both our historical
houses, and that history cannot be properly written with
either bias or counterbias."

—Arthur A. Schomburg

"If you want Negro history you will have to get it from
somebody who wore the shoe, and by and by one to the
other you will get a book."

—an ex-slave

How did American slavery originate?

The world has known and experienced human slavery from
time before recounting: prisoners captured as the booty of war,

a weak group subjugated by a stronger one, unwanted children sold into servitude by poor parents. While occupying the lowest rung in the dominant group's social hierarchy, slaves nonetheless normally had certain rights and privileges. And slave status was not fixed: given the fortunes of war, for example, this year's slaves could be next year's masters.

In British North America, however, a new form of slavery evolved: a system of permanent servitude in which slaves were relegated not to the bottom of society but literally outside of it as non–human beings, and a system from which there could be no escape, because membership was based on a publicly discernible physical characteristic: color. What emerged in North America was a unique kind of slavery, in which slaves were legally defined as chattel, a term related to the words *cattle* and *capital;* that is to say, the slaves were property, not persons, and what the master owned was not merely the slave's labor but his or her body as well.

It seems hard to believe that this was in fact the case just over one hundred years ago in this country, but it is true. **Harriet Beecher Stowe**'s antislavery novel *Uncle Tom's Cabin* was originally subtitled *The Man Who Was a Thing* in order to dramatize that in the eyes of the law, African Americans were not people, but objects, like animals. The animal analogy is in fact a fitting one, as the slaves themselves commented: they were fed like pigs, bred like cows, whipped like horses, worked like mules, and when emancipation finally came, driven off like dogs.

The uniqueness of North American slavery can be seen by comparing it with contemporaneous slavery in South America. Whatever slavery's horrors there, slaves did have certain rights. This was probably the case because of the universalism and internationalism of the Roman Catholic Church. In Protestant North America, in contrast, the churches, because of the nature of the Reformation, were organized on national bases, and thus on racial ones.

It is important to underscore that the chattel slavery system of North America came into existence by evolution. There was nothing natural or inherent or even historical about it. It was something new and it was constructed. This should mean that because it was created, it can be destroyed; because it was learned, it can be unlearned; because it was constructed, it can be destructed. But as we shall see, a powerful ideology was developed to rationalize slavery, and we still live with that ideology three hundred years later. It is called racism.

The Africans who landed in Jamestown, Virginia, in 1619 were purchased as indentured servants, and when they had paid off their contracts by their labor, they assumed their places in the community as free people. An important aspect of the Jamestown situation was the apparent presence soon afterwards of baptized Africans who were not in the original group from the famous Dutch ship. In 1624 there is a record of John Phillip, an African baptized in England. Phillip could not have been a slave, because English law, under which the colony was then governed, forbade the enslaving of Christians.

The first account in Virginia of racial differentiation seems to be in 1630, when Hugh Davis, a white man, was sentenced by the court to a whipping "for defiling his body in lying with a negro." As historian Paul Palmer points out, however, it is not at all clear why this was considered a crime. Was it because Davis was married and thus committing adultery? Or was it because his sexual partner was black? Or because she was not a Christian? Or perhaps the partner was not a woman but a man? The records do not say, but it should not be a surprise that the very earliest account of American law distinguishing between blacks and whites had to do with a sexual relationship.

From 1639 on, there was in Virginia a steady accumulation of cases and laws which made distinctions between African Americans and Euro-Americans, all to the detriment of black people and the chipping away of their rights. In 1639 everyone except blacks was to be armed. In 1640 we see the first case of lifelong servitude, imposed on an African-American servant who ran away but was captured; the two Euro-Americans who ran with him were also captured, but they only had their terms of indenture lengthened as punishment.

In 1641 the Gramere case first opened the question of whether an African's children might be considered the property of the master. It was decided in this instance that they were not, but the issue had been raised and would reappear. In 1656 children of indentured Indians were declared not to be servants, but mulatto children were. While we watch the trend unfold, it is worth noting that at this point in Virginia's history, African labor was becoming much more important as the colony developed a tobacco economy.

While a few African Americans were serving lifelong indentures for one reason or another in the 1640s and '50s, it was not until the early 1660s that Virginia law itself was altered to institutionalize permanent black servitude. The Irish Servant Act of 1655 was repealed in 1660. In '61 perpetual bondage for African Americans became statutory, and the next year saw the first use of the word *slave* in a Virginia law. Quantifiable changes now added up to a qualitative one.

In December 1662 all children were deemed slave or free depending on the status of their mothers, and so, as Palmer points out, "life-long servitude was made self-perpetuating." The law at this point actually used livestock as the model of black people. Adjustments and refinements continued to be made in Virginia law. One of particular importance was the 1667 legislation which declared that baptism did not change a black slave's status. By now it was clear that the slaves were chattel, property, objects, and that they themselves, not just their labor, were owned by the masters.

If a permanent slave status for Africans emerged over time in Virginia, why was it that Africans alone suffered the stigma and fate of perpetual bondage? The answer to the question of the relationship between slavery and racism is an issue of serious debate among scholars. One view is that racism came first and that Virginia's white Englishmen identified blackness with evil, and that they believed Africans were savages. Their fear of the different along with predilection for their own kind predisposed them to a prejudiced view of Africans as their natural inferiors. All these elements were certainly present and active, but were they enough to create the unique American slave system?

It is more likely that, beyond this racial predisposition, slavery in fact came first and produced racism as a consequence. This means that slavery was firstly an economic phenomenon. The large-scale production of staple crops for export, such as sugar, cotton, and tobacco, required an expanding and virtually infinite labor supply. As economist Barbara Solow points out, the Indians had been killed, Asians were too far away, and the Irish were too expensive, but Africans were close, plentiful, cheap, and gave efficient labor. Modern racism followed, then, with its myth of black inferiority to rationalize and justify a highly profitable economic system.

If you want to know more:

Paul C. Palmer. "Servant into Slave: The Evolution of the Legal Status of the Negro Laborer in Colonial Virginia." *South Atlantic Quarterly* (Summer 1966), 355–70.

> "Slavery was the central and determining phenomenon shaping the first centuries of American history."
> —Thomas Holt

> "Alas! and am I born for this?
> To wear the slavish chain?"
> —George Horton

What were the effects of slavery?

Scholars have long argued over the effects of slavery, particularly on black people both as individuals and as a community. One line of argument is that slavery was an all-pervasive, all-encompassing system which robbed people of their humanity, destroyed the family and personal relationships, denied the retention of any identity creating African culture, and turned African Americans into victims of one of the most oppressive and degrading systems in history. This argument has often been used politically to explain the fragmentation of the black family, for example, and to justify social, economic, and governmental action to compensate for slavery's damage.

Another line of argument has held that despite the oppression of slavery, blacks created social space, maintained their humanity by fighting against the slave system in a thousand ways, forged an identity for the present and future using their memory of their home in Africa, and through almost superhuman efforts managed not only to survive slavery but to triumph over it by making and maintaining a unique African-American culture. This is the argument, politically, of the black nationalists and separatists, the advocates of black pride.

The truth probably lies between these two positions. Yes, slavery broke some people and reduced them, but slavery also produced heroes like **Nat Turner** and **Harriet Tubman,** people of infinite courage and vision. Some people became victims of the ultimate form of slavery: a psychological and spiritual servitude which internalized the self-hatred taught by white racism. Racial self-hatred was the result, along with the desire to be like the oppressor, that is, to be white rather than black. Many black people have struggled to escape this mental oppression and analyze the internalized racism still present in African-American life, with the intent of removing the last scars of slavery.

If you want to know more:

Franz Fanon, *The Wretched of the Earth.* New York: Grove Press, 1963.

> "Slavery was the worst days ever seen in the world. There was things past telling, but I got the scars on my body to show till this day."
>
> —Mary Reynolds

"It must be remembered that the oppressed and the oppressor are bound together within the same society; they accept the same criteria, they share the same beliefs, they both alike depend on the same reality."

—James Baldwin

"Even the good part was awful."

—Lucille Clifton

Did the slaves resist?

Most slaves resisted their enslavement. They either ran away or rose up in rebellion, or found innumerable subtle ways to resist the people and the system that held them in permanent and unending bondage. This kind of daily resistance was sophisticated and secret, so it is not well documented. In fact, its very success often depended on slaves' acting ignorant and pretending not to know or understand what was going on. Basically, this form of retaliation was sabotage against the plantation system, and the enslaved found a thousand devices to impede and minimize and undercut their never ending daily rounds of uncompensated work.

One basic strategy throughout the Southern plantation system was setting a slow pace of work and taking as long as possible to get a job done. The strategy took many forms: black slave drivers sometimes intentionally set a pace showing consideration for the oldest and weakest in the crew. Feigned stupidity resulted in slaves going to the wrong workplace, taking the wrong tools, never quite "understanding" how to do the work assigned. A further, more active step involved breaking tools, and this happened so often that special heavy tools had to be made for slaves who were apparently so clumsy they couldn't touch anything without breaking it. Supplies were wasted or mysteriously disappeared ("taking" was differentiated from "stealing"), cotton and tobacco plants were damaged when being hoed, gates were left open and the masters' valuable horses and cattle wandered away.

Slaves often pretended to be sick and were excused from work by overseers afraid that expensive slaves made to labor when they were ill could die and turn into significant financial losses. Women sometimes pretended to be pregnant in order to get more food and be assigned less work. Slaves devised highly creative ways to deceive. When ordered to whip a fellow slave, Solomon Northup flicked the whip a fraction of an inch from the man's body while the intended victim screamed in pretended pain. **Mark Twain** knew a slave who could imitate with his voice the sound of sawing wood, and thereby satisfy his master, who thought he heard work being done.

Resistance could and did take more serious and extreme forms. Slaveowners were sometimes poisoned by slave cooks knowledgeable about lethal plants. Fires of unknown origin could destroy barns, crops, and houses, and in fact there were so many fires that insurance in the South became hard to get. A few slaves even mutilated themselves, deliberately cutting off a hand or foot so they would be permanently useless for work. Some committed suicide rather than face a meaningless life of hard labor.

Perhaps the saddest accounts of all are those of the slave mothers who killed their own children, preferring to give them an early death rather than see them subjected to the horrors of an enslaved life. Toni Morrison used one such historic event as the basis for her extraordinary novel *Beloved*. The perceptions that blacks actually were lazy and slow-moving, careless and stupid were absorbed whole into white culture, proving the effectiveness of this form of slave resistance.

If you want to know more:

Raymond A. Bauer and Alice H. Bauer. "Day to Day Resistance to Slavery." *Journal of Negro History* 27:4 (October 1942), 388–419.

"There was not a day throughout the ten years I belonged to Epps that I did not consult with myself upon the project of escape."

—Solomon Northup

"The overseer rode among them, on a horse, carrying in his hand a raw-hide whip, constantly directing and encouraging them; but, as my companion and I both several times noticed, as often as he visited one line of operations, the hands at the other end would discontinue their labor, until he turned to ride toward them again."

—Frederick Law Olmsted

"Deny the existence of resistance and one negates the dynamic, the soul, the reality of history."

—Herbert Aptheker

"From the careless movements of the individual afflicted with [Dysaesthesia Aethiopica], they are apt to do much mischief, which appears as if intentional, but it is mostly owing to the stupidness of mind and insensibility of the nerves induced by the disease."

—Dr. Cartwright

What was the first protest against slavery?

The traditional answer to this question is the Quaker petition against slavery of 1688 in Germantown, Pennsylvania. However, anything claiming to be "the first" runs a risk of being disproved, because there is a history and precursors to everything. This is especially true for African-American history, because the slaves themselves left few conventional written records and their story has often been ignored or distorted or presumed not to exist. To speak of the first real protest against slavery in this country is of course to speak of the constant struggle of black people against the institution of enslavement from its very beginning, even though these unknown slaves left little of the evidence or documents accessible to the historian. We do know about revolts, insurrections, and mutinies, and can speculate about other forms of resistance.

Another reservation is that there are a number of documents written by white people that are antecedent to the Germantown petition, and these are preserved in records available to historians. These include Roger Williams' criticism of selling Indians as slaves; the 1653 Rhode Island charter granting Africans the same status as European indentured servants; Quaker George Fox's 1676 assertion that Christ died for blacks as well as whites; Pieter Plockhoy's short-lived Mennonite settlement in Delaware whose constitution actually forbade slavery; Puritan theologian Richard Baxter's 1673 pamphlet in which he called slave traders "pirates" and slave owners "incarnate devils"; and William Edmundson's 1676 letter to his fellow Quakers, which states, "For perpetual slavery is an aggravation and an oppression upon the mind," and which seems to question the very nature of the institution.

Within this historical setting, it is possible to say that the Germantown petition is the first known explicit protest against the system itself. It was the work of a small group of settlers who came from the towns of Krefeld and Kriegsheim in the Rhineland in the mid-1680s. They were not actually Germans, though, but Dutch and Swiss whose forebears had left the Netherlands for religious and economic reasons. They had previously been Mennonites, but were now Quakers, and they settled in Germantown, outside Philadelphia. They were weavers by trade. It is likely their opposition to slavery did not come from their being Quakers. The Quakers of the day had reservations about slavery, but were certainly not opposed to the institution and in fact often held slaves. Their opposition may have come from their ethnic and national background, but more likely it is from the Mennonite religious influence under which they still lived. Whatever their motivation, at a church gathering on February 18, 1688, they drafted a petition to send to the Monthly Meeting, the official local Quaker assemblage.

What did they say? The petition is a list of reasons why they opposed "the traffic of Men body." The first is really the Golden Rule: "Is there any that would be done or handled at this manner?" they asked rhetorically. Obviously, no one would, yet "we hear that ye [*i.e.,* the] most part of such Neggers are brought heither against their will and consent." Furthermore, these people are "stollen," and brought to a country where there is liberty of conscience, so "here ought to be lickewise liberty of ye body."

The Germantown Quakers were highly sensitive to the issue of freedom of conscience, because they themselves had emigrated to America to obtain it. But they were distressed to find here a different infringement on human liberty: "In Europe there are many oppressed for Conscience sacke; and here there are those oppressed which are of a black Colour." The racial nature of American slavery astonished them: "Now, tho' they are black, we cannot conceive there is more liberty to have them as slaves, as it is to have other white ones."

An additional reason listed in their petition is that slavery separated wives and husbands and took children from parents and sold them to other men—all creating sexual improprieties counter to Christian behavior. Also, slavery "makes an ill report" in Europe of the Quaker religion when people hear that "ye Quackers doe here handel men licke they handel there ye Cattel." Lastly, the petition raised the question of why the slaves should not join together, rise up, and attack their masters and mistresses, and thus tempt Quakers—who are pacifists—to retaliate. And slave rebellion would be justified: "have these Negers not as much right to fight for their freedom, as you have to keep them slaves?"

The Germantown petition is clear and straightforward and obviously came from the heart. It was directed to the Monthly Meeting and asked fellow Quakers that if they could justify human slavery, please to do so to the satisfaction of the Germantowners as well as to those back in Europe, to whom it is a "terror" that blacks "should be handled so in Pennsylvania."

How was the petition received? It was discussed, but, the clerk reported, it was "so weighty that we think it not Expedient for us to meddle with it here, but do rather commit it to ye consideration of ye Quarterly Meeting." In other words, it was passed on up the line. The Quarterly Meeting evaded the issue in exactly the same way. When the Yearly Meeting received the petition, "It was adjudged not to be so proper for this Meeting," probably because so many Quakers, especially in other colonies, were slaveholders.

And so the Germantown petition came to an inglorious end. It was lost in the files and archives until Nathan Kite, a Philadelphia bookseller, discovered it 156 years later, in 1844, and published it for the first time. But before it got filed away, the petition probably influenced **George Keith,** a schismatic Quaker, who wrote an antislavery protest published in 1693 that is considered the first printed antislavery document. The Quaker establishment and Quaker folk generally then began the slow movement that led to their eventual stand against slavery. When at last they did take their stand, they were a firm, steadfast, and moral light in a dark world. One of the strongest streams of abolitionism, Quaker antislavery sentiment had a modest beginning among a small group of poor weavers in Germantown.

If you want to know more:

J. Herbert Fretz, "The Germantown Anti-Slavery Petition of 1688." *Mennonite Quarterly Review*, 33 (1959) 42–59.

"To bring men hither, or to rob and sell them against their will, we stand against."

—The Germantown Petition

"And while the meeting smothered our poor plea
With cautious phrase, a voice there seemed to be,
'As ye have done to these ye do to me!'"

—John Greenleaf Whittier

"This little leaven helped slowly to work a revolution in the attitude of this great sect."

—W. E. B. Du Bois

Did the spirituals have secret meanings?

The spirituals, also known as the slave songs or plantation songs, were called, by **W. E. B. Du Bois,** "the slave's one articulate message to the world." Little known to white people, the songs were preserved, following the Civil War, because of interest in them created by the Jubilee Singers of Fisk University. The songs are primarily religious in nature, often recounting and retelling Bible stories. It is also true, however, that many of the songs had double meanings and were used by slaves to communicate secretly with one another, sometimes in the very presence of whites.

What made the spirituals do double duty as religious hymns and coded messages was their common themes of slavery, flight, deliverance, and Heaven. One of the best-known, and one of the clearest symbolically, is "Go Down, Moses":

> You may hinder me here, but you can't up there,
> Let my people go.
> He sits in the heavens and answers prayer.
> Let my people go.
> Go down, Moses,
> Way down in Egypt land.
> Tell old Pharaoh
> Let my people go.

While this is a rehearsing of a scriptural narrative, it is also a personal existential expression and a profound statement of social protest.

A song which, on the surface, speaks of death, is also about running away:

No more auction block for me,
No more, no more.
No more auction block for me.
Many thousand gone.

Other lines of this spiritual list additional sufferings that will
be overcome by death (or escape):

No more peck of corn for me.
No more mistress' call for me.
No more hundred lash for me.

A song that Harriet Tubman reportedly sang to signal to
slaves that they should gather in preparation for "stealing away
home":

I'll meet you in the morning
When I reach the Promised Land
On the other side of Jordan
For I'm bound for the Promised Land.

Another, in a similar vein, was

Sweep it clean,
Ain't going to tarry here;
Sweep it clean,
Ain't going to tarry here;
I sweep my house with the gospel broom.

Some of the spirituals convey great poignancy in their expression of the desperation slaves felt facing the terrible dangers of trying to reach the free land of the North or Canada:

I'm running for my life,
I'm running for my life,
If anybody asks you what's the matter with me,
Just tell them I say,
I'm running for my life.

These songs were not all personal, but some articulated important religious truths which also carried radical and egalitarian social and political implications:

> Didn't my Lord deliver Daniel,
> Deliver Daniel, deliver Daniel.
> Didn't my Lord deliver Daniel,
> And why not every man?

Du Bois was quite right that the spirituals were the one means at the slaves' disposal to express themselves to the world. In that light, they are an incredible achievement. They spell out the slaves' deep religious faith and, at the same time, the unique way that that faith was interwoven both with protest against oppression and demonstration on behalf of freedom. The slaves' view of the social order was clearly expressed in the spiritual about Samson in the Temple, in which Samson says, "If I had my way, I'd tear this building down."

If you want to know more:

Charshee Charlotte Lawrence-McIntyre. "The Double Meanings of the Spirituals." *Journal of Black Studies* 17:4 (June 1987), 379–401.

> "Dark and thorny is de pathway
> Where de pilgrim makes his ways.
> But beyond dis vale of sorrow
> Lie de fields of endless days."
> —a spiritual used by Harriet Tubman
> on the Underground Railroad

> "I thought I heard them say
> There were lions on the way.
> I don't expect to stay
> Much longer here.

> Run to Jesus—shun the danger.
> I don't expect to stay
> Much longer here."
> —a spiritual known to Frederick Douglass

What was a slave catechism?

The white Southern churches helped reinforce the slave system by providing ethical, religious, and biblical rationales for human bondage and by behaving in paternalistic ways. The white Northern churches were one of the chief targets of the abolitionists, who were themselves mostly church people but who often withdrew from their congregations because of the churches' complicity with the evil of slavery. Many Southern slaveholders were Episcopalians who believed themselves, as the descendants of the Cavaliers, natural aristocrats. When they provided religious instruction and worship for their slaves, their purpose was really to buttress the status quo.

The following is a portion of a religious catechism written for slaves. It was published in the *Southern Episcopalian* in April 1854:

Q. Who gave you a master and a mistress?
A. God gave them to me.
Q. Who says that you must obey them?
A. God says that I must.
Q. What book tells you these things?
A. The Bible.
Q. How does God do all his work?
A. He always does it right.
Q. Does God love to work?
A. Yes, God is always at work.
Q. Do the angels work?
A. Yes, they do what God tells them.
Q. Do they love to work?

A. Yes, they love to please God.
Q. What does God say about your work?
A. He says that those who will not work shall not eat.
Q. Did Adam and Eve have to work?
A. Yes, they had to keep the garden.
Q. Was it hard to keep that garden?
A. No, it was very easy.
Q. What makes the crops so hard to grow now?
A. Sin makes it.
Q. What makes you lazy?
A. My wicked heart.
Q. How do you know your heart is wicked?
A. I feel it every day.
Q. Who teaches you so many wicked things?
A. The Devil.
Q. Must you let the Devil teach you?
A. No, I must not.

As African Americans accepted Protestant Christianity, they discarded the interpretation represented by this catechism, and emphasized instead the Bible's and Christian theology's image of liberation. They identified with the narrative of Israel in Egyptian bondage, and Jesus' redemptive suffering. In fact, the slaves transformed the established religion of the time and created something new: their own Afro-Protestant folk church.

If you want to know more:

John B. Boles, ed. *Planter and Slave in the House of the Lord: Race and Religion in the American South, 1740–1870.* Lexington: University of Kentucky Press, 1988.

"Indeed, I never heard a sermon to slaves but what made obedience to masters by the slaves the fundamental and supreme law of religion."
— The Reverend Nelson of North Carolina

"There is no parallel instance of an oppressed race thus
sustained by the religious sentiment alone."
                                —Thomas Wentworth Higginson

What was the first published protest against slavery?

The first attack on slavery to appear in print in English was
a small pamphlet written in Philadelphia by George Keith, a
schismatic Quaker, and published in 1693 in New York by William Bradford, that colony's first printer. It was a six-page tract
entitled *An Exhortation and Caution to Friends Concerning Buying
or Keeping of Negroes,* and only one complete copy is now known
to exist. That copy is in the Friends Library, London, where it
was discovered in the nineteenth century by Charles R. Hilde-
burn, an American bibliographer.

Who was the author? George Keith (1638–1716) was a Scots-
man with a degree from the University of Aberdeen who left his
native Presbyterianism to join the Society of Friends, better
known as Quakers. He became an important figure in Friends'
religious circles and an associate of Quaker leaders George Fox
and William Penn. Meanwhile, he migrated to Pennsylvania. At
Fox's death, Keith may well have thought himself a likely successor. Either to establish his own credentials, or because he actually did think the rigor of Quaker purity and practice was
slipping, he began criticizing the Quaker leadership.

Keith was undoubtedly a difficult person who loved a quar-
rel. His early life as a Calvinist made him, in a way, quite unsuited for the less theological and less biblical Quakerism, and
his argumentative and contentious personality clearly made him
unsuited for the peaceful life of a Friend. Keith thought the
Friends ought to concentrate more on the objectivity of the biblical Christ, and less on a subjective inner light. He also thought
the worldliness of the Quaker establishment that ran Pennsylvania was inappropriate.

Keith was disowned for his spirit of discord by the Quakers' official Yearly Meeting, but his criticisms were not his alone: he split the Quaker movement, and many Friends followed him into a schismatic group who called themselves Christian Quakers. The sect did not last long, and Keith himself joined the Church of England and became an Anglican missionary throughout the colonies. He then moved back to England, where he became rector at Edburton. But while it existed, the group of Christian Quakers, with Keith as their articulate and outspoken leader, enunciated their position on several important issues, not least of all on slavery.

Keith's *Exhortation* is a strikingly modern document in one way: amidst all its biblical and religious proof texts and arguments is a surprising statement, "Negroes, Blacks and Taunies are a real part of Mankind . . . and are capable of Salvation, as well as White men." This enlightened anthropological assumption is linked by Keith to the religious belief that Christ came "to ease and deliver the Oppressed and Distressed, and bring them into Liberty both inward and outward." These presuppositions led Keith to conclude not that Quakers should merely be kind to slaves, as William Penn admonished, but that slaves should in fact be set free!

Keith presented five reasons to oppose slavery, all of them rooted in the Bible. The first is simply the Golden Rule, "Do unto others as you would have them do unto you," and who indeed would want to be subjected to lifetime servitude? The second is that the Hebrew Bible rules against buying stolen goods, and slaves not only were stolen but they were people, and therefore the theft was the more serious. Third, the Bible commands that escaped servants should not be returned to their masters, and if this is Mosaic law, the notion of re-enslavement should be even more offensive under the Christian gospel.

Fourth, the money to be made from trafficking in human beings was tainted, especially for Christians, who were supposed to separate themselves from an evil world where slaves are the commercial "Merchandise of Babylon." Lastly, the Book of Deuteronomy cautions against oppressing servants. Keith spelled out the horrors of slavery, and prophetically predicted that "Surely the Lord doth behold their oppression and afflictions, and will further visit for the same by his righteous and just judgment."

Keith's statement made little impact in its day, and it would take a hundred years for the Quakers to take a firm stand against the slavery system. Perhaps Keith was trying to embarrass the Quaker establishment. Perhaps he felt oppressed and so identified with those who were even more oppressed. Perhaps he was building on the 1688 petition of the Germantown Quakers. Perhaps he was truly offended by human enslavement and saw it as a serious impediment to the Friends' attempt to construct a religious colony.

In any event, the contentious and separatist George Keith became a person worth remembering in the antislavery movement. His *Exhortation* is the first printed protest against slavery in British North America. He is one of the earliest white abolitionists. His words may have pricked the Quaker conscience and, when the Keithian schism was safely over, may have led some Friends to ask how they could square slavery with their faith. He leaves us still with the haunting vision of a liberty "both inward and outward."

If you want to know more:

Richard Newman. "The First Printed Protest Against Slavery." *AB: Bookman's Weekly* 93:6 (Feb. 7, 1994), 545–554.

"Therefore, in true Christian Love, we earnestly recommend it to all our Friends and Brethren, Not to buy any Negroes, unless it were on purpose to set them free."
—George Keith

"But these [slaves] have done us no harm, therefore how inhumane it is in us so grievously to oppress them and their children from one Generation to another."
—George Keith

What is the black church?

It has been suggested that African slaves in America achieved two extraordinary accomplishments, one social, one cultural. First, despite the variety of ethnic groups, cultures, languages, and religions the slaves came from in Africa, they welded themselves here into a single people. Second, they transformed the evangelical Protestantism of the American South into a discrete new phenomenon which, despite its important internal differences and divisions, was unified by what historian Laurie Maffly-Kipp calls "shared suffering and deliverance," and which we can call the black church.

The slaves did this both by bringing their own religious sensibility and culture into the world they found and by emphasizing within biblical Protestantism the themes and components most relevant to them and to their own situation. The result was—and it remains—a distinct and unique entity, the Afro-Protestant folk church.

Albert Raboteau, in his classic study, calls the religion of the slaves "the invisible institution" because it flourished in brush arbors near waterfalls or secret praise houses apart from white eyes and ears and where worshipers prayed and sang and shouted into buckets to muffle the sounds. Here African characteristics were able to be preserved: call and response between leaders and congregation, for example, and the ring shout, a shuffling group circle movement. It is easy to see, incidentally, how these characteristics in their secular form also became the basis of African-American music and dance.

One of the more remarkable features of the early black church was its creative appropriation and adaptation of the

Bible, the basis of Protestant authority. Africans identified with the slavery of the children of God in Egypt and Israel's eventual deliverance under Moses. In the New Testament they identified with the birth of Jesus as an innocent child and his unjust humiliation, suffering, and death. In African style, they told the stories of the Bible by turning them into songs, the Negro spirituals. The slaves were largely illiterate, but when the spirituals are strung together, they in fact constitute the entire biblical narrative text.

With good reason, the slavocracy—the slaveholders in the American South—feared the black church as a potential base for insurrection, and tried to control it. By law, for instance, slaves could not gather for worship unless a white person was present, although on lax plantations, a white child occasionally fulfilled the technical requirements. But even with restrictions, the black church developed as the African-American organization least under white control. Therefore it was the institution with the most African retentions, the one in which indigenous leadership could develop, the one most reflective of African-American people and their experience, and the one that became the heart and centerpiece of the black community.

If you want to know more:

Albert J. Raboteau. *Slave Religion: The Invisible Institution in the Antebellum South*. New York: Oxford University Press, 1978.

"The church is the door through which we first walked in Western civilization; religion is the form in which America first allowed our personalities to be expressed."

—Richard Wright

"The black church was the creation of a black people whose daily existence was an encounter with the overwhelming and brutalizing reality of white power."

—James Cone

"Let the church roll on."

—Negro spiritual

What happened in Stono, South Carolina, in 1739?

The major slave revolt in colonial America was the Stono Rebellion of 1739 in South Carolina, where African Americans constituted some two-thirds of the colony's total population of sixty thousand. The uprising took place not only because of the slaves' numerical superiority and their hatred of the system, but also because word had spread rapidly through the slave communities of the recent outbreak of war between England and Spain. The slaves were sympathetic to Spanish interests, partly because their masters were English, partly because Spain had created a haven for fugitives in their own colony of Florida.

The moment seemed ripe for revolt. Under the leadership of a slave, probably from Angola, named **Jemmy,** a dozen Africans chose the morning of Sunday, September 9, 1739, when the planters were in church, to rebel. At Stono Bridge in St. Paul's Parish, some twenty miles from Charleston, they killed store-keepers and collected arms and ammunition. They organized themselves into military formation with a flag and drum, gathered perhaps a hundred recruits along the way, and marched South, presumably towards St. Augustine, Florida, and freedom. They killed nearly twenty whites before stopping in an open field.

A group of planters overtook them there on Sunday afternoon, breaking up the outnumbered rebel army and killing about twenty in the fighting. Forty other blacks who either surrendered or were captured were also killed. The Stono Rebellion had lasted less than one day and was over. The consequences, however, influenced subsequent legal and social development in the South Carolina colony. Whites reacted with panic to the possibilities of further rebellion, and strengthened the codes that controlled slaves' lives and movements. In addition, the ruling whites recruited working-class whites into the colony in an attempt to counter the African Americans' numerical superiority.

If you want to know more:

Peter H. Wood, *Black Majority: Negroes in Colonial South Carolina from 1670 Through the Stono Rebellion.* New York: Norton, 1975.

"As the Protection our deserted slaves have met at that Castle [St. Augustine, Florida], has doubtlessly encouraged others to make the like attempts and even to rise in Rebellion, so the Demolition of that place, would free us from the like Danger for the Future."
　　　　　—William Bull, Lieutenant Governor of South Carolina

Who was the first African-American poet?

During the French and Indian War, **Lucy Terry Prince,** a slave in Deerfield, Massachusetts, composed a poem when Abenaki Indians raided a local hayfield on August 25, 1746, killing a number of white settlers and abducting others. Titled "Bars Fight" (a reference to a common fence around the field), the poem tells a story in the African griot tradition. It is not known when the poem was first written down—other oral versions seem to have existed—but it was not published until 1855 in Josiah Gilbert Holland's *History of Western Massachusetts.*

Prince was born around 1724 in Africa, stolen and enslaved and brought to Bristol, Rhode Island. She was then bought by Ebenezer Wells of Deerfield and baptized in the Deerfield Church on June 15, 1735. She was a slave until 1756, when she married Abijah Prince, a free black man who purchased her freedom. They had seven children. She tried to get one son, Festus, who was born in 1769, admitted to Williams College, and she reportedly argued the case against racial exclusion to the trustees herself, but to no avail.

Prince's verbal fluency went not only into composing rhymes. In 1785, she appealed to Governor Thomas Chittenden of Massachusetts against harassment by white neighbors, and won her case. In Vermont in 1796, she argued a property case before the U.S. Circuit Court, which ruled in her favor. She died in 1821, and **Lemuel Haynes,** the famous African-American minister, preached her funeral sermon. "Bars Fight" is Prince's only known verse, but there were undoubtedly others never written down.

If you want to know more:

David R. Proper. "Lucy Terry Prince: 'Singer of History.'" *Contributions in Black Studies* 9 (1990–1992), 187–214.

> "Oliver Amsden he was slain
> Which caused his friends much grief and pain."
> —Lucy Terry Prince

> "Young Samuel Allen, oh lack-a-day!
> Was taken and carried to Canada."
> —Lucy Terry Prince

> "And shall proud tyrants boast with brazen face,
> Of birth—of genius, over Africa's race?"
> —Lemuel Haynes at Lucy Terry Prince's funeral

Who was the first African American to write a book?

Phillis Wheatley was a slave, bought as a house servant from "a parcel . . . of small Negroes" on a Boston dock in July 1761 by Susannah Wheatley, the wife of John Wheatley, a well-to-do merchant. Phillis was a thin, sickly, naked child, judged by her owners to be seven or eight years old because her front baby teeth were missing. She was for sale cheap because the ship's captain was afraid she was too frail to live. In a humiliating reminder of her condition, she was given the name of the ship that had delivered her into bondage.

It is unknown where Phillis Wheatley came from—perhaps Gambia, perhaps Senegal. She may have come from a literate Islamic people, since she reportedly tried to draw letters at an early age. In any case, she was soon writing English letters and putting them together, and the Wheatley family marveled at her intelligence, her facility with language, and her ability not only to read and write, but to compose poetry. Mrs. Wheatley pampered the young slave, relieved her of some housework, and encouraged her to write.

One evening two men who had escaped a storm off Cape Cod were dinner guests at the Wheatleys', and Phillis overheard and later recounted their dramatic story in a poem that appeared in the *Newport Mercury* of December 21, 1767, her first published work. The poem that made her internationally famous, however, was "On the Death of the Rev. Mr. George Whitefield, 1770," an elegy for the evangelical preacher who had electrified America in the religious revivals of the Great Awakening.

Wheatley wrote enough poems to make a book, but not enough subscribers could be found in Boston to finance publication. Through the international evangelical network, Wheatley came to the attention of Selina Hastings, Countess of Huntingdon, an English noblewoman and philanthropist. With Hastings' support, *Poems on Various Subjects, Moral and Religious,* a collection of thirty-nine poems in stylized heroic couplets, was issued in London in 1773. Its authenticity was verified by prominent Bostonians, who testified it was actually the work of an African-American slave girl. It was the first book by an African American and the second by an American woman, and it has remained in print ever since.

Wheatley traveled with her master to England, where she

was very favorably received and met **Benjamin Franklin,** but Mrs. Wheatley's illness brought them back to Boston before she could meet either the Countess of Huntingdon or King George III, as had been planned. Shamed by comments in England, the Wheatleys gave Phillis her freedom in 1773. Mrs. Wheatley soon died, life was disrupted by the Revolutionary War, and right after John Wheatley's death in 1778, Phillis married John Peters, a free Boston black man.

John Peters has been dealt by history with ambiguity. Some recall him as an intelligent merchant who sometimes functioned as a lawyer. Others claim he was haughty and headstrong and had trouble keeping a job. Whatever the reasons, Phillis Wheatley was finally reduced to working as a cleaning woman in a cheap boardinghouse to pay her rent. Her three babies died in infancy, and Wheatley herself died in Boston on December 5, 1784, at the age of thirty-one. Peters demanded and received from the Wheatley family the three hundred manuscript pages of his wife's unpublished poems and letters. They are now lost.

There were several important influences on Wheatley's thought and work. She was a committed Christian and a member of the Old South Church, whose meetinghouse still stands on the corner of Boston's Milk and Washington streets. Numerous Congregational ministers were her friends, and a Puritan piety and plainness runs through her poems. Her religious faith made her perceive Africa as a pagan place from which divine mercy had delivered her, but she still repeatedly affirmed herself as an "Ethiopian" and proudly spoke of "Africa's blissful plain" as "my nation."

In fact, religion provided a model for Wheatley of radical social equality. Speaking of Christ, she wrote, "Take him, ye Africans, he longs for you / Impartial savior is his title due." Wheatley was also an American patriot when the white Wheatleys and many of their social class were Tories sympathetic to the British crown. Wheatley wrote a poem honoring George Washington, and he met with her privately in his army headquarters in Cambridge in 1775. Thomas Jefferson, in contrast, thought her poems "beneath the dignity of criticism."

Wheatley was not the first to connect the colonists' demand for liberty with the plight of their slaves, and to see the irony of the contradiction. The words "free" and "freedom" occur frequently in her poems, and in her eulogy at the death of the American general David Wooster, she wrote:

> But how, presumptuous shall we hope to find
> Divine acceptance with th'Almighty mind—
> While yet, O deed ungenerous! they disgrace
> And hold in bondage Afric's blameless race?

In spite of her frail health, and behind her meek demeanor and loyal servitude, then, Phillis Wheatley was racially conscious, and deeply opposed to slavery. In a February 1774 letter to her friend, the Native American minister Samson Occom, she wrote, "In every human Breast, God has implanted a Principle, which we call Love of Freedom; it is impatient of Oppression, and pants for Deliverance—and by the leave of our Modern [oppressors] I will assert, that the same Principle lives in us."

If you want to know more:

William H. Robinson. *Phillis Wheatley and Her Writings*. New York: Garland Publishing, 1984.

> "Thy Power, O Liberty, makes strong the weak
> And (wondrous instinct) Ethiopians speak."
> —Phillis Wheatley, "America"

> "Inspiration! Who can sing thy force?
> Or who describe the swiftness of thy course?
> We on thy pinions can surpass the wind,
> And leave the rolling universe behind."
> —Phillis Wheatley, "Imagination"

"You are not to take any Children and Espilly Girls. . . .
I had Rather you would be Two Months longer on the
Coast than to Bring off such a Cargo as Your Last which
were very small."
—Timothy Fitch to Peter Gwin, January 12, 1760.
Fitch was the owner and Gwin the captain of the slave
ship *Phillis*. Fitch's letter criticizes the voyage that
had brought Phillis Wheatley to America.

Who was the first to die for American independence?

The first American to die in the struggle for American independence from Great Britain was **Crispus Attucks,** an African-American slave. On the evening of March 5, 1770, in Boston's King Street near the Custom House, a rowdy gang was taunting British soldiers stationed in the city to enforce the new colonial regulations. According to subsequent testimony, Attucks struck one of the soldiers. In the resulting confusion, the troops fired and five Americans went down. Attucks died on the spot with two musket balls in the chest, the first victim of the Boston Massacre, as the fray was immediately labeled, and the first patriot of the American Revolution.

Actually, little is known of Attucks or his life. He was a six-foot two-inch sailor about fifty years old, and he may have had some Natick Indian ancestry. He was probably a runaway slave who had escaped from Deacon William Brown of Framingham. Even if he was part of what John Adams called "a motley rabble," Attucks became an instant hero in death. Laid to rest in the Granary Burying Ground, he was memorialized in subsequent years by Boston's black and white abolitionists, with a statue in his honor and a memorial day named for him.

Attucks' real significance, however, as the historian **John Hope Franklin** points out, lies first in the paradox that the colonists' struggle for liberty excluded the African Americans they held in bondage, and second in Attucks' ironic role as an unfree symbol of liberty. Many African Americans fought with the colonists in the revolution that followed, but more sided with the British, who offered freedom to the slaves who joined them.

If you want to know more:

Hiller B. Zobel. *The Boston Massacre.* New York: Norton, 1971.

"Few people remember the soldiers' names or Capt. Preston or even that John Adams defended the British soldiers, yet they know Crispus Attucks."

—Hiller Zobel

"[The Americans at the Boston Massacre were] a motley rabble of saucy boys, Negroes and mulattoes, Irish Teagues and outlandish Jack Tars."

—John Adams

CHAPTER 2

~

From Resistance to Reconstruction, 1776–1877

Who wrote an essay against slavery that was not published for two hundred years?

Who founded the first African-American Masonic Lodge?

Does the word *slavery* appear in the U.S. Constitution?

Who founded the first African-American religious denomination?

Who was the first African-American man of science?

Was Thomas Jefferson the father of children by a slave mistress?

What threatened Thomas Jefferson like a "firebell in the night"?

How many slaves escaped on the Underground Railroad?

How many slave revolts were there?

What was the compromise on slavery and did it succeed?

What happened in the African-American community of Christiana, Pennsylvania, in 1851?

Was slavery extended into the new territories?

What were minstrel shows?

Who was the best-known African-American woman of the nineteenth century?

Who was the best-known conductor on the Underground Railroad?

What antislavery book became a publishing phenomenon?

Who was Dred Scott and why was his legal case so important?

Who was the most prominent African-American man of the nineteenth century?

Who is probably the white person most respected by African Americans?

What caused the Civil War?

Did African Americans fight in the Civil War?

What happened at Fort Pillow?

What was Reconstruction?

———————————————

∾

Who wrote an essay against slavery that was not published for two hundred years?

Sometime around 1776, when he was a soldier in the Continental Army, a young African American named **Lemuel Haynes** wrote an essay he called "Liberty Further Extended." He argued that the concept of freedom motivating the colonists' revolution ought to be enlarged and expanded to include the nation's African slaves. His essay did not see the light of day for over two hundred years. Ruth Bogin of Pace University discovered the manuscript in Harvard's Houghton Library and transcribed it for publication in the *William and Mary Quarterly* in 1983.

Lemuel Haynes was born July 18, 1753, in West Hartford, Connecticut, to a white mother and black father, about whom nothing is known except that neither of them wanted him. When he was about five months old, Haynes was indentured to a white family named Rose, who brought him up in exchange for his labor until he came of age. He was a hardworking and serious child who supplemented the limited teaching of the local public school by educating himself, reading by fireside at night. And he fully absorbed the Calvinist piety and theology of the evangelical family that raised him.

Haynes was a Minuteman in the American Revolution who marched out with his neighbors and served in Massachusetts and Vermont. The spirit of freedom in the air led him to use the Declaration of Independence along with biblical texts as background, and laboriously to draft an essay combining the power of logic with great depth of feeling: "Shall a mans Couler Be the Decisive Criterion whereby to Judge of his natural right?" If Haynes' essay had been published at the time, it would have made him an early and effective black abolitionist.

He decided on the ministry as a vocation, studied privately with several clergymen, and was ordained in the Congregational Church on November 9, 1785, probably the first African American to be ordained by a mainstream denomination in the

United States. The slaves, of course, had their own religious leaders, some of whom were elected ministers and set apart in a free church or Baptist tradition before this date. (In Latin America the Roman Catholic Church had long since ordained to the priesthood men of African and mixed-blood descent.)

Haynes served churches in Middle Granville and Torrington, Connecticut, and toward the end of his life in Manchester, Vermont, and Granville, New York. But most of his life was spent in West Rutland, Vermont, where he ministered from 1788 to 1818. He preached 5,500 sermons at Rutland, including 400 funeral sermons, and became a sought-after preacher at ordinations and a popular speaker at public events. He was a lifelong Federalist and political supporter of George Washington, and he was not above making anti-Jeffersonian political speeches.

A good deal of Haynes' reputation came from his ready wit. When the house of the Reverend Ashbel Parmelee burned down, Haynes asked him if he'd lost his sermon manuscripts in the fire. Learning that he had, Haynes said, "Well, don't you think they gave more light than they ever had before?" Haynes once accidentally walked into a hotel dining room where Andrew Jackson's election was being celebrated. He was handed a glass of wine and invited to propose a toast to the new president. "Andrew Jackson: Psalm 109, verse 8," Haynes said promptly, and went on his way. Only afterwards did someone look up the Bible verse to discover the text: "Let his days be few and let another take his office."

Haynes' most famous sermon combined his wit with his Calvinism. In 1805 he responded to a sermon by the Universalist minister Hosea Ballou with a clever rejoinder in which he managed to identify Ballou with the tempting serpent in the Garden of Eden. Haynes' sermon, "Universal Salvation," was so popular it was reprinted in over seventy editions and appeared as late as 1865. This is a publishing phenomenon by any standard, and for an African-American preacher on the Vermont frontier in 1805, it is nothing short of a remarkable achievement.

In later life, Haynes became involved in a sensational murder case. In Manchester, Vermont, two brothers, Stephen and Jesse Boorn, were in prison for the murder of their eccentric brother-in-law, Russell Colvin, who had disappeared. There was no body, but there was strong circumstantial evidence against the Boorns. Haynes visited them daily in jail and became convinced they were innocent. A notice in a local paper turned up Colvin, who was not dead but living in New Jersey. He was brought back immediately to Manchester just before the Boorns' execution in a moment of high local drama. Haynes immediately preached a sermon, "The Prisoner Released," and wrote an account of events, "Mystery Developed," an essay which could pass for a short story. The case itself became significant in American legal history as a warning against dependence on circumstantial evidence, and the British novelist Wilkie Collins picked up the story of "The Boorn Case" and used its "dead-alive" theme in his fiction.

Haynes has been criticized by history and historians for living his entire life surrounded by whites and not identifying with blacks or speaking out against slavery. But that was before the discovery of his manuscript "Liberty Further Extended." A newer discovery is that Haynes was the preacher at the funeral of **Lucy Terry Prince,** America's first black poet, who died in 1821 at the age of ninety-seven. The historian David R. Proper recently located a newspaper account of the funeral, which quotes a poem recited by Haynes, a poem of which he clearly seems to be the author. It contains the lines, "How long must Ethiopia's murder'd race / Be doom'd by man to bondage and disgrace?"

Haynes may have lived his life in the white world, but the twenty-three-year-old soldier who was moved to compose a poem on "The Battle of Lexington" identified himself as "a young Mollato." And the sixty-five-year-old man who was forced out of his Rutland, Vermont, pastorate described what happened with ironic humor: "He lived with the people of Rutland thirty years, and they were so sagacious that at the end of that time they found out he was a nigger, and so turned him away."

If you want to know more:

Richard Newman, ed. *Black Preacher to White America: The Collected Writings of Lemuel Haynes, 1774–1833*. Brooklyn, N.Y.: Carlson Publishing, 1990.

"There is counterfeit gold, and counterfeit silver, counterfeit bills, and counterfeit men."

—Lemuel Haynes

"O! what an Emens Deal of African-Blood hath Been Shed by the inhuman Cruelty of Englishmen!"

—Lemuel Haynes

"What has reduced them [the poor Africans among us] to their present pitiful abject state? Is it any distinction that the God of nature hath made in their formation? Nay, but being subjected to slavery, by the cruel hands of oppressors they have been forced to view themselves as a rank of beings far below others."

—Lemuel Haynes

Who founded the first African-American Masonic Lodge?

The first black Masonic Lodge in America was established just a short time before the Revolutionary War broke out. On March 6, 1775, a British army traveling lodge of Freemasons, the 38th Regiment of Foot in General Gage's troops stationed at Castle William in Boston Harbor, initiated fifteen African Americans into membership. On July 3, 1777, these new Masons founded African Lodge No. 1 in Boston, and received a charter from the Grand Lodge of England on September 29, 1784.

The lodge's leader was **Prince Hall.** His birthplace and date are unknown, but he was born about 1735 and was owned by William Hall of Boston, who manumitted him in 1770. Prince Hall was a leather dresser by trade; he was also a preacher and a prominent leader of Boston's black community. In 1777 he signed a petition to the state legislature urging them to abolish slavery, as it was clearly inconsistent with the spirit of the American Revolution. In 1786 he offered the services of the lodge to the governor to help put down Shay's Rebellion. In 1787 he proposed the creation abroad of a separate black state, perhaps the first organized movement for African colonization. In 1800 Hall set up a school for black children in his home.

Several other African-American lodges grew out of Boston Masonry, including Hiram Lodge in Providence, Rhode Island, in 1797, and a lodge in Philadelphia led by **Absalom Jones** and **Richard Allen.** These associate Prince Hall lodges hark back to his leadership by being named for him. Many white lodges have suggested that the Prince Hall lodges' origin is somehow questionable, but the 1777 charter is indisputable and presently resides safely in a Boston bank vault.

Hall died December 4, 1807, and is buried in Copp's Hill Burying Ground in Boston. The lodge that bears his name was one of many early black self-help organizations, an early part of a strong tradition of black community-building and nurturing, as well as centers of protest against racism and discrimination.

If you want to know more:

Charles H. Wesley, *Prince Hall: Life and Legacy.* Washington, D.C.: United Supreme Council, Southern Justification, Prince Hall Affiliation, 1977.

"I hope you will . . . live in peace and love with your brothers."
> —Prince Hall to the Providence, Rhode Island, lodge

"We therefore must fear for our rising offspring to see them in ignorance in a land of gospel light when there is provision made for them as well as others, and yet [they] can't enjoy and [for] no other reason can be given [for] this [than that] they are black."
> —Prince Hall

Does the word *slavery* appear in the U.S. Constitution?

Despite its importance as a political, legal, and ethical issue in American history, the word *slavery* does not appear in the U.S. Constitution of 1787. The first reference, curiously enough, does not occur until the Thirteenth Amendment, adopted in 1865, which abolished it! Despite the delegates' deliberate avoidance of the term, however, the reality of slavery was the dominating factor in the convention which drafted the Constitution as the fundamental law under which the country would be governed. In the telling phrase of the scholar **Cornel West,** slavery was the serpent coiled around the legs of the table on which the Constitution was drafted.

The basic division between the representatives who met in Philadelphia in the hot summer of 1787 was that some came from states that continued to enslave African Americans, and some from states that no longer did. What united them, besides the hope that they could successfully forge a charter for the new nation, was a deeply conservative belief in the sacredness of private property, and a strongly elitist suspicion of common people, black and white.

The Constitution that came out of the convention specifically forbade Congress from considering the prohibition of the slave trade for another twenty years, that is, until 1808. This obviously placed the trade under government protection, but some opponents of slavery accepted this compromise because they thought Congress would eliminate the trade when it had a chance, and, moreover, they believed the end of the trade would also mean the eventual end of slavery itself.

Another section stated that fugitive slaves were not in fact free if they made their way to the free soil of a free state, but, rather, they remained the property of their masters. This provision was not controversial, and its inclusion was a strong selling point on behalf of the Constitution in the Southern states distrustful of any federal union at all.

The most contested convention question was how to count slaves, who of course could not vote, when representation in the lower house of Congress was to be based on population. At the time, there were some half-million African Americans. They constituted 20 percent of the national population, and 90 percent of them lived in bondage in the Southern states. The compromise, adopted July 12, 1787, was to count each slave as three-fifths of a person.

This decision was momentous, because it gave the white South from the outset an entirely disproportionate strength in the House of Representatives and in the Electoral College, which meant that slaveholders would effectively control the federal government until the Civil War. Northerners' opposed the Southern position, but were willing to compromise in order to get the Constitution approved, and they were not themselves committed to the slaves' interests anyway.

Early white abolitionists, particularly the ideologically purist Garrisonians, perceived the Constitution as an obviously pro-slavery document, and, as a result, often favored dissolving the union. **William Lloyd Garrison** personally burned a copy in Worcester, Massachusetts, at an antislavery rally. Integrationist African Americans, however, struggling for their rights as citizens, tended to look to the Constitution as a great charter of liberty, promising and guaranteeing the rights they were denied, and they held up the Constitution as a promise to be fulfilled. This was clearly the position, for example, of **Frederick Douglass** and **Martin Luther King, Jr.**

If you want to know more:

A. Leon Higginbotham, Jr. *In the Matter of Color, Race, and the American Legal Process.* New York: Oxford University Press, 1978.

"No person held to Service or Labor in one State, under the Laws thereof, escaping into another, shall, in Consequence of any Law or Regulation therein, be discharged from such Service or Labor, but shall be delivered up on Claim of the Party to whom such Service or Labor may be due."

—U.S. Constitution, Article IV, Section 2

"The inhabitant of Georgia or South Carolina who goes to the Coast of Africa, and in defiance of the most scared laws of humanity tears away his fellow creatures from their dearest connections and damns them to the most cruel bondages, shall have more votes in a government instituted for the rights of mankind, than the Citizen of Pennsylvania or New Jersey, who views with a laudable horror, so nefarious a practice."

—Gouverneur Morris of Pennsylvania

"I would have the Constitution torn to shreds and scattered to the four winds of heaven."

—William Wells Brown

Who founded the first African-American religious denomination?

Richard Allen founded and became the first bishop of the African Methodist Episcopal (AME) Church, the first black religious denomination. Allen was born in Philadelphia, Pennsylvania, on February 14, 1760, to a family enslaved by Benjamin Chew, a prominent lawyer, attorney general, and judge. Chew sold the family to an owner named Stockley, whom Allen considered kindly, except Stockley sold off Allen's mother and three of his brothers and sisters, and he never saw or heard from any of them again.

Allen was converted to evangelical Protestantism at age seventeen by a Methodist circuit rider. He became a lifelong Methodist in doctrine, adhering to the Wesleyan belief, in contrast to Calvinism, that men and women could play a role in their own salvation. He adhered, also, to early American Methodism's antislavery stance, though within the white churches this was a position that became severely compromised over the years. A white Methodist evangelist named Freeborn Garretson so moved Allen's owner that he agreed to let Allen buy his freedom—for $2,000.

Allen became an itinerant Methodist lay preacher himself, and may have been present at the historic Christmas Conference of 1784, when American Methodism separated from the Church of England, where it had been an internal evangelical party. Allen preached at St. George's Church, Philadelphia, a racially mixed congregation, and he brought in many new black members. The African Americans requested their own separate church, but were refused. They contributed, therefore, to renovating St. George's to make it large enough to accommodate the new members.

In November 1787, the first Sunday in the new building, the black members found themselves segregated in the balcony. Even here, Allen was astonished to see his friend and colleague Absalom Jones dragged to his feet by an usher during prayer and ordered to leave. Outraged, the black members of St. George's walked out of the service, out of the building, and out of a white-controlled Methodist church. Allen and Jones had already formed the Free African Society, which they intended to turn into a nondenominational church, but many were so disgusted by the Methodists that they constituted themselves as St. Thomas Episcopal Church in 1804 under Jones, who became the first black Episcopal minister.

Allen, however, remained true to Methodist theology and polity. To establish a new house of worship, he moved a building that had housed a blacksmith shop to a lot he owned on the corner of Sixth and Lombard streets. Bishop Francis Asbury dedicated it as a Methodist church on July 29, 1794. In 1799 Allen was ordained deacon. Meanwhile, the black Methodists discovered they had been cheated out of their autonomy by the whites of St. George's, but through a lawsuit they eventually managed to regain control of their property in 1807. On April 9, 1816, a conference was organized which included Daniel Coker of Baltimore and other independent black Methodists. Allen was elected bishop of the new group on April 11, and Jones was among the consecrators.

Allen and the African Methodist Episcopal Church immediately became a center of black institutional life. They supported schools and *Freedom's Journal,* they opposed the Colonization Society, and they petitioned legislatures for an end to slavery. **Denmark Vesey**'s slave uprising in Charleston was planned around the AME Church. The vital place and historic role of African Methodism is summarized in Allen's understatement, "The only place blacks felt they could maintain an element of self-expression was the church."

If you want to know more:

Carol V. R. George. *Segregated Sabbaths: Richard Allen and the Emergence of Independent Black Churches, 1760–1840.* New York: Oxford University Press, 1973.

"We will never separate ourselves voluntarily from the slave population in this country; they are our brethren by the trees of consanguinity, of suffering and of wrong; and we feel there is more virtue in suffering privations with them than fancied advantage for a season."

—Richard Allen

"If you deny us your name [Methodist], you cannot seal up the Scriptures from us, and deny us a name in heaven."

—Richard Allen

Who was the first African-American man of science?

Benjamin Banneker was a self-taught mathematician and astronomer who received international recognition for calculating ephemerides for almanacs for the years 1792 through 1797, almanacs which were published and widely distributed.

Banneker was born in 1731 in Baltimore County, Maryland, to a freed slave named Robert, and to Mary Banneky. Banneky was the daughter of Bannka, a freed slave and an African prince, and an indentured Englishwoman named Molly Welsh. Having no surname of his own, Banneker's father took his wife's name when they were married. He then bought a one-hundred-acre farm with his savings and cleared the land to plant tobacco. It was on this farm that Benjamin Banneker grew up and spent his life. His grandmother, Molly, taught him reading and writing with a Bible that she had brought from England. He went to a nearby school for several seasons as a boy, but received no more formal education. He often read during the leisure hours on his father's farm and, with the few books he could borrow or occasionally buy, he taught himself literature, history, and mathematics.

Banneker had a natural gift for mathematics, and as a boy he collected and invented mathematical puzzles. At twenty-one, after examining a pocket watch, he constructed a successful striking clock without ever having seen one. He began the project because it was a mathematical challenge. He calculated the proper ratio of the gears and wheels and then carved them from wood with a pocketknife. The clock operated for more than forty years, until the time of his death, and people throughout the region remained fascinated by it.

Robert Banneky died in 1759 and left Benjamin to continue to work on the farm, where he lived with his mother and three sisters. Eventually, his sisters married and left home, and in 1775 his mother died. Though his sisters often visited, he lived his life on his farm alone, remote from community life and potential persecution because of his color.

Banneker's great life-turning event happened in 1771, when five Ellicott brothers, Quakers from Pennsylvania, purchased land adjoining his farm and developed it into a major center for the production of wheat and the milling of flour. Banneker was befriended by George Ellicott, who was the young son of one of the founding brothers and who had an interest in the sciences. It was from George that Banneker derived his first interest in astronomy after observing astronomical presentations made by him at the mills. In 1789, Ellicott lent Banneker several astronomy books, instruments, and an old table on which he could study. Without other assistance or guidance, Banneker taught himself astronomy with these borrowed materials. He compiled an ephemeris for 1791 for incorporation into an almanac, but though he submitted it to several printers, no one would publish it.

At the beginning of 1791, President George Washington appointed Major Andrew Ellicott, George Ellicott's cousin, to survey a ten-mile square known as the Federal Territory (now the District of Columbia), in which the new national capital was to be established. Major Ellicott had difficulty finding a competent assistant who could use scientific apparatus, but he learned from his cousin about Banneker and his skills. Ellicott arranged for Banneker to accompany him to work as his scientific assistant for a short period. They began in February 1791, with Banneker making and recording astronomical observations, maintaining the field astronomical clock, and compiling other data as required by the surveyor. At the end of April, after the base lines and initial boundaries had been established, Ellicott's brothers came to assist him, and Banneker returned to his farm.

Banneker's experiences in the Federal Territory increased his interest in astronomy, and after his return he calculated an ephemeris for the following year. Through George Ellicott and his family, Banneker's work was brought to the attention of Pennsylvania and Maryland abolition societies. With their influence, it was published in Baltimore by the printers Goddard and Angell as *Benjamin Banneker's Pennsylvania, Delaware, Maryland and Virginia Almanack and Ephemeris, for the year of Our Lord, 1792; Being Bisextile, or Leap-Year, and the Sixteenth Year of American Independence, which commenced July 4, 1776.*

Shortly before its publication, Banneker sent a manuscript copy of his ephemeris to Thomas Jefferson, then U.S. Secretary of State, with a letter urging the abolition of slavery, an evil he compared to the former enslavement of the American colonies by Britain. Jefferson acknowledged Banneker's letter and manuscript; meanwhile, he forwarded them to the Marquis de Condorcet, secretary of the Académie des Sciences in Paris, as works of little interest but for the fact that they had been done by a black man.

The published almanac featured a biographical sketch of Banneker by Senator James McHenry, who described Banneker's station and achievements as new evidence in support of the end to slavery. Banneker's work sold in great numbers and was very successful.

Encouraged by his achievement, Banneker retired from tobacco farming and devoted all his time to study. He published almanacs for the next five years, and they all enjoyed success. At least twenty-nine separate editions of his almanacs were published during this six-year period, with wide distribution in both the United States and Great Britain. Publication of Banneker's almanacs terminated in 1797, probably as a result of decreasing popularity of the abolition movement.

This disappointment did not quench Banneker's thirst for knowledge. He became interested in writing and produced several short pieces which he described as "dreams." He continued to collect mathematical puzzles. Banneker also wrote brief accounts of natural phenomena that he observed, such as storms, bees, and cicadas.

During the final period of his life, he frequently visited the Ellicotts' Lower Mills, where he discussed current affairs with the Ellicotts and others. Although Banneker was not affiliated with any denomination, he was deeply religious and attended services of various churches, favoring the Society of Friends. He spent the final years of his life living alone in his log house on the farm, pursuing his reading, calculating ephemerides, and producing occasional pieces of original writing.

Benjamin Banneker died October 9, 1806, a month short of his seventy-fifth birthday. The publication of his almanacs brought international acknowledgment to Banneker because of his achievement as a black man. Modern studies confirm that he was a naturally brilliant mathematician, and his ephemerides compare favorably with those compiled for the same years by the outstanding men of science of his same time.

If you want to know more:

Silvio Bedini. *The Life of Benjamin Banneker.* New York: Scribner, 1971.

"In every civilized country we shall find thousands of whites, liberally educated and who have enjoyed greater opportunities for instruction than this Negro [who are] his inferiors in those intellectual achievements and capacities that form the most characteristic features in the human race."

—James McHenry

Was Thomas Jefferson the father of children by a slave mistress?

Although no absolute proof exists, there is little doubt that Thomas Jefferson, the third president of the United States, was involved in a thirty-eight-year-long intimate relationship with Sally Hemings, an African-American slave woman he owned and with whom he fathered seven children. The truth of their relationship is obscured by rumor, legend, political partisanship, and the frantic denials of Jefferson's defenders. Their chief argument is that it would have been out of character for their hero to have been involved in a sexual relationship after his wife's death, especially with a black woman. The historian Dumas Malone, for example, finds the Hemings story simply "inconceivable," though he, and others, fail to explain why Monticello should be any different from the thousands of other Southern plantations that produced mixed-blood children.

What does attest to Jefferson's character, however, is the fact that he never denied his relationship with Sally Hemings, although he paid a political price for his silence and endured vulgar popular songs about "Long Tom" and "Dusky Sally." Unfortunately, there is no portrait of Sally Hemings, though she was said to be beautiful; there is no extant written word to or from her, though she was almost certainly literate; there are no anecdotes about her, though she and her role were well-known; there are no interviews with her, even after Jefferson's death, although only she and he knew the full story of their relationship.

What is known? Sally Hemings was born in Virginia in 1773, the daughter of a white man, John Wayles of Charles City County, and a slave woman, his African-American mistress, with whom Wayles cohabited after the death of his third wife, and with whom he had six children. Her name was Betty Hemings and she was the daughter of a white English ship captain and an African slave. John Wayles' and Betty Hemings' daughter Sally was thus fair-skinned, a Quadroon with long straight hair, light enough to pass for white, and with enough personality and flair to be known in her girlhood as "Dashing Sally."

Sally's father-owner died the year she was born, and she and her mother became the property of Wayles' heir, his white daughter Martha, Sally's half-sister—who was married to Thomas Jefferson. So Sally grew up at Monticello, joining a group of other light-skinned house servants, and in 1782, at age nine, she was present in the room when Martha Jefferson died. Jefferson never remarried. In 1784, he went to France with the commercial mission of John Adams and Benjamin Franklin. Beginning the next year he served as American minister. Jefferson had taken along to Paris his twelve-year-old daughter Martha, and when his youngest child Lucy died back in Virginia, he sent for his nine-year-old daughter Maria, called Polly, to join him as well. She did so in 1787, accompanied by Sally Hemings as her servant-slave, a last-minute replacement for an older slave woman too ill to travel.

Jefferson, meanwhile, had become smitten with Maria Cosway, a married Englishwoman, who apparently proved unwilling to participate in an adulterous affair. Thus in 1789 Jefferson, a forty-six-year-old spurned lover, found himself in the same Parisian household with a beautiful, intelligent, and nubile sixteen-year-old "Dashing Sally." The account books suddenly begin to show large expenditures for clothes for Sally, who already had a French tutor and was being paid an allowance.

Although as a resident on French soil Sally Hemings was technically free, she still looked to Jefferson as her master, and probably looked at herself as a slave subject to his will. Their relationship had its larger model in the whole plantation system, as well as its immediate personal precedent in the liaison between Hemings' mother and Jefferson's father-in-law. Sally Hemings became pregnant, but it is not entirely clear whether the first child, a son named Tom, was born in France or the United States. Most likely he was born at Monticello in December 1789, and worked as a house servant there until early adolescence, when he was permitted (actually encouraged) to run away, pass for white, and disappear into white society in the North.

At Monticello, Hemings had her own room, and no supervisory overseer, and her job seems to have consisted of supervising the care of Jefferson's clothes and bedroom. Their son Madison later claimed that Jefferson had promised her their children would be free if she would return with him to the United States and to slavery. Over the years, she gave birth to six more children: Harriet (1795) and Edy (1796), both of whom died in infancy; a son Beverly (1798) and a second daughter named Harriet (1801), both of whom, like Tom, were allowed to run away (in fact, Harriet was given $50 and a ticket to Philadelphia); and two sons with whom Sally Hemings lived at Jefferson's death, Madison (1805) and Eston (1808).

Jefferson's sexual relationship and African-American children became public knowledge on September 11, 1802, during his first term as president. A political opponent, an unsavory journalist named James Thomson Callender, revealed in the Richmond *Recorder* what the Monticello neighborhood already knew. He broke the Southern taboo of silence surrounding the sexual abuse of slaves by announcing that Jefferson kept a black concubine, "The African Venus," with whom he had several children, including a son, Tom, who waited on tables at Monticello and bore a "striking though sable" resemblance to the president of the United States. Jefferson's political opponents used the story against him, and elaborated it to include the false allegation that a mulatto daughter of his had been sold at auction on the New Orleans slave market. Jefferson made no response to any of it.

At Jefferson's death in 1826, 130 slaves were sold to meet the debts of his bankrupt estate. His will, however, freed Madison and Eston Hemings, but not their mother, who was listed in the estate inventory as an "old woman" and valued at a mere $30. Sally Hemings' manumission would clearly have reopened the scandal, since the Virginia legislature had to be petitioned in order for a freed slave to remain within the state. Sally Hemings was quietly freed by Jefferson's heirs two years later, and she lived unobtrusively with Eston and his family until her death around 1835. The U.S. census conveniently listed them all as white.

Those who insisted that there was no Hemings-Jefferson liaison claim Jefferson was often absent from Monticello as cabinet member, vice president, and president, and that the fathers of Hemings' children were Jefferson's nephews Samuel and Peter Carr—which would also explain the children's obvious physical resemblance to Jefferson. The problem with this argument is that it was the Carr brothers who were usually elsewhere. Jefferson in fact spent his annual August vacation at Monticello, and two of Hemings' children, the second Harriet and Eston, were both born in the month of May, nine months after August. Also, Madison Hemings was born just nine months after Jefferson came home for his white daughter Polly's funeral.

Despite his heralded scientific knowledge and intellectual sophistication, Jefferson was a thoroughgoing racist who considered Africans inferior to Europeans. He believed physical "amalgamation" resulted in white racial "degeneration." He believed mulattos superior to blacks because they had white blood. He claimed to oppose slavery but thought blacks unfit for freedom. He insulted the achievements of Phillis Wheatley and Benjamin Banneker. He believed the races could not live together, and that emancipation, if it came, would have to result in black colonization in Africa, the West Indies, or the western frontier of the United States. Simultaneous with these views, he was Sally Hemings' lover for nearly forty years.

Only because Jefferson was a national figure did the story of his and Sally Hemings' sexual relationship become public, and a convenient means of attacking him publicly. The accounts of the thousands upon thousands of other cases of the sexual abuse of African-American women by their white owners were never told, part of a vast conspiracy of silence about one of the hidden horrors of slavery. Because she is one of the few who is known, however, Sally Hemings has become something of a symbol for her exploited sisters. William Wells Brown published in London in 1853 *Clotel; Or, the President's Daughter: A Narrative of Slave Life in the United States,* long thought to be the first novel by an African American. Barbara Chase-Riboud published *Sally Hemings,* a popular novel, in 1974.

Thomas Jefferson was the author of the Declaration of Independence, a chief intellectual spokesperson for American liberty, and the writer of the classic words, "All men are created equal . . . endowed by their Creator with certain inalienable rights . . . among [which] are life, liberty, and the pursuit of happiness." If Jefferson the architect of freedom cannot be reconciled with Jefferson the enslaver and exploiter, perhaps he can be explained as a product of America's slave culture, a contradiction expressed by Thomas Moore in a poem in 1806:

> The weary statesman for repose hath fled
> From halls of council to his negro's shed,
> Where blest he woos some black Aspasia's grace,
> And dreams of freedom in his slave's embrace.

If you want to know more:

Fawn M. Brodie. *Thomas Jefferson: An Intimate History*. New York: Norton, 1974.

> "Of all the damsels on the green,
> On mountains or in valley,
> A lass so luscious ne'er was seen
> As Monticellian Sally."
>
>   —an anti-Jefferson political ballad

> "Let us bear in mind also that Jefferson expressed extreme aversion to miscegenation many times over the years."
>
>   —Virginius Dabney

> "The whole commerce between master and slave is a perpetual exercise of the most boisterous passions, the most unremitting despotism on the one part, and degrading submissions on the other. Our children see this, and learn to imitate it and, daily exercised in tyranny, cannot but be stamped by it with odious peculiarities."
>
>   —Thomas Jefferson (Paris, 1785)

> "On July 5, 1979, three weeks after the publication of *Sally Hemings,* the curator of Monticello tore out the staircase in Thomas Jefferson's bedroom, mentioned in the novel, which had incited too many questions from tourists."
>
>   —Barbara Chase-Riboud

What threatened Thomas Jefferson like a "firebell in the night"?

Thomas Jefferson used the phrase "a firebell in the night" to describe the fearful alarm set off when Missouri applied to enter the federal union in 1818. There had been a tradition of political equilibrium between free and slave states in the U.S. Senate. Slavery was already well-established in Missouri, but it would clearly upset the balance of power if it were admitted into the union as another slave state. Slavery suddenly became the center of a bitter national debate after being always present—but always ignored—since the Constitutional Convention of 1787.

Rep. **James Tallmadge** of New York proposed an amendment to the bill to admit Missouri which would prohibit the transport of additional slaves into the state and gradually emancipate the ten thousand already present in Missouri's total population of sixty thousand. Tallmadge's amendment passed the House of Representatives where free states held a majority, but the slaveholding South protested strongly, and the Senate insisted on compromise.

The settlement that was worked out called for the admission of Missouri, but it also admitted Maine (recently separated from Massachusetts) as a free state, thus preserving the Senate's equilibrium. Even more important, the new act forbade the extension of slavery north of Missouri's southern border, that is, the line 36 degrees and 30 minutes north latitude. This successfully barred slavery from the North until this Missouri Compromise of 1820 was replaced by the Kansas-Nebraska Act of 1834.

The crisis of confrontation between slavery and freedom was, thanks to compromise, avoided. But all the internal American contradictions remained, so resolution was merely postponed. Jefferson, himself a prominent slaveholder, recognized the battle over Missouri for just what it was, a "firebell in the night," an anxiety-producing wake-up call, sounding the alarm for an inevitable national conflagration.

If you want to know more:

Glover Moore. *The Missouri Compromise, 1819–1821.* Lexington, Ky.: University of Kentucky Press, 1953.

"If a dissolution of the union must take place, let it be so! If civil war, which gentlemen so much threaten, must come, I only say, let it come!"

—James Tallmadge

How many slaves escaped on the Underground Railroad?

The Underground Railroad, the antebellum network of black and white abolitionists and safe houses that provided clandestine escape routes for fugitive Southern slaves on their way to the North and Canada, was secret and illegal. It therefore kept no records. There is no way of knowing, then, just how many African Americans traveled this road from slavery to freedom, but it is generally thought to be at least one hundred thousand. In addition, a great many slaves from Texas and adjoining areas slipped across the border into Mexico, but there is little documentation at all about this route, and many people are still unaware of its having existed.

William Still, a prominent black Underground Railroad conductor in Philadelphia, did keep records of those who passed through his station, and his account, first published in 1871, is a gold mine of stories about the men, women, and children who delivered themselves from bondage. One of the most unusual was Henry Brown of Richmond, Virginia, who had himself nailed into a crate and shipped via the Adams Express Company to Philadelphia. Carried by train, ferry, and wagon for twenty-six hours, the large box arrived at the antislavery office at 107 North Fifth Street. The package was opened, and to an astonished audience, Brown emerged, reached out his hand, and said, "How do you do, gentlemen?" He was forever after known as "Box" Brown.

Perhaps the most dramatic of all slave narratives is that of Ellen and William Craft, a slave couple from Georgia. She was fair-skinned enough to pass for white, and she disguised herself in men's clothes as a young Southern gentleman. William Craft pretended to be her faithful black body servant. Claiming to have a toothache, she wore a scarf to hide her beardless face, and pretending to have a broken wrist, she wore her arm in a sling, since she couldn't write.

They traveled by train and stayed in hotels in Charleston, Richmond, and Baltimore. After several dangerously close calls and almost being detected, they safely crossed out of slave territory into Philadelphia. The Crafts later told their story in a book published in London in 1860 whose title symbolizes the brave and daring enterprise of the 100,000 who risked everything in acts of self-liberation: *Running a Thousand Miles for Freedom.*

If you want to know more:

Charles L. Blockson. *The Underground Railroad: First Person Narratives of Escapes to Freedom in the North.* New York: Prentice-Hall, 1987.

"A fugitive slave while under examination was asked if his master was a Christian, to which he replied: 'No, sir, he was a member of Congress.'"
—*Madison County* (N.Y.) *Journal,* August 7, 1850

"[A fugitive slave is] a living gospel of freedom, bound in black."
—Lydia Maria Child

"[T]here was one of two things I had a right to, liberty or death. If I could not have one, I would have the other, for no man should take me alive."
—Harriet Tubman

"The riverbank will make a very good road.
The dead show you the way.
Left foot, peg foot, travelling on
Follow the drinking gourd."
　　　　　　—"Follow the Drinking Gourd"

How many slave revolts were there?

What we know primarily about African-American slave revolts is that there were many more of them, and they were
much more important, than the conventional history books
generally admit. The planter class played down slave rebellions
for two reasons: theoretically, because revolution contradicted
their myth of contented and docile slaves; and, pragmatically,
because the masters were deeply fearful that news of any one
"servile insurrection," as they were called, might inspire others.

As a result of this silence, it was not until Herbert Aptheker's
pathbreaking 1938 doctoral dissertation at Columbia University,
Negro Slave Revolts in the United States, 1526–1860, that the astonishing fact was established and documented that there were
some 250 substantive rebellions. Historians could thus begin to
correct the official view of the happy and tractable slave. Revolts
were not limited to the plantation South, but took place in the
North—whose slavery was often viewed as less harsh—as well.
There were major "conspiracies" in New York City in 1712 and
again in 1741, for which over sixty African Americans were punished in retaliation by death.

If nothing else, the historical record makes clear the slaves'
detestation of their situation. Of course not every slave was a
revolutionary, and some were even brainwashed and broken
into accepting the system that debased them. But overall, the
desire for freedom was not only never extinguished, it existed
always just below all the surfaces, and it burst into flame over

and over again, including times for which we have no knowledge because there are no records. As Aptheker's inclusive dates indicate, rebellion began as early as 1526 among slaves in a Spanish settlement in what is now South Carolina, and extended until the Civil War some 335 years later.

Aptheker calls attention to the year 1800 as a fateful and crucial one for black revolution: insurrectionists Nat Turner and **John Brown** were both born that year, rebel leader Denmark Vesey won his freedom in a lottery, and **Gabriel Prosser** led a major uprising near Richmond, Virginia.

Born about 1775, Prosser was a tall, dark-complexioned coachman owned by Thomas Prosser, a tavern keeper in Henrico County, Virginia. Influenced by revolt in San Domingo as well as by tensions between the United States and France, Prosser, along with his wife, his two brothers Martin and Solomon, and a friend, Jack Bowler, planned a large-scale rising. At least a thousand slaves, and some estimates of the number of participants ran considerably higher, were to advance in three military columns on August 30, 1800, and take the city of Richmond. The first object was to seize arms and ammunition. Their motto was that of San Domingo: "Death or Liberty." The revolt failed. The slaves were betrayed, and a terrific rainstorm, one of the worst ever to hit the area, made the roads impassable. Some forty African Americans were arrested and killed. Prosser, in hiding, was again betrayed. He was captured and hanged October 7, steadfastly refusing to discuss the insurrection.

One of the slaves who was tried, however, made the following statement to the court:

> I have nothing more to offer than what General Washington would have to offer, had he been taken by the British officers and put to trial by them. I have adventured my life in endeavoring to obtain the liberty of my countrymen and am a willing sacrifice to their cause.

An even larger insurrection, in fact the largest of them all, was planned for Bastille Day 1822 in Charleston, South Carolina, by Denmark Vesey, a onetime slave who had won $1,500 in

a lottery and purchased his freedom for $600. With the rest of
the money he set himself up a business as a carpenter. Vesey's
origins are obscure. He was familiar with Africa and the Caribbean, and may in fact have been born on St. Thomas around
1767. Two influences in particular seem to have inspired Vesey
on his road to rebellion.

One was the Haitian revolution, the victory of black slaves
over their white masters and European armies to secure their
own freedom. Vesey was in communication with San Domingo,
and may in fact have hoped for aid from there. A more immediate influence was the desire for independence on the part of
local black Methodist churches chafing under white control.
Morris Brown of Charleston was ordained by AME bishops in
Philadelphia, and in 1817, along with others, organized an African Association. The next year, some 4,500 black Methodists
withdrew from the white churches to form their own separate
body. Charleston whites reacted by shutting the black house of
worship, an oppressive act Vesey, an ardent Christian, felt
keenly.

Yet a third influence on Vesey was the Bible. He was moved
by the biblical account of God's rescue of the children of Israel
from Egyptian bondage, a story he was known often to read
aloud. In fact, there is a tradition that Vesey was actually the
model for the slave song "Go Down, Moses." Interestingly
enough—in view of Vesey's commitment to Christianity—one of
Vesey's fellow conspirators was "Gullah Jack" Pritchard, a slave
whom whites described as a "sorcerer" and who apparently had
considerable influence over those slaves with ties to African religion.

With a group of slaves, many of them literate and skilled
craftspersons, Vesey now began to plan an armed revolt.
Operating with the utmost secrecy, Vesey and the other leaders
recruited for revolt some 10,000 slaves in and around Charleston, an astonishing number. They avoided sharing their plans
with house servants because they were suspicious of their closer
ties to their white masters. Not unlike other slave plans, this one
was also betrayed, and by a domestic, just as Vesey feared. But
all the others kept silence and Vesey advanced the date from

July 15 to June 16. The crisis might have passed, but they were betrayed again. Over 125 blacks were arrested and hanged, including Denmark Vesey.

Prosser's and Vesey's "conspiracies," as history labels them, reveal the little-known breadth and depth of slave uprisings. Revolts ranged in size from one or two isolated slaves in the countryside to literally thousands in urban areas. While some were undoubtedly reacting to cruel personal treatment, most had a grand and international vision of black liberation. A few revolts were quick and spontaneous, but most were the result of careful thought, intelligent planning, and inspired leadership. Behind them was a full knowledge of the American Revolution and its ideals, as well as the successful struggle of Africans in Haiti. The killing of whites was seldom indiscriminate, with Quakers, Methodists, and others unsympathetic to slavery or decent to slaves spared.

If you want to know more:

Herbert Aptheker. *American Negro Slave Revolts,* 50th anniversary edition. New York: International Publishers, 1993.

"Brethren, arise, arise! Strike for your lives and liberties. Now is the day and the hour. Let every slave throughout the land do this, and the days of slavery are numbered. You cannot be more oppressed than you have been, you cannot suffer greater cruelties than you have already. Rather die freemen than live to be slaves. Remember that you are four million! In the name of God, we ask, are you men? Where is the blood of your fathers? Has it all run out of your veins? Awake, awake! Let your motto be resistance, resistance, resistance!"
—Henry Highland Garnet

"I heard a loud noise in the heavens and the Spirit instantly appeared to me and said the Serpent was loosened, and Christ had laid down the Yoke he had borne for the sins of man, and that I should take it on and fight against the Serpent, for the time was fast approaching when the first should be last and the last should be first."

—Nat Turner

"I can no longer bear what I have borne."

—Martin Prosser

What was the compromise on slavery and did it succeed?

Engineered through Congress by Senator **Henry Clay** of Kentucky, the Compromise of 1850 was an attempt to hold together a country fracturing and dividing over the issue of slavery. It was a poor compromise because it satisfied nobody at the time, and not only did it not work, it strengthened the resolve of both Northern antislavery abolitionists and Southern proslavery fire-eaters. Free black people so hated the Compromise that many armed themselves, pledging not to obey its fugitive slave provision. This provision was the most hated part of the law, because it required people in the free states to cooperate both in the capture of runaways and their return to bondage. To be caught helping a slave escape called for a $1,000 fine and six months in jail.

In the bill's other sections, California was admitted into the union as a free state; Utah and New Mexico were established as territories where the issue of slavery would be decided later by "popular sovereignty"; and the trade in slaves in the District of Columbia was scheduled to be abolished as of January 1, 1851. Southern extremists called for dissolution of the union because of this last provision, which they interpreted as an unwarranted and intrusive restriction on the slave system.

But the fugitive slave law was equally alienating to Northerners, many of whom were radicalized into becoming abolitionists because of it. A federal law requiring free people to aid in the capture of runaways brought "the abomination of slavery to our very door," the prominent minister **Henry Ward Beecher** said. Northerners openly defied the new law by refusing to honor it, and even by helping to rescue from slave catchers its victims, whom they now saw as prisoners of war. The law was so unpopular in the North that, for example, no one in Chicago could be found to serve as its administrator. Boston was so intent on disobeying that President Millard Fillmore threatened to send in federal troops.

If you want to know more:

Stanley W. Campbell. *The Slave Catchers: Enforcement of the Fugitive Slave Law, 1850–1860.* Chapel Hill, N.C.: University of North Carolina Press, 1970.

"The escape of the slave is a legitimate act of hostility against a government to which he owes no allegiance."
—Leonard Bacon

"The Union will not be permanent if the government is to carry out the enslavement of black men in the free cities and towns of the North."
—*New York Independent*

"If a fugitive claims your help, break the law."
—Charles Beecher

What happened in the African-American community of Christiana, Pennsylvania, in 1851?

There was widespread opposition in the North to the Fugitive Slave Law of 1850, with dramatic acts of defiance like the rescue from slave catchers in Syracuse, New York, of an escaped slave named Jerry. But the most significant resistance, and the first bloodshed, came from a small community of militant African Americans on September 11, 1851, in the southeast Pennsylvania village of Christiana, where most of the residents were white Quakers.

Edward Gorsuch, a Methodist class leader but a slave owner in Baltimore County, Maryland, heard through an informer that four slaves who had escaped from his possession were living in Christiana with William and Eliza Ann Parker, both of whom were runaways themselves. Gorsuch obtained a federal warrant under the Fugitive Slave Act in Philadelphia, and with a group of friends and relatives proceeded to Christiana, accompanied by a U.S. marshal.

A friend of William Still, the Philadelphia Underground Railroad conductor, reported Gorsuch's plans to William Parker, who insisted the group stand their ground rather than flee. At the Parkers' house, a Quaker urged Gorsuch to give up and go home, but Gorsuch swore, "I will have my property or go to hell." The confrontation was a standoff, however, until Gorsuch threatened to set fire to the house. At that point Eliza Parker sounded an alarm by blowing the dinner horn. A group of sympathetic black people appeared, fighting broke out, and Gorsuch was shot. He was then stabbed to death by several of the black women.

The paper of nearby Lancaster, Pennsylvania, headlined, "CIVIL WAR—THE FIRST BLOW STRUCK." The Parkers and Gorsuch's runaways quickly departed for Canada, where African-American abolitionist Frederick Douglass helped smuggle them across the border from Rochester to Toronto. President Millard Fillmore dispatched a company of marines to Christiana, along with a posse of 40 Philadelphia policemen. They arrested 38 suspects, 35 of whom were African American. Canada refused to extradite the fugitives.

The state began its case by charging one of the white Quakers, Castner Hanway, with treason, and bringing him to trial, ironically, in a room in Independence Hall in Philadelphia. The defense ridiculed the prosecution by asking just how three pacifist Quakers and a handful of penniless blacks armed with corn cutters could be viewed as conducting war against the United States. The case aroused enormous sympathy among free black people throughout the North, who raised funds for the defense. Hanway was acquitted and the state dropped the charges against everyone else.

In fact, however, "three pacifist Quakers and a handful of penniless blacks" had declared war on the United States through their armed resistance to a law they considered unjust. The "Christiana Riot," as history calls it, infuriated the slave-holding South and strengthened its determination to protect slavery at any price. At the same time, the incident at Christiana radicalized some Northern whites. Most important, it showed many African Americans that only force could guarantee their freedom and safety, and pushed all three groups closer to open warfare.

If you want to know more:

Thomas P. Slaughter. *Bloody Dawn: The Christiana Riot and Racial Violence in the Ante-bellum North.* New York: 1991.

> "My colored brethren, if you have not swords, I say to you, sell your garments and buy one. . . . They said that they cannot take us back to the South, but I say under the present law they can; and now I say unto you, let them only take your dead bodies."
>
> —John Jacobs, an escaped slave

Was slavery extended into the new territories?

The Kansas-Nebraska Act of 1854 was another unhappy compromise in the ongoing effort to reconcile a country that was half slave and half free. What brought the issue to a head in 1854 was the question of the status of enslaved African Americans in newly formed territories. The slaveholding South wanted to expand the area where blacks could be held in bondage. The nonslaveholding North wanted to restrict slavery to the states where it was already established.

The act created the territories of Kansas and Nebraska out of a portion of the Louisiana Purchase of 1803, but it left the question of whether they would be slave or free up to the "popular sovereignty" of the areas' white residents. While this sounded democratic, in fact it repealed the Missouri Compromise of 1820, which had prohibited slavery north of Missouri's southern border. The act therefore opened the possibility that these new territories might later enter the union as slave states. Opponents criticized Congress for relinquishing both its authority to determine where slavery would exist, and its power to stop slavery's spread.

Antislavery people fought hard but unsuccessfully against enactment. Senator Edward Everett of Massachusetts introduced a petition to Congress signed by three thousand ministers opposed to slavery's extension. The act was passed, however, and Kansas soon became a bloody battlefield. Abolitionists from New England started an Emigrant Aid Society to encourage antislavery settlers, while proslavery "Border Ruffians" from Missouri entered the territory to oppose them. In addition to this frontier warfare, on the national scene the act helped split the Democratic Party and so contributed to the rise of the Republicans as an antislavery coalition.

If you want to know more:

Charles Desmond Hart. "The Natural Limits of Slavery Expansion: Kansas-Nebraska, 1854." *Kansas Historical Quarterly* 34:1 (1968), 32–50.

"Women of the free states! the question is not, shall we remonstrate with slavery on its own soil? but are we willing to receive slavery into the free states and territories of the United States?"

—Harriet Beecher Stowe

"[The Kansas-Nebraska Act] converted more men to intransigent free-soil doctrine in two months than Garrison and Phillips had converted to Abolitionism in twenty years."

—Allen Nevins

What were minstrel shows?

Performed by white people wearing "blackface" makeup, minstrel shows began around 1830 and became the most popular form of American entertainment through most of the nineteenth century. "Blackface" was created by applying burnt cork to actors' faces, necks, and hands to make a caricature of a black person. Minstrel shows are, in fact, still performed, and their legacy is still very much with us.

Minstrelsy apparently began when Thomas "Daddy" Rice, a white entertainer who appeared in blackface, saw an old crippled black stable-hand in Cincinnati performing alone for his own amusement an awkward dance and singing a curious song:

Weel about, and turn about
And do jis so.
Ebry time I weel about
I jump Jim Crow.

Rice copied the song, the dance, and the shabby clothes, and introduced them into his act. He became an immediate popular sensation. This beginning established minstrelsy as a national craze, and "Jim Crow" apparently entered the language first as a euphemism for Negro, and later to signify the country's elaborate system of legally and socially enforced racial segregation.

Minstrelsy was influential for a number of reasons. The structure it evolved led to the forms taken later by vaudeville, variety shows, burlesque, and even Broadway musical theater. The minstrel show traditionally opened with the troupe seated in a semicircle with a master of ceremonies or interlocutor presiding over a presentation of songs, jokes, banjo solos, and sentimental ballads. The second part, or olio, consisted of unrelated solo numbers—humorous monologues or sketches, singing quartets, even performing animals. The third part was a singing and dancing skit with a negligible plot, often a Southern plantation scene. The finale, or walk-around, concluded the performance, often with a spirited cakewalk dance by the whole company.

In terms of content, minstrelsy, essentially, was white people imitating their version of the appearance, humor, manner, and speech of black people. The imitation was a vulgar caricature, so minstrels helped institutionalize racism by serving as a mechanism for social definition and control. It portrayed blacks as too ridiculous ever to be taken seriously, or it sentimentally showed them yearning for the happier days of slavery, a condition for which they were demonstrably better suited than they were for freedom and independence.

Minstrelsy had a set of stock characters, all grotesque stereotypes: the infantile, inherently comic, superstitious, lazy, buffoon darkey Sambo; the pretentious, sharply dressed, good-toothed, womanizing urban dude Zip Coon or Jim Dandy; malapropos black preachers and orators who proved that words of more than two syllables were beyond their ability to pronounce; fat mammies and sexy wenches (both acted, interestingly enough, by white men in drag); and stock scenes: nostalgic, idyllic, and carefree days on the old plantation with crooning songs and shuffling dances outside the cozy cabin door.

Tragically, minstrelsy distorted authentic African-American folk music, dance, speech, humor, and style, but it did introduce elements of black culture, however refracted, to white

American audiences. That original culture is obscured by history and perverted by mocking imitation; but historian Constance Rourke claims, "Every plantation had its talented band that could crack jokes, and sing and dance to the accompaniment of banjo and bones." **W. C. Handy,** "The Father of the Blues," who began his career playing the cornet in the band of W. A. Mahara's Minstrels in the 1890s, clearly stated that "Negroes were the origination of this form of entertainment."

One reason for minstrelsy's century-long appeal was its claim to satisfy white people's curiosity about the exotic black strangers in their midst. Minstrels often billed themselves as "Ethiopian delineators" and promised "character studies" and "lifelike" impersonations. At the white blackface singer Al Jolson's 1911 performance in *La Belle Paree,* the *New York Herald* claimed he possessed "genuine Negro unction in his speech and manner."

An irony and additional tragedy is that when African Americans themselves attempted to enter show business, occasionally before the Civil War but more likely toward the end of the century, it was conventional minstrelsy, the nation's established entertainment, in which they had to find a place for themselves—sometimes even wearing cork on their faces. These performers promoted their authentic slave origins, their personal plantation experiences, and they advertised the opportunity for whites to see genuine aspects of the lives of African Americans.

Blackface for white performers was of course a mask behind which whites could act out their racial fears and fantasies as well as be free from their inhibitions (including sexual ones) about blacks, in addition to perpetuating negative stereotypes.

If you want to know more:

Robert G. Toll. *Blacking Up: The Minstrel Show in Nineteenth-Century America.* New York: Oxford University Press, 1974.

"Some form of darkie mimicking has been the strongest musical tradition in pluralized American culture."
—Armond White

> "From 'Oh! Susanna' to Elvis Presley, from circus clowns to Saturday morning cartoons, blackface acts and words have figured significantly in white Imaginary in the United States."
>
> —Eric Lott

Who was the best-known African-American woman of the nineteenth century?

The best-known African-American woman of the nineteenth century was **Sojourner Truth.** She was born in slavery, but she reinvented herself, choosing a name which means "itinerant preacher" to match the new identity she fashioned. Sojourner was a gospel preacher, a member of a strange religious commune, a reformer, an abolitionist, and a pioneering feminist. Through it all she was herself, a tall, rawboned, dark-complexioned, strong and quiet woman, whose direct honesty and unselfconscious outspokenness made her an unforgetting speaker, in her plain Quaker garb, at the religious and reformist meetings she attended through her life.

Truth was born Isabella in Ulster County, near Kingston, New York, toward the end of the eighteenth century. Her slave parents were James and Elizabeth, and Truth grew up speaking Dutch. She later adopted a previous owner's surname, Van Wagenen. From 1810 to 1827 she was owned by John Dumont, with whom she forged a strong lifelong tie despite beatings and sexual abuse on the part of Dumont and his wife. As a young teenager, Truth married a slave named Thomas, with whom she had five children, but little is known of him and she left him as soon as she was free.

Freedom came to Truth in 1827 by New York State law, but she had left Dumont a year earlier. The same year she was converted and joined the Methodist Church in Kingston. In her new-found independence, she also discovered the courage to sue for the return of her son Peter, who had been sold South to avoid New York's emancipation law. In 1828 Truth went to New York City, where she worked as a housekeeper to earn a living, and became involved in evangelical religious circles and activities, including frequent preaching at camp meetings.

In her religious zeal, Truth came under the influence of a radical religious group, the New York Perfectionists, and of Robert Matthews, a charismatic and messianic figure who called himself the Prophet Matthias and established a religious commune in Sing Sing, New York. Truth was a devoted follower, perhaps involved in a sexual relationship with Matthias, and she remained loyal when the commune fell apart under public charges of wife-swapping and other irregularities. Truth seems not to have joined the Millerites, a millenarian group that believed that the world would end in 1843. However, on Pentecost, June 1 of that year, she took the name of Sojourner Truth and left New York City, feeling herself called by God to travel east to preach, largely to Millerites, in Long Island and Connecticut.

Truth spent time at the utopian colony in Northampton, Massachusetts, in the 1840s, and participated in various abolitionist and feminist causes. She could neither read nor write, but in 1850 she dictated her autobiography to Olive Gilbert, who published the *Narrative of Sojourner Truth,* which Truth herself sold to earn an income. Later she also sold photographs of herself, primarily at the many reform meetings she attended. The photographs were printed with the caption sentence, "I sell the shadow to support the substance."

Truth is now best remembered for one of her comments, one of her speeches, and something she did to authenticate herself. In 1850 in Faneuil Hall in Boston, Frederick Douglass, depressed and disturbed by the recent enactment of the Fugitive Slave Law, wondered aloud from the platform if the slaves must now resort to violence in order to free themselves. From the audience, Truth called out, "Frederick, is God dead?"

Her best-known speech, the historical authenticity of which is in doubt, was delivered in Akron, Ohio, in 1851. Hearing a succession of men speak against women's rights because women were considered too delicate for real political life, Truth came to the platform to describe the struggles and sufferings of her own experience, using the rhythmic refrain, "Ar'n't I a woman?" Her strength and appearance led some to doubt if Truth was in fact a woman, and she was asked to bare her breast at a meeting in Silver Lake, Indiana, in 1851. She did so with dignity and without embarrassment and said she had nursed white babies who had grown up to be better people than her detractors.

During the Civil War, Truth worked among the freed people in Washington, D.C., where she also met Abraham Lincoln. In their unusual height, plain speech, and unself-conscious lack of sophistication, they were not unlike, though the president condescended to her. Truth continued her causes and crusades, and died among Hicksite Quakers in Battle Creek, Michigan, in 1883. As historian Nell Painter points out, Truth's creativity found empowerment in the Holy Spirit to deal with and ultimately triumph over the abusive power of the rich and powerful white world.

If you want to know more:

Nell I. Painter, "Representing Truth: Sojourner Truth's Knowing and Becoming Known." *Thus Far by Faith: Readings in African-American Women's Religious Biography.* Edited by Judith Weisenfeld and Richard Newman. New York: Routledge, 1995, pp. 262–299.

"I have plowed and planted and gathered into barns, and no man could head me—and ar'n't I a woman?"
—Sojourner Truth, 1851

"In vindication of her truthfulness, she told them that she would show her breast before them, but to their shame."

—*Boston Liberator*

"If women wants rights, let her take 'em."

—Sojourner Truth

"I felt so tall within, I felt the power of a nation within me."

—Sojourner Truth

"The colored people are going to be a people."

—Sojourner Truth

"You asked me if I was of your race. I am proud to say that I am of the same race that you are, I am colored, thank God for that. I have not the curse of God upon me for enslaving human beings."

—Sojourner Truth

"I cannot read a book but I can read the people."

—Sojourner Truth

Who was the best-known conductor on the Underground Railroad?

Harriet Tubman became the best-known conductor on the clandestine Underground Railroad, making over a dozen dangerous forays into the slave South and shepherding over three hundred African Americans from slavery to freedom in the North and Canada. Illiterate but fully knowledgeable of the Bible, she used scriptural images as cover and referred to the slavocracy as Egypt, while slaves throughout the South knew her by the code name Moses. As the result of her effectiveness as a resistance fighter, the white South put a bounty of $40,000 on her head, but her rescue operations, which sometimes required walking five miles through enemy territory, were so imaginative and so courageously executed that she was never captured.

Tubman knew the secret routes from South to North, and the safe houses of the antislavery people where runaways could be concealed along her perilous journeys. There were warning signs, like colored lanterns, and passwords, like "A friend with friends" as the proper response to "Who's there?" when she knocked on the door of an abolitionist. She traveled in various disguises, and communicated with slaves through double meanings, uncomprehended by whites, in Bible verses and slave song lyrics. She never revealed her plans, knowing that some slaves could be tortured into confessing what they knew about escapes.

Tubman would gather a group of runaways and move out on a Saturday evening, hoping her charges wouldn't be missed until worktime on Monday. She traveled by night. She drugged babies to keep them from crying. She hired children to tear down descriptive "Wanted" posters she couldn't read herself. Under suspicion in a Southern town, she once bought a real railroad ticket, one for a train heading further south! She carried a revolver, not to fight off pursuing slavecatchers, but to threaten any of her own passengers who became too exhausted or too fearful to go on. She would press her pistol against a recalcitrant head, and quietly say, "Live North or die here." They always decided to keep going.

A slightly built, dark-complected woman barely five feet tall, Tubman was born Araminta Ross, sometime around 1820, in Dorchester County, on the Eastern Shore of Maryland. Her parents were Harriet Green and Benjamin Ross, both fully of African blood and owned by Edward Brodas, who bred slaves as a cash crop to sell to the Deep South. Brodas began renting Tubman out when she was five years old. She worked winding yarn, tending trap lines, and splitting rails. She later discovered she had been cheated out of freedom promised her mother, and that there was no legal redress.

As a thirteen-year-old adolescent, Tubman came to the physical defense of a fellow slave being beaten, and received a blow to her own head which nearly killed her. Her recovery took months, and she always carried the scar. As a result of the blow she suffered from blackout seizures for the rest of her life. She claimed to see visions during these sudden deep sleeps, including horrible bloody scenes from the Middle Passage. In 1844 she married John Tubman, a free black man, but he threatened to report her to her master if she ever attempted to carry out her hope for escape from bondage.

Tubman did resolve to run away when she learned that Brodas planned to sell her South, where he had sent other members of her family and where slaves were soon worked to death under unspeakable conditions. After one unsuccessful attempt (which failed because the men involved turned back), Tubman took off on her own. In 1849 she ran away, carefully working her way the ninety miles from Maryland to Pennsylvania. When she walked over the state line onto free soil, she said, "There was a glory over everything."

The Fugitive Slave Act the next year made running away far more dangerous, and advocates of freedom had literally to fight to rescue and protect those who escaped, as well as violate federal law. Tubman immediately put herself in the service of the cause. She was a radical who identified completely with John Brown, the white Calvinist extremist who plotted a war of insurrection and liberation. He always referred to her as General Tubman. Only illness kept her from participating in the Harpers Ferry raid of 1859, and at Brown's execution, Tubman called him "Christ . . . the savior of our people."

As the Civil War broke out, Tubman made her last rescue mission, but in 1861 she went South again, this time to work with the contrabands, that is, the thousands of slaves who ran away to link up with the Union army. She also served as a federal spy. On June 2, 1863, Tubman literally exercised her military generalship by helping command a Union gunboat campaign on the Combahee River in South Carolina. It was an astonishing expedition which destroyed a million dollars' worth of rebel stores, cotton, and property, and liberated over eight hundred slaves.

Tubman served Colonel Robert Gould Shaw his last meal before the great assault of the Massachusetts 54th Regiment on

Fort Wagner, July 18, 1863. She watched the battle, in which African-American troops proved their courage and worth, and she helped care for the dead and dying. The United States government never recognized Tubman's extraordinary contributions to the war, but Britain's Queen Victoria read of her exploits and sent her a silver medal.

In 1869 Tubman married Nelson Davis, a black army veteran twenty-two years her junior. She retired to her home in Auburn, New York, a house purchased inexpensively from another of her admirers, Secretary of State William Seward. She devoted herself to the AME Zion Church, of which she was a member, and the needs of the African-American aged. She died in Auburn on March 10, 1913.

Thomas Wentworth Higginson, one of the most articulate and uncompromising leaders of the abolitionist movement, said that it was meeting men and women brought out of slavery by Harriet Tubman that taught him how to be an orator. "I learned to speak," he wrote, "because their presence made silence impossible."

If you want to know more:

Earl Conrad. "I Bring You General Tubman: Sesquicentennial of Harriet Tubman's Birth," *Black Scholar* 1:3–4 (1970), 2–7.

"I never ran my train off the track and I never lost a passenger."

—Harriet Tubman

"Every time I saw a white man I was afraid of being carried away. . . . Slavery is the next thing to hell."

—Harriet Tubman

"[Harriet Tubman felt no fear] for she said she ventured only where God sent her."

—Thomas Garrett

"She was a woman of no pretensions; indeed, a more ordinary specimen of humanity could hardly be found among the most unfortunate-looking farm hands of the South. Yet in point of courage, shrewdness, and disinterested exertions to rescue her fellow-man, she was without equal."

—William Still

"Now Moses took the people by the hand,
And led them all to the promised land.
Pharaoh's army got drownded;
Oh, Mary, don't you weep."

—Negro Spiritual

"I's gwine to the free country where there ain't no slaves. I travels all that day and night up the river and follow the North Star. . . . I's hoping and praying all that time I meets up with that Harriet Tubman woman."

—Thomas Cole

"And then we saw the lightning, and that was the guns; and then we heard the thunder, and that was the big guns; and then we heard the rain falling, and that was the drops of blood falling; and when we came to get in the crops, it was dead men that we reaped."

—Harriet Tubman, on the Battle of Fort Wagner

What antislavery book became a publishing phenomenon?

Harriet Beecher Stowe's novel *Uncle Tom's Cabin*, which appeared in 1852, not only radically altered the world's view of Southern slavery, but made publishing history by becoming the most popular title of the nineteenth century. Stowe (1811–

1896) was a member of a prominent family of Congregational ministers. Her father, Lyman Beecher, was a firebrand for Calvinism; her brother, **Henry Ward Beecher,** pastor of Brooklyn's fashionable Church of the Pilgrims, was probably the most notable orator of the day; other brothers and sisters were involved in churches, schools, and abolitionism; and her husband, Calvin Stowe, was a noted biblical scholar.

Clearly, Stowe came from a family and social environment that was responsible, religious, and reformist. The whole family, according to critic Orestes Brownson, was somehow able to anticipate popular trends and appear as public leaders, a phenomenon he even labeled "Beecherism." Stowe got her idea for *Uncle Tom's Cabin* during a service of Holy Communion in a Congregational Church in Brunswick, Maine. She saw a vision of a bleeding slave, and as a Calvinist who believed that salvation could never be achieved by human striving, perceived that God would send his Kingdom only through the suffering of the oppressed.

Motivated also by outrage at the Fugitive Slave Law, and in pain over the recent death of her child, Stowe began to write. *Uncle Tom's Cabin* appeared in weekly installments in the *National Era* from June 5, 1851, to April 1, 1852. It was published in book form in two volumes by John P. Jewett of Boston, on March 22, 1852, in an edition of 5,000 copies. They sold out in two days. In the next eight weeks, sales rose to 50,000. Three power presses worked twenty-four hours a day and over a hundred binders labored to try to meet the public demand for books. By September, sales were at 150,000, and by year's end at 300,000.

Overseas, the reception was even more remarkable. In England, close to a million and a half books were sold the first year, more than three times as many copies sold as in the United States. A special Sunday school edition priced at a shilling put copies in the hands of British children. In a few years, *Uncle Tom's Cabin* had been translated into over forty languages, including Armenian, Icelandic, Welsh, and Low Dutch (for Dutch-dialect-speaking residents of the Spice Islands). There were sixty-seven known editions in Italian alone. There were also *Uncle Tom's Cabin* songs (twenty in 1852) and thirty proslavery novels written in rejoinder, and as a play *Uncle Tom* was performed somewhere every year all over the world well into the twentieth century.

From a modern perspective, *Uncle Tom's Cabin* is a sentimental novel of Victorian piety, and Uncle Tom himself has become a symbol of Negro subservience. How is it possible that no other book before or since has ever had the social impact of Stowe's novel? The arrogance of the slave South, particularly after the Fugitive Slave Law, stirred in the North and West a sense of basic injustice. Stowe's story, perhaps because of its melodrama, struck a chord about the cruelty of the slave system, even among white people who had no particular sympathy for black people, slave or free. White people began to comprehend that slavery was a moral evil, and not merely a necessary economic system, particularly in a supposedly free and democratic society. Speaking to the dehumanization of chattel slavery, the book's first subtitle was *The Man Who Was a Thing*, which became *Life Among the Lowly*.

Also, the novel was written in a more religious time. Uncle Tom appeared in the 1850s not as weak but as a Christian and a Stoic martyr who triumphed, Christ-like, through his acceptance of his suffering. He appeared as heroic to many people until George Alexander McGuire, a black nationalist, first identified him with servility in a 1920 speech calling for black consciousness, militancy, and nationalism. "The Uncle Tom nigger has to go!" McGuire said. Uncle Tom, ever since, has been synonymous not only with submissiveness and humility, but with accommodationism and the perpetuation of a servile mentality among African Americans.

The South reacted to *Uncle Tom's Cabin* with indignation, claiming Stowe's portrait of slavery was untrue. Stowe countered with *A Key to Uncle Tom's Cabin,* a book which documented the facts of her story. The South responded by publicly burning copies of her novel and arresting anyone caught with a copy. Stowe wrote another novel, *Dred, A Tale of the Great Dismal Swamp,* published in 1856, based on the life of the great slave insurrectionist Nat Turner, but that book is little known or read today, and as an author Stowe is as relegated to a reputation for melodrama as Uncle Tom is to subservience.

But Stowe should not be entirely disparaged, given what she accomplished in her own time in her own way. While slavery still existed, she helped millions of white Americans see its horrors, and she supplied white people with a view of the moral basis which led to slavery's overthrow. The international popularity of *Uncle Tom's Cabin* helped keep foreign nations on the side of the Union during the Civil War. What actual role did she and her famous book have in ending the slave system? When Stowe visited the White House in 1862 to meet President Abraham Lincoln, his first words reportedly were, "So you're the little woman who wrote the book that started this great war!"

If you want to know more:

Joan Hendrick, *Harriet Beecher Stowe: A Life*. New York: Oxford University Press, 1994.

"It is humiliating to think that there should be in the church of Christ men and ministers who should need to be reminded that the laws of their Master are above human laws which come in conflict with them."
　　　　　　　　　　　　　　　　—Harriet Beecher Stowe

"No ruler of Great Britain or of France could have recognized a Confederacy whose corner-stone rested on the mutilated body of 'Uncle Tom.'"
　　　　　　　　　　　　　　　　—Edward Channing

"My view of Christianity is such that I think no man can consistently profess it without throwing the whole weight of his being against this monstrous system of injustice that lies at the foundation of all our society."
　　　　　　　　　　　　　　　　—Harriet Beecher Stowe

> "*Uncle Tom's Cabin* did more than any other one thing to arouse the fears of the Southerners and impel them to fight for independence. On the other hand, the Northern boys who read it in the fifties were among those who voted for Abraham Lincoln in 1860 and followed the flag of the Union from Bull Run to Appomattox."
>
> —Edward Channing

Who was Dred Scott and why was his legal case so important?

Dred Scott was born to slave parents in Southampton County, Virginia, around 1795, where he was owned by Captain Peter Blow. Over the years, Scott was sold several times, and he traveled with one of his masters, Dr. John Emerson, to the free state of Illinois and the free territory of Wisconsin. Because of his travels, antislavery activists decided to use Scott to test legally the popularly held notion "once free, always free," that is, the belief that as soon as a slave sets foot on free soil he automatically became free forever, even if he was later returned to a slave state.

Therefore, in April 1846 a suit for Scott's freedom was filed in the Circuit Court of St. Louis, Missouri. Scott, a dark-complexioned man less than five feet tall, was illiterate and signed the necessary papers with his mark, an X. The case took its time moving through various courts, but *Scott* v. *Sandford* was finally decided on March 6, 1857, when Chief Justice Roger B. Taney of the U.S. Supreme Court delivered the opinion of the justices, a majority of whom were proslavery Southern Democrats.

Taney announced that the federal courts had no jurisdiction over Scott because as a slave of African descent, he was not a citizen of the United States. So his bid for freedom was denied. But the Court went further: it said Scott had in fact remained a slave even when he entered a free state, the reason being that the Missouri Compromise of 1820 was unconstitutional. Congress had no right to limit the expansion of slavery into the territories, the Court held, and slave owners' rights to their slave property were protected by the Constitution, even though Congress had voted to outlaw slavery north of Missouri.

In his decision, Taney wrote:

> [Slaves] had for more than a century before been regarded as beings of an inferior order, and altogether unfit to associate with the white race, either in social or political relations; and so far inferior that they had no rights the white man was bound to respect.

The Court's decision created a national sensation. Abolitionists were furious because the case nullified a compromise and opened the entire country to slavery's expansion. The proslavery South now wanted legislation to protect slavery everywhere. The division between Northern and Southern Democrats led directly to Lincoln's election in 1860 and Southern secession.

African Americans reacted to the *Dred Scott* decision with anger and alarm. The State Convention of Ohio Colored Men voted the statement: "If the Dred Scott dictum be the true expression of the law of the land, then are the founders of the American Republic convicted by their descendants of base hypocrisy, and colored men absolved from all allegiance to a government which withdraws all protection."

Dred Scott himself died of tuberculosis in St. Louis the next year, on September 17, 1858, fully aware that the case bearing his name had exploded like a bombshell all around the country. But he died too soon to see the bombshells of Civil War, which, unlike the fond hopes for the Missouri Compromise, were required to settle the issue of slavery once and for all.

If you want to know more:

Walter Ehrlich. "The Origins of the Dred Scott Case." *Journal of Negro History* 59:2 (1974), 132–142.

"This very attempt to blot out forever the hope of an enslaved people may be one necessary link in the chain of events preparatory for the complete overthrow of the whole slave system."

—Frederick Douglass

"[In Chief Justice Taney's] zeal to prove that the Fathers of our country held the Negro to have 'no rights which the white man is bound to respect,' he has not only denied the rights of man and the liberties of mankind, but has not left a foothold for the liberty of the white man to rest upon."

—The *New York Anti-Slavery Standard*

"The Supreme Court has made Illinois a slave state."

—Abraham Lincoln

Who was the most prominent African-American man of the nineteenth century?

As the African-American leader of both the antebellum abolitionist movement and of the struggle for black rights following the Civil War, Frederick Douglass was the most prominent African-American of the nineteenth century. He was an orator of unmatched eloquence, his autobiography represents the slave narrative at its best, and he always stayed true to principle despite the cost, including his unqualified support for women's rights and women's suffrage.

Douglass was born a slave, probably in 1818, in Tuckahoe, Maryland. He took February 14 as his birthday because he recalled, as a child, his mother referring to him as her valentine. His mother was a slave who visited him only infrequently, and apparently died young. His father was an unknown white man, perhaps Anthony Aaron, manager of the ten-thousand-acre Edward Lloyd plantation, or perhaps Lloyd himself. "Slavery has no recognition of fathers," Douglass once remarked, "as none of families." Douglass was raised by Betsy Bailey, his strong and resourceful maternal grandmother.

In 1825 Douglass was sent to Baltimore to the household of Anthony Aaron's daughter, Sophia Auld. She was kind to the child, recognized his intelligence, and taught him to read, an achievement crucial to his development. Her husband, Hugh Auld, always ambivalent about Douglass, was entirely correct in predicting that "if you teach [him] . . . how to read the Bible, there will be no keeping him."

Sent back to the plantation, Douglass' independent spirit led his owner to hire him out to Edward Covey, a notorious "breaker" of recalcitrant slaves. Douglass endured the pressures and systematic beatings until one day in 1834, when he took on Covey in an epic wrestling match. Standing up for himself and fighting back was, Douglass said, "the turning point" in his life as a slave: "I was nothing before; I am a man now." Having discovered how to be a man, his next step was to discover how to become a free one.

Disguised as a sailor, Douglass escaped on September 3, 1838, and made his way via New York to New Bedford, Massachusetts. He married Anna Murray, an illiterate free black woman who had provided money to aid his flight. Taking the name Douglass to avoid recognition and possible capture as a runaway, he settled in as a laborer until a fateful day, August 16, 1841, when he attended a meeting on Nantucket of the Massachusetts Anti-Slavery Society. Douglass was invited to the platform, where his simple speech telling his own personal story and his firsthand accounts mesmerized **William Lloyd Garrison** and the other white abolitionist leaders. More important, Douglass began to find his own voice as one of the great orators of the century as he discovered immediately that his true vocation was to be a spokesperson for the millions of his brothers and sisters still in bondage.

It was a natural extension of Douglass' public speaking as an agent of the Massachusetts Anti-Slavery Society for him to tell his story in a book. *The Narrative of the Life of Frederick Douglass, An American Slave* was published in 1845 and sold for 50 cents.

It was the first of his three autobiographies, each written as his thinking developed and as he felt able to reveal more. Some who heard the magnificent-looking and magnificent-sounding Douglass doubted that he could be a product of the slave system, and the book was a response to their doubts. The *Narrative* was an immediate success, selling thirty thousand copies in five years. It was also published in Britain, and translated into French.

The book, however, left Douglass the escaped slave more visible and thus more vulnerable. As soon as it was published, he prudently set sail away from the United States for the United Kingdom, where he was lionized by reformers and abolitionists, and where he personally experienced the freer air of a less racist society. British friends arranged to buy Douglass' freedom for $750, and they also raised money to fulfill his hope to establish his own newspaper.

The North Star, founded by Douglass in Rochester, New York, in 1847, with Martin R. Delany, was his declaration of independence both personally and intellectually. He had found a mentor in William Lloyd Garrison, editor of the abolitionist *Liberator,* a publication which had a place in his heart "second only to the Bible." Also, he had found a philosophy he could follow in the idealistic Garrisonian disavowal of corrupt and corrupting politics, along with a contempt for the U.S. Constitution as a proslavery document. Now, however, coming under the influence of the equally liberal but more political abolitionist Gerrit Smith, Douglass began to see politics as a viable way to change things, and to perceive the Constitution, if correctly interpreted, as a charter for human justice which slavery had violated. The white abolitionist establishment that first befriended Douglass soon found him not quite humble enough to their taste, and so his move to even greater self-determination was not everywhere appreciated, but he knew the antislavery movement had to be black-led.

Douglass' switch to political activism immediately involved him in a variety of movements. In 1848 he was present at Seneca Falls, New York, for the women's rights conference, where he became one of the few men to support enfranchising women, a position which cost him some influence as an abolitionist. In 1852 he supported the Free Soil Party, forerunner of the antislavery Republicans, and on July 4 that year he made one of his most memorable speeches, asserting the emptiness that America's Fourth of July independence commemoration had for African Americans. He was active in the Underground Railroad, and at least four hundred escaped slaves passed through his station in Rochester, one of the last American stops before Canada and freedom.

Douglass was well acquainted with John Brown, but Brown failed to convince him to join the slave insurrection he expected to ignite when he attacked the federal arsenal at Harpers Ferry. At Brown's capture and arrest, the governor of Virginia requested that President James Buchanan send Douglass to Virginia for trial. Douglass wired his son to destroy incriminating papers in his desk in Rochester. He slipped into Canada and sailed for England, till the outbreak of war left Brown's trial forgotten, though Brown's body was vividly remembered in the Union army's most compelling marching song.

Douglass was enthusiastic in his support of the war, especially for raising black regiments and enlisting colored troops. "Men of color, to arms!" became his familiar battle cry. His own sons enrolled in the Massachusetts 54th, and Douglass hoped for an officer's commission, but none came; the Union army was not yet ready to accept African Americans as officers.

When the war was won and slavery abolished, Garrison disbanded his Anti-Slavery Society, believing its work was done. But Douglass, who had never separated the issues of slavery and civil rights, knew that the freed slaves were powerless without political enfranchisement. He believed, with most Americans, that the democratic power to vote was determinative, and that with it, the freed slaves would be secure in shaping their own destinies. Douglass was the quintessential integrationist, opposing emigration and nationalism, and always fighting for black people to secure their full rights as American citizens.

In 1872 Douglass moved to Washington, where he received several governmental appointments from the Republican Party, which he served faithfully. "The Republican Party is the ship," he said, "all else is the sea." He was Marshal of the District of Columbia, Recorder of Deeds in the District, and then U.S. minister to Haiti. Douglass felt that none of these roles was quite worthy of his ability and distinction, but the higher recognition and accolades he looked for never came.

Douglass had always been close to women, and at least two of his fellow abolitionists, the Englishwoman Julia Griffiths and the German Ottilia Assing, were undoubtedly his lovers as well as his compatriots. After Anna Douglass' death, Douglass in 1884 married Helen Pitts, a white woman, despite criticism from both the black and white communities. Frederick Douglass died in Washington on February 20, 1895.

If you want to know more:

William S. McFeely. *Frederick Douglass.* New York: Norton, 1991.

"Who would be free must themselves strike the blow."
—Frederick Douglass

"I stand here tonight to advance in my humble way, the unrestricted and complete Emancipation of every slave in the United States whether claimed by loyal or disloyal masters. This is the lesson the Hour."
—Frederick Douglass, 1862

"To those who have suffered in slavery, I can say, I, too, have suffered. . . . To those who have battled for liberty, brotherhood, and citizenship I can say, I, too, have battled."
—Frederick Douglass

"If there is no struggle, there is no progress."
—Frederick Douglass

"Those who profess to favor freedom, and yet deprecate agitation, are men who want crops without plowing up the ground."

—Frederick Douglass

Who is probably the white person most respected by African Americans?

Only exceptional white Americans have gained the full respect of African Americans over the years: William Lloyd Garrison, leader of the white antislavery movement; **Thaddeus Stevens** in the House of Representatives and **Charles Sumner** in the U.S. Senate, both of them abolitionists and leaders of the Radical Republican fight for black rights during Reconstruction; **Eleanor Roosevelt,** who pressured the federal government on behalf of black interests beginning in the 1930s. All were important leaders in the struggle for social justice.

But the white person probably most respected, even revered, by African Americans has been John Brown, a single-minded religious zealot, a converted pacifist who came to believe that only violence could put down the Slave Power. Brown led an unsuccessful armed revolt against the federal arsenal in Harpers Ferry, Virginia, in 1859, hoping and intending to ignite a massive slave uprising throughout the South.

Brown was born May 9, 1800, in East Torrington, Connecticut, to Owen Brown, a cobbler, and Ruth Mills Brown. Both were strict Calvinists who were imbued with strong antislavery convictions from New England Congregational ministers, including Jonathan Edwards, Jr., who believed slavery was a sin against God. This was a view that came both to define and to motivate John Brown's life.

A few months after Brown's birth, his family joined the Torrington church where Lemuel Haynes, an African American, had once served as minister. Brown was a belligerent child and a poor student, perhaps because of his mother's early death. He grew up austere and humorless, as serious as only the product of a Puritan culture can be. An eye inflammation kept him from pursuing private studies necessary to prepare him for Amherst College and study for the ministry.

Brown's adult life was a consistent financial disaster, as he failed at the myriad of business speculations and enterprises he undertook. At one point he was forced to declare bankruptcy, and all the federal court left him were a few personal possessions, but these included eleven Bibles. In terms of antislavery, Brown admired Garrison's radical abolitionism, particularly his opposition to colonization, but as both a student and an adherent of Reformed theology, he rejected Garrisonian perfectionism as naively ignoring the doctrines of sin and election.

John Brown consulted with black activists like **Henry Highland Garnet** and Frederick Douglass, and seemed to be one of the few white abolitionists who dealt personally with African Americans on a basis of true social equality. He was living in the Adirondacks in upstate New York in a racially integrated settlement, on land acquired from **Gerrit Smith,** his fellow abolitionist, when he was confronted by the Kansas-Nebraska Act of 1854. With the presidency, the U.S. Senate, and the Supreme Court all in proslavery hands, Brown believed the Act to be part of a Southern conspiracy to open the American West to the expansion of slavery.

In Kansas, law-abiding free-soil advocates, many of whom were sent out by the New England Emigrant Aid Society, clashed bitterly with proslavery "Border Ruffians" who invaded from Missouri. "The great drama will open here," one of Brown's sons accurately predicted, and Brown himself traveled to the territory eager to do what he perceived to be the Lord's work. A bogus Kansas legislature declared that only proslavery men could sit on juries, and further decreed that circulating abolitionist literature would be punished by hard labor in prison. When Missouri terrorists sacked the abolitionist town of Lawrence, Kansas, and when news arrived of the vicious beating on the floor of the U.S. Senate of Charles Sumner of Massachusetts by proslavery Preston Brooks of South Carolina, Brown could contain himself no longer.

Along the Pottawatomie Creek, near the settlement of Osawatomie, Kansas, on May 23 through 26, 1856, Brown and a small band of followers killed five proslavery men, one less than the six abolitionists who had been murdered earlier. There was now open guerrilla warfare in southeast Kansas, and John Brown emerged as the Puritan warrior-saint, God's avenging angel of death on a grim mission to destroy the evil of slavery with the sword of righteousness. In the words of **W. E. B. Du Bois,** the old man's "blow freed Kansas by plunging it into civil war, and compelling men to fight for freedom which they had vainly hoped to gain by political diplomacy."

President James Buchanan offered a reward of $250 for Brown's capture, but no officer of the law dared arrest him, owing to the vast popular support he enjoyed after his next move: an incursion into Missouri, from where he brought out a family of slaves. Concealing his role in the Kansas killings, Brown next persuaded wealthy but high-minded Boston brahmins to support his secret plan to carry the antislavery war into the South itself. The plan evolved through several forms. He envisioned the Allegheny Mountains as a "Subterranean Pass Way," apparently a kind of wholesale Underground Railroad. In a covert meeting in Canada, he drew up a constitution for a revolutionary government, presumably for a new state in the mountains of what is now West Virginia, a state to be populated by slaves as they fled the plantations. All the tinder needed, he believed, was the spark.

The old man himself lit the flame. Gathering a Provisional Army of 21 recruits, consisting of 5 blacks and 16 whites, Brown seized the federal arsenal at Harpers Ferry at four A.M. on Sunday, October 16, 1859. Several people were killed on both sides. Dangerfield Newby, an escaped slave who hoped to free his wife and children, had the ears cut off his dead body as souvenirs by whites driven to frenzy by the idea of black people with guns. Brown's assault stalled. The slaves did not rise up. The governor of Virginia hurried Marines to Harpers Ferry, under Colonel Robert E. Lee and his aide J. E. B. Stuart. Brown was wounded and captured.

At this point an extraordinary thing happened. John Brown

suddenly realized he could do even more for his sacred cause by speaking to the national audience now focused on his trial, and, given its inevitable outcome, by dying bravely as a martyr for the slaves' freedom. Brown's rhetoric in court was eloquent, powerful, and alive with moral fervor:

> I believe that to interfere as I have done—as I have always freely admitted I have done—in behalf of His despised poor, was not wrong, but right. Now if it is deemed necessary that I should forfeit my life for the furtherance of the ends of justice, and mingle my blood further with the blood of my children and with the blood of millions in this slave country whose rights are disregarded by wicked, cruel, and unjust enactment, I say let it be done.

As Du Bois points out, Brown turned the tables and put the South and slavery on trial. At first, an attempt was made by his supporters to convince the court that he was insane, in the hope of saving his life. Unfortunately, this is a myth which continues to be repeated by those who cannot imagine his single-mindedness. Brown may well have been fanatic, self-righteous, even messianic, but he was not crazy. His calm demeanor, as if he had been born for this trial and execution, forced white people in the North, after they had caught their breath, into a raised level of consciousness about what was now required. "The slave will be delivered by the shedding of blood," **Gerrit Smith** now realized.

On December 2, 1859, the day of Brown's hanging, Aaron Stevens, one of his followers, said, "Good-by, Captain, you are going to a better land." Brown replied, "I know I am." He was escorted to a wagon that bore his coffin, and he sat on the coffin as he was driven to the gallows. In abolitionist communities in the North, businesses were closed, flags were flown at half-mast, church bells were rung, and memorial services were conducted. In Concord, Massachusetts, Henry David Thoreau organized "Services for the Death of a Martyr," just at two o'clock, the hour of execution, and said, "Let us honor you by our admiration, rather than by short-lived praises, and, if nature aid us, by our emulation of you."

Because of John Brown, the stakes for the abolition of slavery were now different—and higher. The war that was necessary to end slavery and that Brown had prophesied soon came, and though he did not live to see it, his name was heard over and over through the course of the Civil War. The 33rd Massachusetts, a company of white troops, was one of the provost guard regiments that was the last to leave Atlanta when Sherman made retreat impossible by burning his bridges and setting off on the momentous march to the sea. As the whole city of Atlanta went up in flames and smoke in a grand spectacle of fiery destruction, the 33rd's band struck up the Federal army's most popular song, "John Brown's Body."

If you want to know more:

Stephen B. Oates. *To Purge This Land with Blood: A Biography of John Brown.* New York: Harper and Row, 1970.

> "Talk! Talk! Talk! That will not free the slaves. . . . What is needed is action! Action!"
>
> —John Brown

> "If I were asked to point out . . . the man in all this world I think most truly a Christian, I would point to John Brown."
>
> —Gerrit Smith

> "You may dispose of me very easily—I am nearly disposed of now; but this question—this Negro question, I mean; the end of that is not yet."
>
> —John Brown, at his trial

> "Harpers Ferry is the Lexington of today."
>
> —Wendell Phillips

"I guess I'll go with the old man."
> —Shields Green, a fugitive slave, when Frederick Douglass tried to talk him out of accompanying Brown to Harpers Ferry

"I, John Brown, am now quite certain that the crimes of this guilty land will never be purged away but with blood."
> —John Brown's last message, written the day he died.

"[John Brown, a white man] is, in sympathy, a black man, and as deeply interested in our cause as though his own soul had been pierced with the iron of slavery."
> —Frederick Douglass

"It was not John Brown that died at Charles Town. It was Christ, it was the savior of our people."
> —Harriet Tubman

What caused the Civil War?

The Civil War was a defining moment in African-American history. Although President Abraham Lincoln and most of the white population of the North stated clearly, and wanted to believe, that the single purpose of the war was to preserve the federal union, black people knew that the South's unyielding commitment to chattel slavery was the real reason underlying its claims to states' rights, independence, and Southern "freedom." They knew, also, well before the administration and the white public knew, that the two sections of the country could never be reconciled unless the war destroyed the entire slave system.

When Lincoln became president on the Republican ticket in 1860, Southerners, who had essentially controlled the federal government since the nation's inception, simply refused to accept an administration they disagreed with, even though it had been elected to office legally and democratically. As a momentous consequence, the state legislature of South Carolina met on December 20, 1860, and voted unanimously to secede from the United States. On February 4, 1861, in Montgomery, Alabama, representatives of the six cotton-producing states—Alabama, Georgia, Florida, Louisiana, Mississippi, and South Carolina—agreed to organize themselves into a new nation, the Confederate States of America.

Historians have long debated the causes of this break, whether it was necessary and inevitable, whether it was "an irrepressible conflict." They proposed all kinds of reasons for the war: the competition to control the West and thus the future of the country; the North's small farmers versus the South's large plantations; the North's growing industrial capitalism versus the South's unchanging agricultural economy; the democratic culture of Northern puritanism versus the aristocratic culture of Southern cavaliers—all unresolved contradictions which sprang not only from America's own origins, but from the two sides in the English Civil War from which both were descended.

All theoretical discussions became academic on April 12, 1861, however, when South Carolinians opened fire on Fort Sumter, the United States' installation in Charleston Harbor. Firing on the American flag, troops, and fortifications was an act of open treason, and President Lincoln could only respond accordingly, even though his reaction cost more defections from the Union.

What the dissolution of the Union, the creation of the Confederacy, and the war were all fundamentally about was spelled out by Alexander Stephens, the Confederacy's vice president, in a speech in March 1861, a month after the Montgomery meeting and a month before Fort Sumter:

> The Confederacy's foundations are laid, its cornerstone rests on the great truth, that the Negro is not equal to the white man; that slavery subordination to a superior race is his natural and moral condition. This, our new government, is the first, in the history of the world, based upon this great physical, philosophical, and moral truth.

Southern partisans called it "The War of Northern Aggression." Abolitionists called it "The War of the Slaveholders' Rebellion." Those who pretended the conflict was value-free called it simply "The War Between the States." However the Civil War's name reflects the assumptions of those doing the naming, Stephens' statement makes clear that while the North may have believed it was fighting to preserve the Union, the South, like African Americans both slave and free, knew better than Lincoln himself that the nation could not exist "half slave and half free."

If you want to know more:

David Blight. *Frederick Douglass' Civil War: Keeping Faith in Jubilee.* Baton Rouge: Louisiana State University Press, 1989.

> "Some speak as if abolition of slavery were the object, but putting down the gigantic conspiracy against the government is it. That and nothing else."
> —*New York Tribune,* July 7, 1861

> "Our national sin has found us out."
> —*Douglass' Monthly,* May 1861

> "I come from another field—the country of the slave. They have got their liberty—so much good luck to have slavery partly destroyed; not entirely. I want it root and branch destroyed."
> —Sojourner Truth

Did African Americans fight in the Civil War?

The North's attitude toward black soldiers reflected the national intolerance and racism concerning people of color, along with its ambivalent views on the future of slavery as an institution. At the beginning of the Civil War, therefore, African Americans were not allowed in the U.S. Army at all, even though black men had fought in the American Revolution. By the war's end, however, there were nearly 200,000 black soldiers, and 10,000 black sailors, over 10 percent of the Union's fighting force. And they did fight: 16 African-American enlisted men received the Medal of Honor, and 8 won the Navy Medal of Honor.

Direct black involvement in the military began a month after South Carolinians fired on the federal installation at Fort Sumter. Official government policy was to return escaped slaves to their owners. At Fortress Monroe, near Norfolk, Virginia, in May 1861, however, three escaped slaves made their way to the Union encampment. General Benjamin Butler, a radical abolitionist, took the South at its word that these men were merely property, and so he declared that as such they were the legitimate contraband of war. Also, with a degree of irony, Butler took Virginia at its word that it was a foreign country, and so he argued that the Fugitive Slave Law did not apply. Butler put the three "contrabands" to work in the camp bakery. By July the gates were open, and over a thousand slaves had found refuge behind Union lines.

The government at first declared that contrabands be returned to their masters, largely because President Abraham Lincoln was obsessed with trying to keep the border states from joining the Confederacy, which he believed they would do if the federal government held a strong antislavery position. As the war progressed, however, blacks by the thousands—men, women, and children—fled for freedom to Yankee lines wherever they could find them. This created problems of housing, rations, health, and sometimes most difficult of all, clogged roads.

Each Union army below the Mason-Dixon line had, in effect, then, its own attendant army of blacks. The most sympathetic and progressive commanders enlisted the men into military units. Others put men and women to work as laborers, cooks, laundresses, and teamsters. The unsympathetic tried to ignore them all, and sometimes actually abandoned these escaped slaves to Confederate capture—or worse.

The earliest African-American unit seems to have been the 1st South Carolina Volunteer Infantry (African Descent), raised by General David Hunter in May 1862. Hunter commanded the Department of the South and urgently needed soldiers on the Sea Islands. Lincoln reprimanded Hunter, and these runaway, freed, and confiscated slaves in Federal uniforms were disbanded by presidential order. Out of the remnant, however, came the first black regiment actually mustered into the U.S. Army. It was commanded by the remarkable **Thomas Wentworth Higginson:** Unitarian minister, abolitionist, supporter of John Brown, and, after the war, confidant of poet Emily Dickinson.

The first organized black troops to engage the enemy were apparently the 1st Regiment of Kansas Colored Infantry in an October 1862 skirmish in Missouri. That fall, Ben Butler created three battalions of Louisiana Native Guards out of the Corps d'Afrique. These scattered forces were eventually regularized and reorganized into the United States Colored Troops (USCT). They were all segregated units under white officers, although as a rule, the noncommissioned officers were African American.

Two shifts in Northern thinking affected what happened next. First, it became clear that the war was not going to end quickly or easily, and that its outcome might well depend on a lengthy confrontation between the men and matériel of both sides. If it came to that test, the North could win simply by hanging on long enough. It could afford to sustain more losses—of matériel because it was more industrialized, of men because it had a larger population, especially if one added the numerous black men who were eager to fight the slavocracy.

The second shift, not unrelated to the first, was Lincoln's decision to make freeing the slaves a war aim in addition to the preservation of constitutional government. Lincoln himself was personally a gradualist on the slavery question, believing owners should be compensated for their loss of property, and he was a conservative on the question of race, believing freed blacks should be colonized in Africa.

Under ideological pressure from abolitionists, however, and in an attempt to undermine the Confederacy by weakening its labor supply, Lincoln, in his capacity not as president but as commander-in-chief, issued an Emancipation Proclamation on January 1, 1863. It was in many ways a hollow document, since it claimed to free slaves in the rebellious states, over which the president at that point had no authority! In other words, the proclamation in fact freed nobody, and the many thousands of slaves who left their homes under circumstances of great danger in fact freed themselves in the nation's greatest historical act of self-liberation.

The proclamation did specifically open the U.S. armed forces to black men. The first governor to call for an African-American regiment was John A. Andrew of Massachusetts, and he did so just days after the president's proclamation. Andrew fully understood the symbolic importance of what he was doing, because many white people did not believe black men could or would fight. The first regiment of free blacks organized in the North was the 54th Massachusetts, well-known now because the film *Glory* showed its valiant attack on Fort Wagner in Charleston Harbor on July 18, 1863. The battle for Fort Wagner proved African Americans' fighting ability, but it was a truth that would have to be re-established in World Wars I and II.

African-American soldiers performed well in such Civil War battles as Overton Hill and Chafin's Farm in Virginia; Honey Hill, South Carolina; Nashville, Tennessee; and the infamous debacle at the Crater outside Petersburg, Virginia. Women played roles: Susie King Taylor of South Carolina was a nurse, laundress, and teacher. Elizabeth Bowser of Richmond, a slave in the Confederate White House, was actually a Union spy. The war had its high moments: Martin R. Delany, physician, novelist, and emigrationist, was promoted to the rank of major, the first black field officer. And there were low moments: Sergeant William Walker of the 3rd South Carolina Colored Troops protested the fact that black soldiers were paid only $7 a month while white soldiers were getting $13. He said he could no longer serve. Walker was court-martialed and shot.

The very existence of black troops created several effects. Free blacks in the North felt pride at their involvement in the war. White Northerners, if not modified in their racism, were grateful for the black contribution. White Southerners were outraged at the black military presence and never forgave the North for what they called an imposition of Negro rule. The African-American soldiers themselves experienced a new sense of dignity and worth, not only at smashing slavery but in restoring constitutional government, under which they hoped to see changes following the war.

But perhaps most affected were the South's four million slaves. To see liberators was one thing. To see liberators in the blue uniforms of the United States Army was another. But to see government liberators with black faces was a deeply emotional experience for all African Americans whether slave or free. What the war meant was dramatized in its closing days when U.S. Colored Troops marched smartly into Richmond, the Confederate capital, singing "John Brown's Body." They halted at the city's slave pens, where black men, women, and children for sale had been herded like cattle. The soldiers were surrounded by slaves who spontaneously broke into song, a spiritual whose double meaning became actualized at that very moment, "Slavery Chain Done Broke at Last."

If you want to know more:

Benjamin Quarles, *The Negro in the Civil War.* Boston: Little, Brown, 1953.

"As soon as we took a slave from his claimant, and placed a musket in his hand, he began to fight for the freedom of others."
—Colonel Oliver T. Beard, 48th New York Infantry

"Boys, the old flag never touched the ground."
—Sergeant William Carney of the 54th Massachusetts,
awarded the Medal of Honor for bravery
at the Battle of Fort Wagner

Oh, we're the bully soldiers
Of the First of Arkansas.
We are fighting for the Union,
We are fighting for the law.
We can hit a Rebel further
Than a white man ever saw.
As we go marching on.

We are done with hoeing cotton,
We are done with hoeing corn;
We are Colored Yankee soldiers now,
As sure as you are born.
When the master hears us shouting
He will think it's Gabriel's horn.
As we go marching on.
—1st Arkansas Colored Regiment's marching song

"Blood was water, money was leaves, and life was only common air until one flag floated over a Republic without a master and without a slave."
—Robert Ingersoll

"So rally, boys, rally, let us never mind the past.
We had a hard road to travel, but our day is coming at last.
For God is for the right, and we have no need to fear.
The Union must be saved by the colored volunteer."
—"Give Us a Flag"

"While Lincoln continued to hesitate about the legal, constitutional, moral, and military aspects of the matter, the relentless movement of the self-liberated fugitives into the Union lines [meant the slaves] took their freedom into their own hands."
—Vincent Harding

What happened at Fort Pillow?

Fort Pillow was a small earthwork on a bluff overlooking the Mississippi River, about sixty miles north of Memphis by meandering waterway, or thirty miles in a straight line. In 1864 the fort was held by a small Federal force of some six hundred men about evenly divided between black and white troops. The whites were 13th Tennessee Volunteer Cavalry, the African Americans were mainly 6th U.S. Heavy Artillery with some from the 2nd U.S. Light Artillery. Most had only recently been freed from slavery.

The fort was attacked on April 12 at 5:30 A.M. by a Confederate force of 1,500 men under Gen. James R. Chalmers, who served under the notoriously tough and able rebel General Nathan Bedford Forrest. The Union soldiers hung on, but it was clear they would have to yield to overwhelming numbers. Forrest himself arrived with the rest of his cavalry at about 10 o'clock, and that afternoon sent the fort a message demanding surrender. Many interpreted his words as a threat: "Should my demand be refused, I cannot be responsible for the fate of your command." The fort's commander replied, "I will not surrender."

What happened next is disputed, but the evidence indicates that as the Confederates stormed Fort Pillow, having moved their troops during truce talks, they literally slaughtered the black soldiers who surrendered. Reports stated that the cursing Southerners shouted "No quarter" and burned some blacks alive by setting fire to the tents of the wounded. Several African-American sergeants were singled out, nailed to logs, and set afire. When it was over, 231 Union soldiers had been killed; Confederate deaths numbered only 14. Of the remaining Union prisoners, most of whom were wounded, 168 were white and only 58 black.

The Federal government's Joint Committee on the Conduct of the War immediately investigated and determined that what had happened at Fort Pillow was a racial massacre. A deposition by Private William J. Mays described one incident:

There were also two Negro women and three little children standing within 25 steps of me, when a rebel stepped up to them, and said, "Yes, God damn you, you thought you were free, did you?" and shot them all. They all fell but one child, when he knocked it in the head with the breech of his gun.

President Abraham Lincoln ordered the Union army to retaliate, but nothing was ever done. Word of the murders spread quickly through the Northern army's black troops, and "Remember Fort Pillow" became a rallying battle cry. Union general Edward W. Hinks requested that colored troops under his command be issued repeating rifles rather than the old muzzle loaders they carried because, as he said, his men "cannot afford to be beaten and will not be taken." His request was refused.

Confederates denied that anything wrong had taken place at Fort Pillow. The South's official policy, issued in 1862 by President Jefferson Davis, was that captured black soldiers should be considered slaves and returned to the states they came from, and free blacks should be sold into slavery. The Union insisted that black soldiers be treated as prisoners of war, and refused to exchange captured troops because the South would not recognize African Americans as such. It should be said that the North was not entirely motivated by an enlightened racial policy, but the government was eager to restrict prisoner exchanges, since the South was already so outnumbered in terms of manpower.

The rebel general Nathan Bedford Forrest was undoubtedly a brave soldier; in one engagement, three horses were shot out from under him. But he had once been a slave dealer in Memphis, and after the war he was not only involved in organizing the Ku Klux Klan, but probably served as its first Grand Wizard. His attitude toward blacks was clear, both during and after the war. Today Fort Pillow State Park is located seventeen miles west of Henning, Tennessee, and tourists can visit the remains of the fort.

If you want to know more:

Albert Castel. "The Fort Pillow Massacre: A Fresh Examination of the Evidence." *Civil War History* 4:1 (March 1958), pp. 38–50.

"If human testimony ever did or can establish anything, then [Fort Pillow] is proved a case of deliberate, wholesale massacre of prisoners of war after they had surrendered."

—Horace Greeley

"I with several of the others tried to stop the butchery and at one time had partially succeeded but Gen. Forrest ordered them shot down like dogs and the carnage continued."

—a Confederate sergeant

"Of course Forrest and all Southerners will kill them and their white officers; we all know that."

—General William Tecumseh Sherman

"Twenty-three of the Rebs surrendered but the boys asked them if they remembered Fort Pillow and killed them all."

—John Brobst of the 25th Wisconsin (a white regiment)

What was Reconstruction?

The Civil War began with the single purpose of preserving the integrity of the federal union from the withdrawal of eleven Southern states into the Confederacy. It soon became clear, however, that the "peculiar institution" of chattel slavery on which the South's whole economic, political, and social life was based was the real issue underlying its claim for independence.

Thus, setting free African Americans became one of the North's war aims. When General Robert E. Lee surrendered the demoralized Confederate Army of Virginia in the spring of 1865, the United States had officially won the war, but the complex questions of peace, reunion, and reconciliation had to be faced. Above all, the nation, North and South, had to deal with Abraham Lincoln's plaintive question, "But what shall we do with the Negroes after they are free?"

Lincoln's policy for Reconstruction—that is—what should be the terms and conditions for remaking a broken country— was essentially a plan of great tolerance and generosity for the defeated South. His Proclamation of Amnesty and Reconstruction of December 8, 1863, simply required oaths of allegiance to the United States, oaths from which only a few high-level Confederates were excluded. This meant Southern whites could and would soon regain the franchise and local control over the areas subdued by the Union army. African Americans were to be excluded from voting, although Lincoln tentatively suggested that perhaps a few particularly qualified blacks in Louisiana might be allowed the ballot experimentally. Congress reacted with the Wade-Davis Bill, in July 1864, calling for much stricter terms for allowing the rebellious states back into the union.

What began as a substantive disagreement over the terms of reunion, soon turned into a jurisdictional dispute between the White House and Capitol Hill over whether the president or the Congress was going to determine the course of Reconstruction. The question was heightened by the assassination of President Lincoln six days after Lee's surrender at Appomattox Courthouse. Andrew Johnson, a tailor whose wife had taught him to read, was now president. As a poor white, he hated the aristocratic Southern planter class, but he was perhaps even less sympathetic to the country's nearly four million free African-American men, women, and children than even Lincoln had been. The stage was set for a political confrontation as titanic as the military encounter the war had been.

Essentially, the question went back to the nature of secession itself. At the war's conclusion, North and South seemed to switch definitions. The South had claimed its national sovereignty with regard to the United States, having lost the war, it now said it had never really left the union after all. Therefore the Southern states, they said, should be readmitted easily and allowed to conduct their local business as usual. The North, on the other hand, originally claimed the union to be indissoluble, but it now said the Confederacy was to be taken at its word as a foreign country, but now one occupied by the Federal army. The rebellious states could therefore be reabsorbed into the United States only on terms laid down by the victorious national government. Just as slavery was the hidden issue underlying the war, so the fate of the African-American freedpeople was the real issue underlying the terms of peace.

Many whites in the North were originally inclined to tolerance about Reconstruction, like Lincoln and Johnson. But Johnson began to annoy the public with his wholesale pardon of prominent Confederates, particularly the wives of former officers, who lined up outside his office. It was said that the working-class Johnson enjoyed the subservient begging by his social superiors. Even more aggravating was the blatant arrogance of the white South in defeat. The South elected to the Thirty-ninth Congress, which met in December 1865, the former vice president of the Confederacy, along with fifty-seven Confederate congressmen, six Confederate cabinet members, and four Confederate generals. The North began to wonder what it had meant to win the war.

Reconstruction is one of the most misrepresented and misunderstood, but determinative, periods in American history. Johnson's bitter conflict with Congress led to his impeachment, the first for an American president, but conviction failed by one vote. The Radical Republicans, led by Charles Sumner of Massachusetts in the Senate and Thaddeus Stevens of Pennsylvania in the House, took control of Reconstruction. They divided the South into military districts and set up democratic criteria for reinstatement into the union, and they passed legislation to protect the freedpeople. The Freedmen's Bureau, for example, established forty hospitals and in only a few years distributed twenty-one million rations to hungry people.

The fundamental issue of Reconstruction remained the question of local control within the former Confederate states, a code phrase for white supremacy. Would power remain in the hands of white people, where it had exclusively resided before the war, or would political, social, and economic power be extended to include the newly freed African Americans? If the latter, then it was clear a reconstructed South would have to be both created and maintained by the federal government.

Led by the Radical Republicans, the national government engineered passage of the 13th, 14th, and 15th amendments to the U.S. Constitution which ended slavery, made African Americans citizens, and enfranchised black men. Dominated by Republicans and including black members, Southern state legislatures enacted significant legislation establishing public schools, reducing the number of capital crimes, and generally advancing a progressive agenda.

The white Southern backlash was ruthless, powerful, and ultimately successful. Peonage and sharecropping came to replace slave labor. Locally enforced "vagrancy" charges sent many blacks literally back to their former masters to work off "public" sentences. Unusual taxes kept blacks from many jobs. Grandfather clauses and the white primary first reduced then virtually eliminated black voters. Jim Crow laws segregated transportation and other public facilities, and social control segregated private life. Most important, extreme and extensive white violence through murder and systematic terrorism by the Ku Klux Klan and other racially supremacist secret organizations intimidated many freedpeople and their few white allies into inactivity.

The tension between the integrationist and progressive Republican national government, with its black and tan Southern adherents, and white Southern Democrats bent on local "redemption" continued until the Republicans lost interest in the issues, perhaps beguiled by the new issues brought by prosperity and the Gilded Age of the end of the century. The moral zeal of abolitionism and the ethical movement to make the freedpeople full American citizens was abandoned by liberal whites, and African Americans were left powerless to fend for themselves.

The usual date and event given for the end of Reconstruction is the Compromise of 1877. The presidential contest of 1876 between Republican Rutherford B. Hayes and Democrat Samuel J. Tilden was disputed because of rival Democratic and Republican claims to members of the electoral college in three Southern states. In fact, Tilden had won the popular vote.

The Republicans were interested primarily in holding on to the office of the presidency. The Democrats were interested primarily in local autonomy and racial hegemony in the former Confederacy. To satisfy both groups, a deal was struck at a secret meeting in Washington's Wormley Hotel, ironically an African-American–owned establishment. The Democrats traded their claims to electoral college votes to the Republicans in exchange for the withdrawal of federal troops from the South, and, in effect, the government's turning state and regional power over to white racists and racism.

The consequences in the South were predictable and disastrous. African Americans' last hopes in the federal government were destroyed with the striking down of civil rights legislation by the U.S. Supreme Court. Most decisive was the *Plessy* v. *Ferguson* decision of 1896. Here the doctrine of racially "separate but equal" as compatible with the Constitution was handed down by the court, and the era of racial segregation was legitimized for the next fifty years. The unique, dramatic, even revolutionary attempt to democratize the American South, where 90 percent of all black people lived, had failed.

If you want to know more:

Eric Foner. *Reconstruction: America's Unfinished Revolution, 1836–1877.* New York: Harper and Row, 1988.

"The elite Negroes tended to place primary emphasis on civil and political rights, but what the ex-slaves wanted most of all was land of their own to cultivate and the opportunity to secure an education."

—August Meier and Elliott M. Rudwick

"If we do not furnish [the freedpeople] with homesteads, and hedge them about with protective laws; if we leave them to the legislation of their late masters, we had better have left them in bondage."

—Thaddeus Stevens

"[The state Republican governments] abolished the whipping post, the branding iron, the stock and other barbarous forms of punishment which had up to that time prevailed."

—Albion W. Tourgee

"Although the freedman is no longer considered the property of the individual master, he is considered the slave of society."

—Carl Shurtz

"The unending tragedy of Reconstruction is the utter inability of the American mind to grasp its real significance, its national and worldwide implications. It was vain for Sumner and Stevens to hammer in the ears of the people that this problem involved the very foundations of American democracy, both political and economic."

—W. E. B. Du Bois

CHAPTER 3

❧

From the Nadir to the New Negro, 1878–1919

Who was the leading African-American landscape painter of the nineteenth century?

How were the spirituals preserved?

What sport was once dominated by African Americans?

Who were the Healys?

Where did the blues come from?

Who led the fight against lynching?

Who was the first musician to play jazz?

What was the cakewalk?

Where did ragtime music originate?

Where did jazz come from?

Who was the first African-American artist to achieve international recognition?

What is the most influential book written by an African American?

Who founded the leading African-American Pentecostal denomination?

Who was the King of Ragtime?

Who was the Wizard of Tuskegee?

What was the American Negro Academy?

Who said, "God is a Negro"?

Who was the Mother of the Blues?

What film most influenced popular views of African Americans?

What was an unexpected by-product of World War I?

~

Who was the leading African-American landscape painter of the nineteenth century?

Edward Mitchell Bannister, a leading artist of rustic motifs and the American wilderness, added his own sense of tranquillity to his portrayal of regional landscape. He was born in St. Andrews, Nova Scotia, Canada, around 1828. His father, Edward, was an African American, reportedly from Barbados, and his mother was Hannah Alexander. Her race is unknown, but presumably she was white. Both parents died early in Bannister's life, and after a stint at sea he moved to Boston, where he became a barber and a photographer.

Bannister began sketching and painting as a child and continued to paint in Boston, specializing in portraits because they were marketable. In 1857 he married Christiana Cardeaux, a successful hairdresser and wigmaker from North Kingston, Rhode Island, who was part black and part Narragansett Indian. Together they participated in Boston's large and politically active free black community. Bannister sang tenor in the Crispus Attucks Choir, and he and Cardeaux may in fact have met at the Histrionic Club, a black dramatic group. His studio was near that of the important African-American sculptor Edmonia Lewis.

Bannister and his wife were particularly involved in the abolitionist movement and in spiriting escaped slaves to Canada and freedom on the Underground Railroad. They boarded with Lewis Hayden, Boston's antislavery and Underground Railroad leader. Bannister was secretary of the Union Progressive Association, which sponsored the famous meeting in Boston's Tremont Temple on January 1, 1863, to hear the news of President Lincoln's Emancipation Proclamation, and at which **Frederick Douglass, William Wells Brown,** and **William Cooper Nell** spoke.

In 1870, following the Civil War, the Bannisters moved to Providence, Rhode Island, perhaps to escape Boston's growing racism. By this time Bannister's work was more widely known. In 1876 he submitted a large landscape, *Under the Oaks,* to the show at Philadelphia's Centennial Exposition, where it received a first-prize bronze medal and made Bannister the first African American to win a national award for art. Guards tried to keep him out of the exhibition where his work was on display, and when officials discovered he was black, they tried to revoke the prize. *Under the Oaks* sold for $1,500, a large sum at the time, but, like much of Bannister's work, it is now lost. Only a few of his pieces survive.

Bannister's style was influenced by Millet and the Barbizon and Hudson River schools, but he added his own distinctive touch to rural and wooded American landscape. In Providence he was a founder in 1880 of the Providence Art Club, which evolved into the present Rhode Island School of Design. Bannister died on January 9, 1901, just after offering prayer at a midweek service at Elmwood Avenue Baptist Church.

If you want to know more:

Juanita Marie Holland. *The Life and Work of Edward Mitchell Bannister (1828–1901).* New York: Kenkeleba House, 1992.

> "Art is a moral power . . . revealing to us a glimpse of the absolute ideal of perfect harmony."
> —Edward Mitchell Bannister, *The Artist and His Critics*, 1886.
>
> "This pure and lofty soul who, while he portrayed nature, walked with God."
>   —inscription on Bannister's tombstone
>
> "All that I would do—that is, all I could say in art—simply from lack of training, but with God's help I hope to deliver the message he entrusted to me."
>   —Edward Mitchell Bannister

How were the spirituals preserved?

The songs of slavery, often called Negro spirituals, might well have been lost if it had not been for a black choral group from Fisk University called the Jubilee Singers. When the Civil War ended, the plantation hymns had never been written down, most of the newly freed people identified the songs with slavery and thus as a part of their collective life they wanted to forget and move beyond, and most white people had never heard them. The fact that the songs were preserved at all is the result of a remarkable moment in history.

In 1866 a school for freed slaves was opened by the American Missionary Association in an abandoned Union army hospital barracks in Nashville, Tennessee. What soon became Fisk University was named for Clinton B. Fisk, a former U.S. Army officer, who became head of the Freedmen's Bureau in Kentucky and Tennessee. There was no public education, so the school filled a real need. It was an immediate success, drawing a thousand students a day, most of whom came to learn elementary skills like reading and writing. As soon as they learned, however, the Fisk students themselves went out to teach, and were soon reaching ten thousand African-American children a year.

The former slaves' hunger for education put enormous pressures on the young school, so its financial stability was precarious from the beginning. Chains from Nashville's slave pens were sold as scrap iron, and the money went to buy spelling books. George L. White, another Union army veteran, was both the college's treasurer and its teacher of voice. He organized a choir that performed some local concerts, and he hit upon the idea of taking the choir on a tour to raise funds for the school. Eleven young men and women students using borrowed money headed north on October 6, 1871, for the Congregational and Presbyterian churches of Ohio.

The group lived hand to mouth, often didn't even meet expenses, and suffered the indignities of racial prejudice and discrimination, especially in the hotels and restaurants that refused them service. They sang anthems, ballads, opera, and temperance songs wherever there was a hall open to them, and at least proved to skeptics (who had doubted it) that African Americans could sing Euro-American music. Jennie Jackson soloed, for example, with "Old Folks at Home," and Isaac P. Dickson with "Temperance Medley." Their first major success came November 15, 1871, at the National Council of Congregational Churches meeting at Oberlin College, a group of churches that were constituent members of the association that had founded Fisk.

However, what made the Jubilee Singers so successful was not their renditions of European and European-American songs, but singing the slave hymns that came to be known as

Negro spirituals. At first the choir sang only one or two in a concert, but whites were touched by the haunting melodies and powerful lyrics. The more spirituals the choir sang, the more enthusiastic their audiences became. The popular Congregational minister **Henry Ward Beecher** invited the Jubilee Singers to his Brooklyn church and called them "living representatives of the only true native school of American music."

The group sang spirituals that are now familiar, like "Swing Low, Sweet Chariot," "Nobody Knows the Trouble I Seen," "Roll, Jordan, Roll," "Old Ship of Zion," and "Ride On, King Jesus." They also sang spirituals that for slaves had had double meanings: "Children, We Shall Be Free," "Steal Away," "Go Down, Moses," "Many Thousand Gone," "Didn't the Lord Deliver Daniel?" Perhaps most often, they sang the stirring antislavery song "John Brown's Body," a hymn that moved the hearts of the veteran abolitionists who came out to hear them.

The choir was a smashing success in Massachusetts and Connecticut. They sang for President Ulysses S. Grant in Washington, and then sailed for the British Isles, where they were even more enthusiastically received and where they raised even more money for Fisk. They sang "Go Down, Moses" and "Steal Away" for Queen Victoria. William Gladstone, the prime minister, invited them to lunch, and Mrs. Gladstone asked them to sing "John Brown's Body" for one of the guests, the Grand Duchess Maria Fyodorovna, the czarevna, whose father-in-law had liberated the Russian serfs. The students sang for common people as well as aristocrats, though, appearing with Dwight L. Moody and Ira Sankey's evangelistic campaign and at the London tabernacle of the popular nonconformist preacher Charles H. Spurgeon.

In 1875 Fisk University graduated its first college class and completed its first permanent building, Jubilee Hall, named for the traveling band of singers who had raised the thousands of dollars required to build it. Negro spirituals became an important part of the nation's musical life and subsequently the base for much of American music with its strong African-American influences. George White led the choir, Prof. T. F. Seward first wrote down the songs, and Ella Sheppard, a young black woman whose father had bought her freedom during slavery for $350, was the pianist, but the legacy and heritage of the spirituals was preserved by the Jubilee Singers themselves. The slave composers will never be known.

If you want to know more:

J. B. Marsh. *The Story of the Jubilee Singers with Their Songs.* Reprint of 1880 ed. New York: AMS Pr.

> "If anybody asks you
> What's the matter with me,
> Just tell him I say,
> I'm running for my life."
> —"I'm Running for My Life"

> "I'm a-rolling,
> I'm a-rolling,
> I'm a-rolling
> Through an unfriendly world."
> —"I'm A-Rolling"

> "Hypocrites and concubines,
> Living among the swine,
> They run to God with lips and tongue
> And leave all the heart behind."
> —"The Hypocrite and the Concubine"

> "Mary set the table
> In spite of all her foes;
> King Jesus sat at the center place
> And cups did overflow."
> —"Children, Did You Hear When Jesus Rose?"

"When the preacher, the preacher done give me over,
King Jesus is my only friend.
When my house, my house becomes a public hall,
King Jesus is my only friend.
When my face, my face becomes a looking glass,
King Jesus is my only friend."
—"King Jesus Is My Only Friend"

What sport was once dominated by African Americans?

Thoroughbred horse racing is a sport that was once dominated by African Americans as jockeys and trainers. **Oliver Lewis,** a black jockey, won the first Kentucky Derby, on May 17, 1875, riding Aristides and competing against fourteen other riders, thirteen of whom were black. The English had introduced racing to America, but they were not the only ones who knew horses; many Africans brought to America as slaves were skilled horsemen, horses having been used in West Africa, as in Europe and Asia, for transportation, cavalry, and sport. On Southern plantations, young slave boys made ideal riders because of their light weight.

Isaac "Honest Ike" Murphy was probably the greatest of the African-American jockeys. Born around January 1, 1861, in Lexington, Kentucky, Murphy was the son of a Union soldier who had died in a Confederate prison. Murphy piled up an impressive record of racing achievements. He was the only jockey to win the Derby, the Kentucky Oaks, and the Clark Stakes as well. In 1882, in Saratoga, he won 49 out of the 51 races he entered. He rode 1,412 races during his career and came in first in 628 of them. He was the first to win successive Derbys, 1890 and 1891.

An ingenious rider and masterful judge of pace, Murphy was a "hand" rider, using only his heels and hands on his horses and saving a display of the whip only to please the crowd. He retired from racing in 1895, and died a year later, on February 12, 1896, of pneumonia brought on by the weak physical health he suffered because of the constant dieting necessary to keep his weight down. Isaac Murphy was one of the first people voted into the Jockey Hall of Fame in Saratoga Springs, New York, when it opened in 1955.

Jimmy Winkfield, also born near Lexington, Kentucky, might have rivaled Murphy for preeminence, since he won the Derby twice, but he received a threatening letter from the Ku Klux Klan, and left the United States. In Europe, Winkfield won the Grand Prix de Baden, the Polish Derby, the Moscow Derby, and other major races. The Bolshevik Revolution drove him out of Russia, and World War II forced him to leave France, but he was able to return after the war, where he continued to breed horses. He rode the winner, Alan-a-Dale, in the last Derby won by an African-American jockey.

The last African American to compete in the Kentucky Derby was Henry King, who rode Planet in 1921. There had been considerable discrimination and harassment over the years against black jockeys, who were, for example, pushed into accidents or cut. When thoroughbred racing turned into serious money for jockeys, blacks were forced out completely. In 1894 the Jockey Club denied them membership. The same happened to black trainers. When Edward Dudley Brown grew too heavy to ride, he became a trainer and was responsible for four Derby winners: Baden-Baden in 1877, Hindoo in 1881, Ben Brush in 1896, and Plaudit in 1898. Today only a few black jockeys, like Wayne Barnett, remain, and a few trainers, like rap star **Hammer's** father, Lewis Burell.

If you want to know more:

Arthur Ashe. *A Hard Road to a History of African-Americans 1619– 1918.* New York: Warner Books, 1980.

"You just ride to win."

—Isaac Murphy

Who were the Healys?

The Healys were one of the most extraordinary African-American families of the nineteenth century. The unusual circumstances of their origins and lives, however, have obscured them in history rather than making them remembered for their achievements. The family began when Michael Morris Healy of County Roscommon, Ireland, deserted from the British army in Canada during the War of 1812 and made his way by 1818 to rural Georgia. Through land speculation and the acquisition of plantations, he built a considerable estate, including numerous slaves.

With one of his slaves, a mulatto woman named Elisa, Healy fathered ten children, seven sons and three daughters. Healy recognized Elisa in his will as "my trusty woman"—marriage between blacks and whites being illegal—and he provided that at his death she be paid an annuity and be transported to a free state. (She was to predecease him, however.) He also recognized his children, although by Georgia law they continued to be slaves, and he worried about getting them out of Jones County.

Healy's solution in the 1840s was to send the older children to a Quaker school in New York State. In 1844, however, an accidental meeting with Roman Catholic bishop John B. Fitzpatrick of Boston led him to enroll the boys in the newly founded College of the Holy Cross, a Jesuit school in Worcester, Massachusetts. The eldest daughter, Martha, was sent to the Notre Dame Sisters school in Boston. The children were well received in the Catholic community, where their family background was known. They were all baptized and became actively religious.

The older boys gravitated to the priesthood. The eldest, James (1830–1900), was in the first class to graduate from Holy Cross in 1849, and since he could not be admitted to a Catholic seminary in the United States because of his race, he went to the Sulpician Seminary in Montreal, and then the Sulpician Seminary in Paris. He was ordained on June 10, 1854, in Paris' Notre Dame Cathedral. Though a man could not be ordained

a Catholic priest if he was illegitimate, it appears Bishop Fitzpatrick in Boston falsified the records.

Healy became chancellor of the diocese of Boston and secretary to his benefactor, Bishop Fitzpatrick. He was appointed rector of the cathedral and then pastor of St. James, the largest
parish in Boston. There were whisperings about his race, but he
was accepted and apparently respected by his largely immigrant
Irish parishioners. In 1875 Healy was named bishop of Portland,
Maine, where he diligently constructed churches, schools, mis-
sions, and convents until his death on August 5, 1900.

While never unaware of his mixed heritage, Healy and the
rest of his family never publicly identified themselves as black,
and as bishop he declined to address the five African-American
Catholic conferences held between 1889 and 1894. There are
no letters to or from his mother, who was probably illiterate,
and she died in Georgia, still legally a slave, on May 19, 1850,
aged about thirty-seven. While a student Bishop Healy mentioned having a daguerreotype photograph of her, but it is now
lost.

James Healy's brothers and sisters led equally interesting
lives. Patrick (1834–1910) also went to Holy Cross and then entered the novitiate of the Society of Jesus. He studied in France
and Belgium, again because race made it impossible for him to
be enrolled in an American school. He received a Ph.D. at Louvain, probably the first African American to earn a doctorate.
He was ordained in Belgium in 1865 and took his final vows as
a Jesuit in 1867.

Patrick Healy then joined the faculty at Georgetown University in Washington, where he held a number of teaching and
administrative posts before he became Georgetown's president
in 1874. He literally transformed the school, turning a college
into a university, modernizing and upgrading standards, and
constructing a building, modeled after Louvain, which still
stands and which bears his name. Today few realize Healy Hall
was named for an African American. His impact on Georgetown
was so great that he is commonly referred to as the university's
second founder. The stress of overwork weakened Patrick Healy's health. He retired as president and died January 10, 1910.

Named for her mother, Eliza Healy, born December 23, 1846, was orphaned at age three, as her father died just a few months after her mother, in 1850. She was brought to New York, baptized, and sent to school in Quebec with her sister Martha. She entered the Congregation of Notre Dame and became a nun, taking the name Sister Mary Magdalene. She taught in various Canadian schools and then became superior at Villa Barlow in St. Albans, Vermont, and the superior of the Academy of Our Lady of the Blessed Sacrament in Staten Island. She died on September 13, 1919.

Perhaps the most intellectual of the Healys was Sherwood (1836–1875). He, too, attended Holy Cross as well as Sulpician seminaries in Montreal and Paris. He was ordained in Rome, where he received a doctorate in canon law. He was considered for the rectorship of the North American College then being established in Rome, but his patron, Bishop Fitzpatrick of Boston, wrote to Archbishop John Hughes of New York: "It would be useless to recommend him. He has African blood and it shows distinctly in his exterior."

Alexander Healy followed James as chancellor of the diocese of Boston, but then went to St. Joseph's, the new provincial seminary at Troy, New York, where he was vice president, professor of moral theology, and also taught rubrics and church music. John J. Williams, Fitzpatrick's successor as bishop of Boston, appointed Healy his personal theologian for the First Vatican Council in 1870, and Healy counseled the bishop as he voted on the council's various decrees. Sherwood Healy served as rector for the cathedral in Boston, while James was in charge of the neighboring St. James. Always a victim of poor health, he died October 21, 1875.

Perhaps the most interesting of all the Healy family, however, was Michael (1839–1904). He did not follow his brothers and sisters into a religious vocation and, in fact, ran away from several Catholic schools in which he was placed. In 1865 he joined the U.S. Revenue Cutter Service, now the Coast Guard. He became well known as the captain of several famous ships, particularly the *Bear* and the *Thomas Corwin,* which he commanded in several dangerous and adventurous voyages in the North Pacific and the Arctic.

Healy became known as "Hell Roaring" Mike, fond of strong language and stronger drink, not always liked by his colleagues, but respected by Native Americans in the North for whom he represented the full power of the United States government. He survived a court-martial, and now his portrait hangs in the Coast Guard Museum. Healy is said to have been the model for the protagonist of Jack London's novel, *The Sea Wolf.* He died in 1904.

Unlike the religious members of his family, Michael Healy married. His wife was an Irish-American woman named Mary Jane Roach, with whom he had a son, Frederick (1870–1914) who became a San Francisco journalist. Michael Healy was fully aware of his racial heritage and reportedly participated in buying his mother's sister out of slavery. But he was light-skinned like his brother Patrick and probably passed for white. In the 1930's, Hollywood was interested in a film version of his life and approached his daughter-in-law concerning Healy's unpublished four-volume diary. She had not read it before. When she did and discovered her husband's grandmother had been a black slave, she burned the entire manuscript.

If you want to know more:

Albert S. Foley. *Bishop Healy: Beloved Outcaste.* Reprint. New York: Arno Press, 1969.

"Remarks are sometimes made which wound my very heart. You know to what I refer. I have with me a younger brother, Michael. He is obliged to go through the same ordeal."

—Patrick Healy, at Holy Cross

"[T]he said Elisa shall not be bartered or sold or disposed of in any way or manner whatever."

—Michael M. Healy, Sr.'s, last will and testament

"I remember Father Healy. He was a colored man, and I remember it was quite well known and talked about that he was one. But if he had any such thing as an inferiority complex concealed about his person, his Irish congregation never discovered it, for he ruled them— and they were not easy to rule."
— a parishioner of St. James Church, Boston

Where did the blues come from?

The origin of the blues is lost somewhere in the unaccompanied work songs, ring shouts, field hollers, and religious call-and-response rituals of the slave South. However these songs may have evolved, the blues express the timeless sadness and melancholy of people struggling with the "blue devils" of despair. Sometimes performed by wandering singers, the music-poetry of the blues is traditionally simple, earthy, ironic, and often highly humorous. The blues were improvised because they were created by people who did not read music.

With great personal intensity, blues deal with such themes as mistreatment and abandonment by lovers, bad luck, loneliness, the penitentiary, poverty, drink, and escape. They are often raucously sexual, full of clever if vulgar meanings and sexual euphemisms. Beneath the sorrow, however, is often another theme: the wisdom of survivors who perceive the incongruity of their situation. They "squeeze from it," as **Ralph Ellison** says, "a near tragic, near comic lyricism," and so transcend their victimization to endure with strength and dignity, and even hope.

The blues seem to have been born in the Mississippi Delta, the Georgia coast, and rural Texas, areas where the large black population was often poorest and most isolated. John Jacob Niles, the folklorist, mentions hearing of Ophelia Simpson, a shouter and moaner in Dr. Parker's Medicine Show. She performed "Black Alfalfa's Jail-House Shouting Blues" in 1898.

Blues composer **W. C. Handy** first encountered the blues, "the weirdest music I had ever heard," around the turn of the century in the Tutwiler, Mississippi, railroad station. An old black hobo was picking a primitive guitar with a knife and singing "Goin' where the Southern cross the Dog," referring to the site of the Moorhead, Alabama, penitentiary, where two rail lines, the Great Southern and the Yazoo Delta, known as the Yellow Dog, meet. Handy said, "The tune stayed in my head," and he understood from the outset that blues were born in aching hearts.

Ferdinand "Jelly Roll" Morton recalled a prostitute named Mamie Desdunes singing a blues song in New Orleans around 1902: "If you can't give me a dollar/Give me a lousy dime./I want to feed/That hungry man of mine."

Whatever its antecedents, the blues as a discrete form did not emerge until the late nineteenth century. African-American men were probably the earliest blues singers, usually self-accompanied on a guitar or harmonica. Their rural laments are generally considered the most basic expression of the blues. Singers like "Papa Charlie" Jackson, **"Blind Lemon" Jefferson,** "Blind Willie" Jackson, and **"Leadbelly" (Huddie Ledbetter)** are now well known as masters of country blues. Middle-class black people quite correctly associated the blues with low-life folk and gut-bucket dives. As a child, W. C. Handy was ordered by his parents to get rid of the guitar he had bought with his own money, since they considered it "a sinful thing brought into a Christian home."

Handy was the first to write and popularize a blues composition, "Memphis Blues: A Southern Rag" in 1912. He published "St. Louis Blues" in 1914, and the song became so popular during World War I it was said Europeans believed it was the American national anthem. A somewhat more sophisticated urban or classic blues style emerged as the early country songs were influenced by Euro-American ballads and instruments as well as by black vaudeville, spirituals, popular theater, and traveling musical shows. Classic blues were usually sung by black women accompanied by a piano or jazz band.

Versions of the blues that were presented to whites became

even more stylized and diluted. Yet even with this homogenization, the blues had generated an impressive array of vocalists by the 1920s, many of them enormously talented: Ida "the Sepia Mae West" Cox, Lucille Hegamin, Bertha "Chippie" Hill, Alberta Hunter, **Gertrude "Ma" Rainey, Bessie Smith, Clara "Queen of the Moaners" Smith,** "Trixie" Smith, "Queen Victoria" Spivey, Beulah "Sippy" Wallace, and Edith Wilson.

If you want to know more:

Francis Davis. *The History of the Blues.* New York: Hyperion, 1995.

> "Going North, child, where I can be free,
> Where there's no hardship, like in Tennessee.
> Going where they don't have Jim Crow laws.
> Don't have to work there like in Arkansas."
> —"North Bound Blues"

> "I'm going to chew my bacca
> I'm going to spit my juice.
> I'm going to save my thing
> For my particular use."
> —"What's the Matter?"

> "People is raving about hard times,
> Tell me what it's all about.
> Hard times don't worry me,
> I was broke when it started out."
> —"Hard Times Ain't Gone No Where"

> "Some men crave high yellow
> But give me black or brown.
> Cause I can't tell the difference
> When the sun goes down."
> —"Good Woman Blues"

Who led the fight against lynching?

Lynching is murder by mob violence. It was largely directed in this country against African Americans in the South as an extralegal way of maintaining and enforcing white supremacy. Every African American knew that any violation—real, perceived, or contrived—of written or unwritten customs or laws could result in assault and death without protection from police, courts, press, or government. In fact, representatives of these agencies were themselves sometimes actively involved in lynchings. Between 1882 and 1968, at least 4,743 people were lynched in America, 3,446 blacks and 1,297 whites. The number of black victims, and therefore the totals, are undoubtedly higher due to unreported or questionably defined cases.

The worst period for lynching was the 1880s and '90s, as white Americans vehemently reacted against the gains of African Americans during Reconstruction and sought, successfully, to regain by force total white political, social, and economic control. The worst year was 1892, when more than four black people were lynched a week. The total annual number of lynchings stayed in the triple digits until 1902, when it dropped to double digits, and not until 1936 did it drop to a single digit. The states with the highest numbers of lynchings from 1882 to 1968 were Mississippi, with a total of 581, then Georgia, with 531, and Texas, with 493.

The federal government, presidents, Congress, and courts refused to intervene in what they called local or state affairs. George H. White, a black congressman from North Carolina, introduced the first of many antilynching bills in the U.S. House of Representatives in 1900, but it never got out of committee. The NAACP campaigned vigorously against lynching. The Department of Records and Research at Tuskegee Institute kept scrupulously detailed records of racial murders, and the shocking accuracy of their reporting did exert some influence on public opinion.

If any person can be said to have led the crusade against lynching, it was **Ida B. Wells-Barnett,** a militant African-American journalist. Wells-Barnett was born in slavery on July 16, 1862, in Holly Springs, Mississippi, to James Wells and Elizabeth Warrenton Wells. Her mother had an Indian father, and her father's father, not untypically, was his mother's slavemaster. Ida attended Rust University in Holly Springs, a school sponsored by Methodists, where she was accompanied by her mother, who wanted to learn to read and write. Both parents died in a yellow fever epidemic, and Ida supported her brothers and sisters by teaching in rural schools for $25 a month.

Moving to Memphis, Tennessee, she taught in the city's segregated school system until she criticized the school board and was fired. She wrote for the local black press, and became an editor of the *Free Speech and Headlight* with the Reverend Taylor Nightingale of Beale Street Baptist Church. In 1884 she sued the Chesapeake, Ohio and Southwestern Railroad for refusing her a seat. She won in the lower court, but on appeal the Tennessee Supreme Court ruled in the company's favor, saying Wells-Barnett's only purpose was to harass the railroad.

In 1892 several African-American men opened the People's Grocery on "The Curve," in a black Memphis neighborhood where the streetcar turned from Mississippi Avenue to Walker Avenue. They were soon doing better business than the white-owned grocery store across the street. The white owner retaliated, and three of the men, Thomas Moss, Calvin McDowell, and Henry Stewart, were lynched by a white mob which included, reportedly, the local criminal-court judge. In shock and anger, black people boycotted the streetcars, and over two thousand African Americans left Memphis for the Oklahoma Territory.

Wells strongly criticized the lynching in her newspaper, but she went further and dared say something in print that was well known in the black community but never publicly expressed. It was generally thought by whites that most black men who were lynched were killed because they had raped white women. But in truth, charges of rape, untried and unproven, constituted only 25 percent of the alleged crimes of which lynching victims were accused. The secret Wells revealed was that sexual relationships with black men were sometimes initiated by white women, who held absolute power by being able at any moment to cry "rape," and thus protect themselves while condemning black men to death.

Wells wrote of this on May 25, 1892:

Nobody in this section of the country believes the old threadbare lie that Negro men rape white women. If Southern white men are not careful, they will over-reach themselves and public sentiment will have a reaction; a conclusion will then be reached which will be very damaging to the moral reputation of their women.

Wells had spoken the unspeakable. Luckily, she was out of Memphis at the time her editorial appeared, attending the AME General Conference in Philadelphia. The office and press of the *Free Speech* were destroyed by a mob, and Wells was threatened with death if she returned to the city.

She moved to Chicago, where she spent her life crusading against lynching and involving herself in civic, settlement-house, suffragist, political, and women's movements. She participated, in London, in founding the Anti-Lynching Committee, the first of its kind. She was one of the signers of the 1909 call that led to the formation of the National Association for the Advancement of Colored People, but she was too radical to be accepted as one of its leaders. Ida B. Wells-Barnett died on March 25, 1931.

If you want to know more:

Mildred I. Thompson. *Ida B. Wells-Barnett: An Exploratory Study of an American Black Woman.* Brooklyn: Carlson Publishing, 1990.

"No savage nation can exceed the atrocities which are often heralded through the country and accepted by many as an incidental consequence. Men are hung, shot, and burnt by bands of murderers who are most invariably represented as the most influential and respectable citizens, while the evidence of guilt of what is charged against the victim is never established in any court."

—Henry McNeal Turner

"Lynching is a practical demonstration of racial hysteria; it is actuated through fear, a guilty conscience, or a retributive foreboding."

—Amy Jacques Garvey

"I had already determined to sell my life as dearly as possible if attacked. I felt if I could take one lyncher with me, this would even up the score a little bit."

—Ida B. Wells-Barnett

Who was the first musician to play jazz?

Other bands had "ragged" music for parades, but around 1895, **Buddy Bolden,** a New Orleans cornetist and bandleader, was apparently the first to rag music for dancing by syncopating the beat, adding improvised embellishments, and playing uptempo and loud. People loved it, and Bolden's band, it is believed, was the first to play "hot blues," a new sound that came to be called jazz, and which changed the nature of musical culture all around the world. **Willie "Bunk" Johnson,** who was there, claims it was Bolden who was the first to play true jazz.

Charles Joseph "Buddy" Bolden was born in New Orleans at 319 Howard Street on September 7, 1877, the year of the political compromise that ended black American hopes for Reconstruction. His family was brown-skinned, but not members of the city's Creole elite, and his father worked for a local white drayage company. Buddy Bolden went to school, learned to read and write, took lessons on the cornet, and probably learned to read music. New Orleans was a city full of music; bands played for parades, picnics, dances, social club parties, and funerals. The Boldens were members of St. John Fourth Baptist Church, which had its own special reputation for swinging music.

Bolden was such a good musician that he apparently never worked at anything else, except for a short stint as a plasterer. His band played at outings in Lincoln and Johnson parks, in the honky-tonk black dives of South Rampart and Perdito streets, and at dances in Masons and Odd Fellows Hall as well as in Union Sons Hall, which became so identified with Bolden it was called Funky Butt Hall, after one of his most popular numbers. Bands didn't play in either the black or white whore-houses, which had only pianos, but they did play in black Story-ville, a wide-open and rough carnival of alcohol, narcotics, sex, and violence that ran full blast, twenty-four hours a day. Jelly Roll Morton remembered that ten killings on a Saturday night was about average for the district.

A slender, handsome man idolized for his music, Bolden received the titles "Kid," then "King." He drank all the whiskey he could get, was fought over by teenage prostitutes, and was always surrounded by attractive women, one carrying his coat, one carrying his handkerchief, one carrying his comb. No one, however, was allowed to touch his cornet; he carried that him-self. He was hero-worshiped by music-loving people for his abil-ity to improvise and embellish; for the sweet, moaning, low-down sound of his blues; and especially for the rough loud music he could create for fast dances.

Bolden also liked to hear the sound of shuffling feet as back-ground to his music and would tell his band during a slow blues number:

> 'Way down, 'way down low,
> So I can hear them whores
> Drag their feet across the floor.

Bolden's band made a musical sound that had never been heard before. His generation of New Orleans musicians produced giants: "Big Eye" Louis Nelson, Bunk Johnson, Alcide "Slow Drag" Pavageau, **Edward "Kid" Ory,** John Robichaux (who was Bolden's chief rival), and Freddie Keppard, whose sound was said to be the most like Bolden's. Bolden's hot style became New Orleans jazz. He could get low and play sweet, especially on waltzes and blues, but it was the loud and rough low-down music people loved to dance to that changed musical history. It broke the restrictive rules of classical playing and introduced spontaneous feeling and freedom.

Bolden's band played everything from rags to hymns, adapting popular tunes to their own unique performance. "Funky Butt Blues" became his theme song. "Make Me a Pallet on the Floor" was a great favorite, as was "If You Don't Shake It, You Don't Get No Cake," along with the well-known New Orleans standbys "Panama," "Tiger Rag," and "Didn't He Ramble."

There is now no one alive who actually heard Buddy Bolden play. A persistent rumor that the band cut an old-fashioned cylinder record is most likely only wishful thinking, although the hope remains that it will someday turn up on a dusty shelf.

Buddy Bolden was at the peak of his popularity and musical influence in 1905, when he began to show signs of depression, erratic behavior, and paranoia. After several arrests for violence, he was committed to a segregated state mental hospital at Jackson, Louisiana, at the age of twenty-nine and lived there in an unreal world for another twenty-five years. The hospital had a black patients' band, but it is unclear whether Bolden ever played in it. The cause of his illness was diagnosed as alcoholism.

If you want to know more:

Donald M. Marquis. *In Search of Buddy Bolden: First Man of Jazz.* Baton Rouge: Louisiana State University Press, 1978.

"Make me a pallet on the floor,
Make me a pallet on the floor.
Make it soft, make it low
So your sweet man will never know."
                                        —Buddy Bolden

What was the cakewalk?

At the turn of the century, although African Americans had
lost Reconstruction's battle for political, economic, and social
democracy, they began, curiously enough, to exert an unprece-
dented influence on mainstream American popular culture. It
is not clear why white America consistently appropriated black
artistry. Perhaps it was because blacks had been so effectively
relegated to the margins of mainstream society that white people felt it "safe" to imitate appealing aspects of African-American life. Perhaps there was a genuine curiosity about black
people, characteristically part of the strange fascination of the
oppressor for the oppressed. Perhaps it was simply that black
culture was itself a more appropriate medium for expressing
the new, more sophisticated and faster-paced urban life of the
Gilded Age.

In any event, a new black musical style and an old black
dance permeated the 1890s and contributed significantly to
making the decade "gay," as it was called when *gay* meant
bright, lively, and joyous. The new music was ragtime, the old
dance was the cakewalk. The cakewalk probably originated on
Southern plantations when black slaves imitated the fancy ball
dances of white people. The cakewalk's movements were exaggerated, and whites who watched with amusement never knew
that their own formal cotillions were being mimicked and
mocked more than they were being imitated.

The cakewalk was essentially an improvised promenade.
Wearing fancy dress, dancers folded their arms across their

chests, threw back their heads, arched their bodies backwards, and strutted to syncopated ragtime. Before the dance became sophisticated and stylized, dancers sometimes carried a pitcher of water on their heads, which they tried to carry without spilling. The name came from the cake awarded in competitive "cutting" contests to the couple showing the best style and receiving the most applause from the audience, which was always the final judge.

Blackface minstrelsy had used a form of the cakewalk in its grand finale, where it was known as the walk-around. This means that when the dance re-emerged in the 1890s, it was performed by blacks imitating whites who had been imitating blacks imitating whites. White people who threw themselves into the new pleasures of the Gilded Age learned the strutting cakewalk, just as whites in the 1920s would act out their new freedom by dancing another fast-moving step with working-class black origins, the Charleston.

If you want to know more:

Marshall and Jean Stearns. *Jazz Dance: The Story of American Vernacular Dance.* New York: Schirmer Books, 1968.

"We must never forget that the dance is the cradle of Negro music."

—Alain Locke

"Dance is our Negritude. It's us and we shouldn't try to deny that."

—Spike Lee

Where did ragtime music originate?

Ragtime music transformed American popular culture at the turn of the century, but nobody really knows for sure how it originated. It may well have started in the better black sporting houses and honky-tonks which often employed piano players. Sometime before 1900, the classical musician Ignacy Paderewski was taken by a *Post-Dispatch* reporter to Babe Connors' St. Louis, Missouri, bordello, which featured octoroon "Creole" girls who danced nearly naked, wearing only stockings, and where Mammy Lou sang to the accompaniment of a blind pianist "Ta-ra-ra-boom-de-ay" and other songs as yet unknown to the white world. If not technically ragtime, this was at least an early form of a distinctive African-American music about to explode onto the vernacular white entertainment scene.

In 1896, **Scott Joplin,** the greatest of the ragtime composers, was touring with his Texas Medley Quartet, publishing his first piano compositions ("Please Say You Will" and "A Picture of Her Face"), and living, studying, and playing in Sedalia, Missouri. As Vera Brodsky Lawrence points out, this was a critical moment for black music. Ragtime was taking a "definite, potentially classic" shape, but it stood in real danger of being lost: "were it to survive with enough time for full fruition, it needed to be heard throughout white America and it needed to be preserved in printed scores."

Exactly this breakthrough came the same year, 1896, when Ben Harney, a black musician passing for white (or was he a white musician passing for a black musician passing for a white?), introduced ragtime as "jig piano" at Tony Pastor's Theatre in New York. It was an immediate hit. The word *ragtime* apparently first appeared in **Bert Williams'** 1896 song, "Oh, I Don't Know, You're Not So Warm." And William Krell, a white Chicago bandleader, copyrighted "Mississippi Rag" the next year, quickly followed by the first black-authored rag to see print, **Tom Turpin**'s "Harlem Rag."

Meanwhile, the growing popularity of ragtime not only gave Joplin the impetus he needed to publish his own ragtime compositions, but prepared the public to recognize his genius. Joplin's "Maple Leaf Rag" came out in 1899, raising the genre to classic proportions, and forever identifying ragtime as a black art form. The fledgling white music industry, however, concerned with money rather than art, forced most of the best rags

. to the sidelines or even out completely, in favor of simple, homogenized tunes white people could comprehend; hence the great popularity of something like Irving Berlin's "Alexander's Ragtime Band" and other pseudo-rags. But Joplin's compositions were too remarkable to be ignored or displaced.

One reason for ragtime's success was its appropriateness for the cakewalk, the black plantation dance the white middle class discovered simultaneously with ragtime. The cakewalk has no set steps, and its improvised struts, prances, and kicks can be done perfectly to ragtime's syncopation, where the left hand plays a steady bass beat and the right hand plays the melody. The melody's strong accents intentionally match the weak accents of the left-hand rhythm.

Ragtime was not universally appreciated. Advocates in both races of a "higher" class of European music found it vulgar. The *Negro Music Journal* in 1902 said, "Let us take a united stand against the Ragtime Evil as we would against bad literature." But something extremely important for world culture was fermenting here. J. B. Priestley wrote, "Out of this ragtime came the fragmentary outlines of the menace to old Europe, the domination of America, the emergence of Africa, the end of confidence and any feeling of security, the nervous excitement, the feeling of modern times."

If you want to know more:

Rudi Blesh and Harriet Janis. *They All Played Ragtime,* revised edition. New York: Music Sales.

"In Paris they call [ragtime] American music."
—James Weldon Johnson

"The American 'rag time' . . . is symbolic of the primitive morality and perceptible moral limitations of the negro type. With the latter[,] sexual restraint is almost

> unknown, and the widest latitude of moral uncertainty
> is conceded."
>
> —Walter Winston Kenilworth,
> in the *Musical Courier*, May 28, 1913

Where did jazz come from?

Jazz grew out of the same ingredients as the blues: a meld of
European musical forms and complex African percussive
rhythms. The poet **Amiri Baraka** suggests that jazz is even based
on the blues: unlike "correctly" played music, jazz imitates the
human voice and is a spontaneous, improvisatory art in which
the performer rather than the composer is the real creator. Jazz
is intense and immediate; it is, in Frederick Turner's phrase,
"the sound of life being lived at the limits."

It is impossible today to sort out jazz's various historical components, which include plantation brass bands, nonunison-
shouting Baptist hymns, Caribbean cult rituals, "the Spanish
tinge" (as Jelly Roll Morton called it), the accents of syncopated
ragtime piano, the shape-note singing of white gospel. But each
of these made a contribution to what became America's most
distinctive indigenous music. Even the meaning of the word *jazz*
itself is lost, although it most likely originated as an African-
American slang term for the rhythmic abandon of sexual inter-
course.

Jazz as we know it emerged in New Orleans around the turn
of the century. It came from the city's marching bands, dance
hall orchestras, riverboat entertainment, advertising wagons,
and sporting-house pianos. New Orleans was—and is—a unique
American city in its blend of races, different cultural traditions,
and sophisticated openness. Unlike other cities, it allowed black
people to gather on Sundays for their own remembered African
music and bamboula, or drum, dances in Congo Square. Also,
the slave trade continued to bring Africans to New Orleans,
often via the West Indies, after the traffic had been stopped

along the Atlantic seaboard. So it can be argued that African influences were stronger in New Orleans than elsewhere.

A libertine, pleasure-seeking French-like city, New Orleans was alive with dance and music—"drenched" in music, historian James Lincoln Collier says. For blacks, there were the street bands belting out "Didn't He Ramble" in the funeral parades back from the cemeteries; the Storyville sporting houses where, Charles E. Smith says, "they wanted the blues slow and mean, and the rags fast and dirty." Also, there were the dances at Johnson Park, where the legendary **Buddy Bolden** would say, "Let's call the children home," put his cornet out the hall window and blow. According to Edward "Kid" Ory, working-class black people from Uptown would come running.

Bunk Johnson says the reason Bolden's band played the best jazz was that none of its members could read music. Old influences were therefore retained, the band was not restricted by conventional musical rules, and its uninhibited members were free to play what they felt. Some New Orleans musicians preferred to "fake" reading music, it is said, and refused to learn for fear it would destroy their ability to play.

It is important to note that in 1894 New Orleans tightened the city's segregation laws, and the middle-class, mixed-blood, French-speaking Creoles, whose trained musicians could indeed read music, were thrown together with the darker-skinned and lower-class African Americans. As a result, there was undoubtedly a mixing of Creole classical training with more "authentic" African-American folk music traditions.

Jazz developed and flourished in Storyville, the legalized red-light district established by the New Orleans City Council in 1897 to contain and control the city's extensive prostitution. Jokingly named after Alderman Sidney Story, it was always called simply the District by residents. There was a white Storyville, some twenty blocks adjoining the French Quarter, and a black Storyville of ten blocks across Canal Street. Black women worked in both places, but black men had access to white Storyville houses only as musicians or other workers, like the young **Louis Armstrong** selling coal from a wagon. According to Al Rose, in 1914 Storyville contained 750 prostitutes (down from an earlier peak of 2,000), 300 pimps, 200 musicians, 500 domestics, and 150 saloon employees. He estimates that 12,000 people lived off the District's income.

Both Storyvilles were wild and wide-open places, though the black district was rougher and poorer. The saloons had no doors, because the drinking and gambling never ceased. Drugs were easily available, and everybody was hustling something or somebody. Drunkenness, robbery, and violence were routine events. The dance halls were so rowdy the musicians played from balconies so they—and their instruments—could be reasonably safe from frequent brawls. The honky-tonks provided constant music, and a musician could earn a dollar a night. Yet in spite of the wildness, Storyville was a neighborhood and community where people lived, raised their families, and remembered with affection each other and the colorful characters drawn to the district.

New Orleans was the home of scores of bawdy houses, from the elegant five-dollar *maisons joies* with mirrored parlors and octoroon women, to the sordid ten-cent shuttered "cribs" that fronted directly on the streets and where adolescent girls wearing see-through teddies worked day and night shifts. The better brothels had pianos, and a good "perfessor" could make big money in tips, as much as $100 a night.

Countess Willie Piazza's fancy Basin Street bordello was supposedly the first to hire a pianist, a legendary rag player remembered only as John the Baptist. Lulu White's famous house was immortalized in **Clarence Williams'** "Mahogany Hall Stomp." When the U.S. Navy closed down Storyville in 1917, the party was over, the jobs in the Tenderloin were gone, and many musicians left New Orleans, following the black emigration routes northward to Kansas City, St. Louis, and, preeminently, Chicago.

New Orleans produced an extraordinary roster of men who could "play hot," as they described the new music. Among the best was Ferdinand "Jelly Roll" Morton, who sported a diamond filling in his front tooth and whose nickname testified to his sexual prowess. He was a hustler, and like other pianists with access to bawdy-house residents, a sometime pimp who often traveled with a retinue of ladies.

Morton was a Creole of color who disliked black people and liked to think of himself as white. He always claimed he "invented" jazz himself in 1902, and that everything significant in the music had been stolen from him. He certainly was a brilliant pianist, the first conscious jazz theorist and composer, and the first to arrange jazz music without sacrificing its spontaneity. His "Jelly Roll Blues" of 1915 was the first published jazz arrangement, and he was the first black to record with a white band, the New Orleans Rhythm Kings, in 1923.

If you want to know more:

Nat Shapiro and Nat Hentoff, eds. *Hear Me Talkin' to Ya: The Story of Jazz as Told by the Men Who Made It.* New York: Dover, 1955.

"Man, if you gotta ask, you'll never know."
— Louis Armstrong

"It [jazz] is the only music that is able to describe the present period in the history of the world."
— Duke Ellington

"Music is your own experience, your thoughts, your wisdom. If you don't live it, it won't come out of your horn."
— Charlie Parker

"The best sound usually comes the first time you do something. If it's spontaneous, it's going to be rough, not clean, but it's going to have the spirit which is the essence of jazz."
— Dave Brubeck

Who was the first African-American artist to achieve international recognition?

James A. Porter, the Howard University art historian and critic, said that **Henry Ossawa Tanner** was "the first genius among Negro artists." Tanner was certainly the first black artist whose talents were recognized around the world. He was born in Pittsburgh, Pennsylvania, June 21, 1859, the son of Benjamin Tucker Tanner and Sarah Miller Tanner. Sarah Tanner was a former slave whose mixed-blood father was the son of a Virginia plantation owner; she had escaped to the North on the Underground Railroad. Benjamin Tanner was a bishop in the African Methodist Episcopal Church and the founder of the AME Church Review, a leading black periodical of the day. He gave his son the middle name "Ossawa," after John Brown of the Osawatomie, Kansas, antislavery raid who was martyred the year Tanner was born.

Tanner studied art at the Pennsylvania Academy of Fine Arts in Philadelphia under Thomas Eakins, who was to remain a major influence on his work. He operated a photograph gallery and taught at Clark College. To escape American racism, both personal and professional, he traveled to Africa and the Middle East and moved to Paris, where he studied at the Académie Julien and where he lived and worked the rest of his life. In 1899 he married Jessie Macaulay Olsson, a white opera singer from San Francisco. They had one son, Jesse Ossawa.

In the 1890s Tanner produced some of his most memorable work, notably *The Banjo Lesson* (1893) and *The Thankful Poor* (1894). In 1895 with *Daniel in the Lion's Den,* he began the paintings with biblical themes for which he is now best remembered. His work displays a unique use of color and, with its dream-like quality, clearly pre-figures the symbolist and impressionist movements. His *Salome* is a decidedly modern picture.

Tanner helped make American art independent of Europe, and he, unlike Bannister and others, used African-American subjects, especially at the beginning of his career. Tanner died in Paris on May 25, 1937. He was known during his lifetime, but he came to greater prominence as time went by, notably by his inclusion in the first large all-black show in this country, at the 135th Street branch of the New York Public Library in 1921. In 1969 there was a major one-person show of his work at the Smithsonian Institution in Washington, D.C.

If you want to know more:

Henry Ossawa Tanner. Philadelphia: Philadelphia Museum of Art, 1991.

> "I believe it, the Negro blood counts and counts to my advantage."
>
> —Henry O. Tanner

> "Four generations were required to produce the first genius among Negro artists. But the interval prepared the way for Henry O. Tanner."
>
> —James A. Porter

> "Tanner tells us much of what he thinks about the world and of man's place in it. This kind of self-exploration when integrated by a personality of real proportions can be both vital and transcendent."
>
> —Romare Bearden

What is the most influential book written by an African-American?

Probably the most influential book by an African American, at least the one most reflective of the African-American experience itself, is **William E. B. Du Bois**'s *The Souls of Black Folk,* published in 1903. Du Bois (1868–1963) was born in Great

Barrington, Massachusetts, and educated at Fisk and Harvard universities as an undergraduate. He took a Ph.D. at Harvard, the first African American to earn a doctorate there, and studied with Max Weber in Berlin at Friedrich Wilhelm University. In 1896 he published his Harvard thesis, *The Suppression of the African Slave Trade,* and was on his way to becoming the international political and intellectual spokesperson for black America, and for other oppressed people as well.

Du Bois published a staggering number of books and articles over his long life, and he wrote in every discipline, from fiction to philosophy, and in every format, from poetry to treatise. His best form, though, was probably the essay, and *The Souls of Black Folk,* written when he was thirty-five years old, is a collection of fourteen essays that artfully combine personal impressions with social data. The result was a book that expressed and communicated to the world, perhaps better than anything before or since, the spirit of the black American. It decidedly shaped the African-American literature that followed.

The Souls of Black Folk contains writing of Du Bois' that has lasted over the years, that is still read and quoted today, and that sustains its original dramatic impact:

> The problem of the twentieth century is the problem of the color line,—the relation of the darker to the lighter races of men in Asia and Africa, in America and the islands of the sea.

Du Bois spoke not only for himself, but articulated the experience of every African American and explicated that experience to nonblacks:

> One ever feels his two-ness,—an American, a Negro; two souls, two thoughts, two unreconciled strivings; two warring ideals in one dark body, whose dogged strength alone keeps it from being torn asunder.

In a moving essay on education and discrimination, Du Bois wrote

From out the caves of evening that swing between the strong-limbed earth and the tracery of the stars, I summon Aristotle and Aurelius and what soul I will, and they come all graciously with no scorn nor condescension. So, wed, with Truth, I dwell above the Veil. Is this the life you grudge us, O knightly America?

If you want to know more:

W. E. B. Du Bois, *The Souls of Black Folk.* Introduction by Henry Louis Gates, Jr. New York: Bantam Books, 1989.

"Would America have been America without her Negro people?"

—W. E. B. Du Bois

"The Nation has not yet found peace from its sin; the freedman has not yet found his promised land."

—W. E. B. Du Bois

Who founded the leading African-American Pentecostal denomination?

Charles H. Mason was born in 1866 near Memphis, Tennessee, to a family of sharecroppers recently freed from slavery. Influenced by the prayer tradition of slave religion, he was healed from sickness in 1880 and baptized in Mount Olive Missionary Baptist Church near Plumersville, Arkansas. An advocate of radical Wesleyanism, he preached the sinless perfection of sanctification subsequent to conversion as a second work of grace. Ordained in 1893, he joined forces with **Charles Price Jones,** who shared his views, but their holiness beliefs resulted in their being disfellowshiped from the Baptist Church.

A new body was formed, with Jones as overseer. Mason said

he heard God speak to him in 1897 in Little Rock, Arkansas, giving him the name Church of God in Christ. In 1907 Jones sent Mason to Los Angeles to investigate the explosive Azusa Street Revival led by William J. Seymour. Mason was literally lifted from his chair by the power he experienced. He combined healing and speaking in tongues with holiness, but he and Jones split over these new doctrines. Jones went on to found the Church of Christ (Holiness) USA, and under Mason's leadership the Church of God in Christ, now with more than 3,500,000 members in over 11,000 local churches, has become the largest African-American Pentecostal denomination.

The early days of the Church of God in Christ were clearly interracial. The first credentials issued to white Assembly of God preachers, for example, were signed by Mason. Interestingly, Mason was a pacifist who attempted, unsuccessfully, to obtain conscientious objector status for members of his church during World War I and was investigated by the FBI. Worldwide Pentecostalism is probably the most important religious phenomenon of the twentieth century. Its African-American roots through Seymour and Mason are clear.

If you want to know more:

Harvey Cox. *Fire from Heaven: The Rise of Pentecostal Spirituality and the Reshaping of Religion in the Twenty-First Century.* Reading, Mass.: Addison-Wesley, 1995.

"It is clear that Mason and his followers felt it to be of far-reaching significance that one of the great religious movements of the twentieth century was founded by a member of the African race."

—F.B.I. files

"I prayed earnestly that God would give me above all things a religion like the one I had heard about from the old slaves and seen demonstrated in their lives."

—Charles H. Mason

Who was the King of Ragtime?

Scott Joplin was known during his lifetime as the King of
Ragtime, a title of honor that continues to be attached to his
name, both because of the brilliance of his piano compositions,
and, after years of neglect, because of the assured place he
holds now in the history of American music. Joplin was born,
perhaps on November 24, 1868, near Texarkana, Texas. His father, Giles, a tenant farmer and railroad worker, was a former
slave from North Carolina who played the violin. His mother,
Florence Givens, was from Kentucky and played the banjo. Joplin displayed extraordinary musical talent as a child, so much so
that his mother, a domestic who cleaned the houses of white
people, took him with her to work and persuaded her employers to let him practice on their pianos.

Joplin traveled as a young man, playing in black saloons and
whorehouses from Texas to Missouri and the adjacent states. In
St. Louis in 1885 he worked in the red-light district at the Silver
Dollar Saloon owned by Honest John Turpin, a fellow composer
and pianist whose son Tom Turpin wrote the first ragtime tune,
"Harlem Rag," in 1892. The club was a meeting place and employment office for pianists; one of the young women from the
sporting houses would appear and announce that they had a
customer and needed a professor.

In 1893 Joplin went to the World's Columbian Exposition in
Chicago, where he organized and led a band and discovered
that white people liked and appreciated his music. He settled
in Sedalia, Missouri, where he played at the Maple Leaf Club at
121 East Main Street and studied music at the George R. Smith
College for Negroes. By this time ragtime was becoming popular across the country, and Joplin, who had already published a
few ballads and marches, decided to try and sell a composition
in the style in which he composed and played best. There are
many stories about how "Maple Leaf Rag" got published. One
is that Joplin took it to the white music publisher John Stark.
He also took along a small boy, whose job was to dance while

Joplin played the piece, so Stark could see that "Maple Leaf Rag" was a danceable tune.

Stark was so impressed he not only accepted the rag for publication, but agreed to pay royalties instead of the usual procedure of merely buying the piece outright for a few dollars. Joplin was to receive one cent per copy on sheet music that sold for 50 cents. The first year, 1899, Stark sold 400 copies, so Joplin made $4. But in 1900, "Maple Leaf Rag" became a national sensation, the first great instrumental sheet music hit, and Stark received orders for so many copies he had to stop printing anything else. It sold a million copies, made Joplin famous and Stark rich, and changed the face of American popular music.

Joplin continued to write successful rags, but as the genre became even more popular, he shifted his interest toward making ragtime more respectable and even classical. He composed *The Ragtime Dance,* a ballet using the popular black dances of the day, including the slow drag and the dude walk. He then created *A Guest of Honor,* a ragtime opera that was well received in a 1902 St. Louis performance, but which John Stark thought unmarketable and refused to publish. The manuscript is now lost.

Increasingly committed to legitimizing the ragtime music of African Americans, Joplin composed pieces like "The Chrysanthemum: An Afro-Intermezzo," and in 1908 issued a manual called *The School of Ragtime,* instructions on how to play the music correctly. Profoundly critical of ragtime's vulgar imitations and cheap commercialization, he included clear instructions on his sheet music: "Do not play this piece fast."

Moving to New York, Joplin wrote *Treemonisha,* a 230-page, three-act ragtime grand opera that he was finally forced to publish himself in 1911. Unable to find support or backing, depressed and short of money, Joplin rented Harlem's Lincoln Theatre in 1915 and put on a trial performance. Unable to afford an orchestra, he played the entire score himself on the piano. *Treemonisha* was not a success, and there was not a full production of this uniquely indigenous American opera until 1972 in Atlanta, Georgia.

A critical incident in the evolution of *Treemonisha*—and of ragtime itself—concerned the "Marching Onward" section of "A Real Slow Drag" in the finale of Joplin's opera. He took the manuscript to several publishers, including Crown-Seminary-Snyder, all of whom turned it down. All of a sudden, a new popular song stole the show in *The Merry Whirl,* a revue that opened May 30, 1910. *Variety* called it, "the musical sensation of the decade." It sold a million sheet music copies the first year, and earned a phenomenal $30,000 in royalties. Joplin immediately recognized the theme of "Alexander's Ragtime Band" by Irving Berlin as his own tune.

Berlin was working at Crown-Seminary-Snyder and had rejected *Treemonisha* when Joplin submitted it there. Belief that he had stolen the song was so widespread that Berlin felt obliged to write an article publicly denying it. Joplin rewrote that section of his work, but the similarities can still be heard. Ironically, "Alexander's Ragtime Band" is only a weak, nonsyncopated imitation of a rag, but it was homogenized enough to enter the white American musical mainstream, where it became a classic. Even more ironically, it won for Berlin the title "King of Ragtime," even though he once admitted, "I never did find out what ragtime was."

Ill with syphilis, Joplin entered Manhattan State Hospital in New York, where he died April 1, 1917. Ragtime's syncopation helped form the basis for jazz, a new African-American music that began its national impact and influence just at the time of Joplin's death. Jazz soon totally eclipsed ragtime as a popular musical form. Ragtime had several rebirths, though. One major resurrection was in 1970 at the successful re-recording of Joplin's rags by Joshua Rifkin. His performance was responsible for the use of several Joplin rags, including "The Entertainer" in the soundtrack of the Academy Award–winning 1973 film *The Sting* with Paul Newman and Robert Redford. Joplin's dream for the recognition and legitimization of ragtime as a uniquely American and distinctively African-American music, which had eluded him in his lifetime, did come true at last.

If you want to know more:

Edward A. Berlin. *King of Ragtime: Scott Joplin and His Era.* New York: Oxford University Press, 1994.

> "Oh go 'way man
> I can hypnotize dis nation
> I can shake de earth's foundation
> Wid de Maple Leaf Rag."
> —Sydney Brown, "The Maple Leaf Rag Song"

> "He wanted to free his people from poverty, ignorance, and superstition, just like the heroine of his ragtime opera, *Treemonisha*."
> —Lottie Joplin, Scott Joplin's wife

> "*[Treemonisha]* is not . . . an 'opera' in any conventional sense; indeed, it is something much more interesting: it is what Joplin conceived an opera as being."
> —William J. Schafer and Johannes Riedel

Who was the Wizard of Tuskegee?

Booker T. Washington (1856–1915) was called the "Wizard of Tuskegee" because of the power and influence he wielded both within the African-American community and as a power broker between blacks and the white elite who controlled government, education, and philanthropy. Frederick Douglass, the chief African-American spokesperson of the century and a tireless advocate of civil rights, died February 20, 1895. On September 18, only seven months later, Washington made a speech at the Cotton States and International Exposition at Atlanta that brought him to national attention and led to his anointing by the white establishment as the nation's leading Negro.

The mid-1890s were probably the most desperate years for African Americans since the end of slavery. Attempts at political and economic Reconstruction were being successfully beaten back by a white South bent on "redeeming" their states from any attempt to construct a democratic society. Murder, arson, rape, looting, and intimidation were used without any fear of justice; many blacks were reduced to the economic peonage of tenant farming and sharecropping, institutions hardly different from slavery; and the states enacted without federal hindrance legislation to segregate African Americans into second-class citizenship. A black person was lynched on an average of one every other day.

Into the midst of this disaster stepped Booker T. Washington, with an address at Atlanta which, for all practical purposes, agreed to accept the new white domination. "Cast down your bucket where you are," he advised black people—that is, assume responsibility for your own situation and for improving it. "In all things that are purely social," he said to white people, "we can be as separate as the fingers, yet one as the hand in all things essential to mutual progress." In one sentence Washington thus accommodated black America to racial segregation, and his speech became known, appropriately, as the Atlanta Compromise. It was a sad repudiation of the fighting spirit of Douglass.

Booker T. Washington was born in slavery on April 5, 1856, in rural Virginia, to Jane Ferguson, a plantation cook. His father was an unknown white man. The family moved to Malden, West Virginia, where Washington at age nine worked with his stepfather in the salt mines, and from ages ten to twelve in coal mines. He first learned to read by memorizing the numbers on the underground containers he and his father filled with coal. At age sixteen Washington walked five hundred miles to Hampton Normal and Agricultural Institute with $1.50 in his pocket. He became a student in this school for blacks founded by the American Missionary Association and headed by Samuel Chapman Armstrong, the first of several white father-figures in Washington's life.

In 1881 Washington had an unusual opportunity: to become founding principal of the Tuskegee Normal School for Colored Youth, established in Alabama by the state legislature, which appropriated $2,000 for salaries. He opened the school with 30 students in an AME Zion church. However, when Washington died in 1915, Tuskegee had a $2,000,000 endowment, a staff of

200, plus 2,000 regular students and 2,000 more in extension classes. He built Tuskegee on racial and educational principles he had learned at Hampton: hard work, good manners, cleanliness, thrift, self-reliance, practicality, and above all, subservience to the white power structure.

In 1901 Washington published his inspirational autobiography, *Up from Slavery*, actually ghostwritten by Max Thrasher, a white man. The book became a best-seller, with its simple narrative, its story of success, and its humility. These same qualities endeared Washington to prominent whites: northern philanthropists showered him with money, and presidents of the United States consulted him on their few black appointments. Theodore Roosevelt shocked the country by actually inviting Washington to lunch at the White House.

The Wizard of Tuskegee built a power base that came to be known as the Tuskegee Machine. Civil rights advocates like William Monroe Trotter of Boston and intellectuals like W. E. B. Du Bois, who criticized industrial education at the expense of the liberal arts, became Washington's enemies and the subjects of secret opposition. With large sums of money at his disposal, Washington paid black newspapers to glorify his Tuskegee "idea" and to disparage those who disagreed with it. He seemed sincerely to believe that by picking themselves up economically by their own bootstraps and living middle-class lives of respectability, black people would so impress white people that they would simply abandon their racist beliefs and practices and grant political rights and social equality to African Americans.

In spite of his opposition to civil rights and intellectuals, though, Washington did use some of his secret money to lobby behind the scenes for black civil rights. He sent his own son to Fisk University, the center of black academic education, instead of Tuskegee, the center of the vocational training he championed. His philosophy of black self-reliance did inspire nationalists and militants like **Marcus Garvey,** and continues to motivate those who believe in a "do-it-yourself" philosophy. Perhaps the best that can be said for Washington's accommodationism is that it was a practical necessity at the time, when overt opposition to Southern racism would have been suicidal.

If you want to know more:

Booker T. Washington. *Up from Slavery*. Edited, with an introduction by William L. Andrews. New York: Oxford University Press, 1995.

> "The wisest among my race understand that the agitation of questions of social equality is the extremest folly."
>
> —Booker T. Washington
>
> "At the bottom of education, at the bottom of politics, even at the bottom of religion, there must be for our race economic independence."
>
> —Booker T. Washington
>
> "No race can prosper till it learns that there is as much dignity in tilling a field as in writing a poem."
>
> —Booker T. Washington
>
> "Character, not circumstances, makes the man."
>
> —Booker T. Washington
>
> "No student is permitted to remain [at Tuskegee] who does not keep and use a tooth-brush."
>
> —Booker T. Washington

What was the American Negro Academy?

The American Negro Academy was the first, and most important, African-American learned society, but it has always been a neglected institution, generally ignored by the public, both black and white, during its existence (1897–1928), treated slightly by many of its own members in its lifetime, and often ignored by historians since. Yet the Academy included some of the most significant African-American men (it essentially excluded women) of its day: **Alexander Crummell, W. E. B. Du Bois, Archibald Grimke, John W. Cromwell,** and **Arthur A. Schomburg** all served as presidents.

The Academy grew out of the period historian Rayford Logan aptly called "the betrayal of the Negro." Leon Litwack and other scholars have described how a combination of factors created a nadir for black Americans: the failure of Reconstruction; disfranchisement; the codification of Jim Crow segregation laws under the blessing of the U.S. Supreme Court; "scientific" racism on the part of the leading white scholars, which "proved" black inferiority; and economic repression by northern Republican industrialist-philanthropists rationalized by the philosophy of Booker T. Washington.

As a result of this total onslaught, African Americans forced out of all aspects of mainstream America began to build more self-sufficient communities of their own. The American Negro Academy sought to be a community of black intellectuals, leading and protecting their people by opposing racism on truly scientific grounds, encouraging prideful consciousness of black history and culture, and demonstrating that people of color were fully capable of scholarly achievement on a level with whites.

From the outset, the Academy manifested the tension between, on the one hand, assimilationism, which included an elevated distance from black folk culture, and a certain intellectual elitism, and, on the other hand, a perspective that valued a distinct African-American ethnic identity and supported a definition of American nationality that could encompass it. Two of the important addresses to the Academy wrestled with these themes: Alexander Crummell's "Civilization, the Primal Need of the Negro Race," and W. E. B. Du Bois's "The Conservation of the Races."

The Academy intended to produce a journal, aid talented

young people, establish a library, have a full complement of fifty members, and exert influence on educated people both black and white. It never accomplished these goals, partly because, being in Washington, D.C., it was somewhat isolated, partly because many of its members were already overcommitted and involved in other activities, and partly because Booker T. Washington was opposed to it.

There was a strong positive side, though. The Academy attracted attention and publicity from its exhibitions of rare African-American books. It supported Howard University scholar Kelly Miller's effort to have Howard University establish a special library collection of African and African-American material. Perhaps most important was the Academy's publication of the papers delivered at its own meetings. There were five monographs and twenty-two occasional papers, all significant intellectual contributions, and a lasting tribute to the successful achievement of the idea of a learned society.

The American Negro Academy faded out of existence just at the time of the arrival of the New Negro and the Harlem Renaissance, when black art, music, literature, and dance began to capture the national imagination. Perhaps the reason for the success of the Renaissance is that it drew upon the uniqueness and vitality of the black folk tradition and not on the model of a European scholarly tradition, which of course was the basis of the Academy. At any rate, the "sophisticated and regenerative" culture of which Crummell spoke came into existence, and Du Bois' hope for "the great message we have for humanity" began to be realized in ways neither of them expected, and the Academy disappeared.

If you want to know more:

Alfred A. Moss. *The American Negro Academy: Voice of the Talented Tenth.* Baton Rouge, La.: Louisiana State University Press, 1981.

"For the development of Negro genius, of Negro literature and art, of Negro spirit, only Negroes bound and welded together, Negroes inspired by one vast ideal, can work out in its fullness the great message we have for humanity."

—W. E. B. Du Bois

Who said, "God is a Negro"?

Henry McNeal Turner, a bishop of the African Methodist Episcopal Church, was a leading advocate of African colonization because he believed racism foreclosed any meaningful future for black people in America. His radicalism made him a predecessor of Malcolm X and the militant black nationalist tradition. He was born in 1834 to free parents, Hardy and Sarah Green Turner, near Alberta, South Carolina. He managed to learn to read and write.

Turner was converted in a white Methodist camp meeting, but he abandoned what he discovered to be a paternalistic and controlling denomination for an independent black church. When he became a minister, his congregation was a recruiting station for black troops in the Civil War, and he served as a Union army chaplain with the 1st U.S. Colored Troops, the first black army chaplain. He was elected to the Georgia legislature, but, like **Julian Bond** later, he was denied his seat because of his race. He recruited AME ministers by asking, "Can you preach?" and by filling out licenses on street corners and on railroad cars. He saw AME church membership shift from north to south, providing a refuge from white hostility to black freedom following Reconstruction, and creating a truly national institution. He was president of Morris Brown College in Atlanta.

Turner ordained a woman, Sarah Ann Hughes, to the ministry (although the denomination later overruled him). He received into the AME Church the Ethiopian Church of Mangena

Mokone in South Africa. He was high church in ritual and evangelical in theology. He said, "God is a Negro," and advocated retranslating the Bible from an African-American perspective. He wrote, "A man must believe he is somebody before he is acknowledged as somebody . . . Respect black." He said, "Hell is an improvement over the United States where the Negro is concerned," and managed to die across the border in Windsor, Ontario, Canada, on May 8, 1915.

If you want to know more:

Stephen Ward Angell. *Bishop Henry McNeal Turner and African-American Religion in the South.* Knoxville, Tenn.: University of Tennessee Press, 1992.

"A man who loves a country that hates him is a human dog and not a man."
—Henry McNeal Turner

"We have as much right biblically and otherwise to believe that God is a Negro as white people have to believe that God is a fine-looking, symmetrical and ornamental white man."
—Henry McNeal Turner

"No one can say, who has any respect for the truth, that the United States is a civilized nation, especially if we take the daily papers and inspect them for a few moments and see the deeds of horror."
—Henry McNeal Turner

Who was the Mother of the Blues?

Gertrude Pridgett "Ma" Rainey was a traveling vaudeville and tent show performer who first heard a blues song in Missouri in 1902 and added it to her act. It was so popular with her audiences she developed a repertoire of blues songs, influenced somewhat by then popular tunes of the day as well as by jazz and folk music, and she became the first of the great women singers of classic urban blues. Rainey was a short, heavyset, dark-skinned woman with a contralto voice who made a flamboyant appearance on stage, with her necklace of $20 gold pieces, her gold-capped teeth, and her diamond jewelry, sequined dresses, and ostrich plumes. Other performers said she had "the ugliest face in show business," but common people loved her style, her raucous humor, and her plaintive blues songs, which spoke of their own lives and experiences.

Rainey was born in Columbus, Georgia, on April 26, 1886, the daughter of Thomas and Ella Allen Pridgett. Her parents may have been minstrel performers, and Rainey herself was in a local show called *A Bunch of Blackberries* at the age of fourteen. In 1904 she married William Rainey, also a performer, and they toured in various shows such as the famous "Foots" (i.e., the Rabbit Foot Minstrels) and the Florida Cotton Blossoms.

Rainey was called "Ma" not because she was older, but as an abbreviation of "Mama," an affectionate term for a sensuous lover. Her chorus line women were also full-figured and dark, and Rainey was said never to hire a chorus girl lighter than she was. Her shows were full of low-down humor and sexual innuendo, and the show stopper featured Rainey and the entire cast doing a wild singing and dancing version of **Georgia Tom Dorsey**'s "It's Tight Like That."

Like many other black female performers of her day, Rainey was bisexual. She liked young chorus girls as much as she liked young men. Several of her songs had overtly homosexual themes, like "Prove It On Me":

> I went out last night with a couple of my friends,
> It must have been womens 'cause I don't like men.

Or these lines from "Sissy Blues":

> My man's got a sissy,
> His name is Miss Kate.
> He shook that thing
> Like jelly on a plate.

Rainey's most memorable records, like those of Bessie Smith, were with Louis Armstrong's accompaniment. She and Armstrong turned "See See Rider Blues," which Rainey was the first to record, into a classic. Starting in 1923, all in all, she recorded ninety-two sides. Rainey retired in 1935, and bought theaters in two Georgia cities, Rome and Columbus. She died in Rome on December 22, 1939. Though memory of her tended to fade after her death, she was dramatically brought back to life by August Wilson's play *Ma Rainey's Black Bottom* (the title of one of her double-entendre songs). The play opened at the Yale Repertory Theatre in New Haven, Connecticut, on April 6, 1984, with Theresa Merritt playing the lead.

If you want to know more:

Sandra Lieb. *Mother of the Blues: A Study of Ma Rainey*. Amherst, Mass.: University of Massachusetts Press, 1981.

> "I talked to a fellow, an' the fellow say,
> 'She jes' catch hold of us, somekindaway.' "
> —Sterling Brown, "Ma Rainey," 1932

> "Chains on my feet
> Padlocks on my hands
> It's all on account
> Of stealin' another gal's man."
> —Ma Rainey, "Chain Gang Blues"

What film most influenced popular views of African Americans?

Artistically and technically, **D. W. Griffith**'s *Birth of a Nation*, his epic film on the Civil War and Reconstruction, is considered a masterpiece of moviemaking. In terms of vividly presenting life on the screen, it was not only the first true spectacular, but it has been called the greatest movie ever made. In terms of content, however, its portrayal of American history is so distorted and its view of African Americans so biased that probably no other film has done so much damage both to black people and to the truth of the historical record. The high quality of *The Birth of a Nation* as a film made its negative impact all the more influential.

On the positive side, *The Birth of a Nation* is an innovative film that has strongly influenced movie directors ever since. Its sweep is daring; its twelve reels run for three hours, while other films of the day were only two or three reels long. It experimented with a number of techniques now commonplace: the close-up, the split screen, the moving camera, night photography, and creative lighting and editing. It was the first film to have a special orchestral score. It took two years to make and cost a whopping $100,000, an extraordinary sum for the time.

The Birth of a Nation was based on two novels by Thomas Dixon, Jr., a North Carolina state representative: *The Leopard's Spots: A Romance of the White Man's Burden* and *The Clansman: A Historical Romance of the Ku Klux Klan*, which he wrote to counter a stage version he'd seen of Harriet Beecher Stowe's *Uncle Tom's Cabin*. In fact, the film's first title was *The Clansman*. Griffith, the director, was born in Kentucky, the son of a Confederate war hero. Dixon earned an astounding $750,000 in royalties, the highest amount ever generated by a silent film.

The movie tells the interwoven story of two families, the Southern Camerons and the Northern Stonemans. The character of Austin Stoneman was based on the life of Thaddeus Stevens, the Pennsylvania congressman, abolitionist, civil rights advocate, and leader of the Radical Republicans in the House of Representatives. The story follows the two families through the Civil War and Reconstruction. There were no African Americans in the film; their roles were played by white actors in blackface.

In its view of history, *The Birth of a Nation* portrays an extreme Southern interpretation of Reconstruction: the freed slaves were childlike creatures better off under benevolent slavery, or beasts recently removed from the jungle who needed to be restrained by the slave system. The film depicted a political stranglehold on the defeated white South, where drunken and illiterate black legislators leered at white women in the balcony while resting their bare feet on the South Carolina state house desks.

When it was suggested there were inaccuracies, Griffith offered $10,000 to anyone who could prove that anything in the film was not historical. The president of the NAACP, Moorfield Storey, asked what African-American lieutenant governor had bound and gagged a white woman in order to force her into marriage. Of course there had been none, but Griffith never paid.

The Birth of a Nation was apparently the first film shown in the White House. No documentation exists, but President Woodrow Wilson, a historian of note and a former president of Princeton University, is reputed to have said, "It's like writing history with lightning, and my one regret is that it is all so terribly true." Wilson was a Southern Democrat, born in Virginia, whose administration systematically resegregated government offices and bathrooms for the first time since the Civil War and began to eliminate African Americans from government service.

If the film's presentation of history was more myth and rationalization than fact, its portrayal of individual black people was insidious, utilizing every stereotype: "toms, coons, mulattos, mammies, and bucks," to borrow film writer Donald Bogle's famous list. The movie was especially interested in "bucks" and sex. Perhaps its most dramatic sequence is the stalking through the woods of the virginal white "Little Sister" Cameron by Gus, a wild-eyed, sex-crazed Negro whose mouth was foaming with lust—an effect created by a mouthwash of hydrogen peroxide.

Today this all seems absurd enough to be amusing. But in 1915, the historical distortions and racial stereotypes, which served the ends of Southern white supremacists, were through the power and popularity of the film established as truth in the public mind, North as well as South. People saw the film and actually believed that Reconstruction had been a mistake and that people of color were savages. The NAACP and other liberal groups attempted to stop the film from being shown, but their protest brought a rejoinder of censorship and probably only contributed to the film's notoriety.

John Hope Franklin, the distinguished historian, points out that the black rule pictured in *The Birth of a Nation* never took place anywhere, and he blames the film more than any other source for the popular perception that blacks could not be trusted with the ballot. It thus helped promote justification of the systematic disfranchisement of blacks by whites until the Voting Rights Act of 1965.

Even more serious is the film's contention that violence was and is justified in regaining and maintaining white supremacy. In the film, Gus' castrated corpse is thrown on the porch of the mulatto lieutenant governor by the Ku Klux Klan as a rightful punishment for his rape of Little Sister. The white-sheeted Klan are the film's true heroes, restoring the rule of the superior master class, riding to rescue from black federal troops a group of whites "united in defense of their common Aryan birthright." At the movie's premiere in Los Angeles on February 8, 1915, the audience stood up and cheered.

If you want to know more:

Robert Lang, ed. *The Birth of a Nation*. New Brunswick, N.J.: Rutgers University Press, 1994.

"[This film] tends to prevent the lowering of the standard of our citizenship by its mixture with Negro blood."

—Thomas Dixon

"[*The Birth of a Nation*] in its first eleven months in New York City had 6,266 showings and was seen by an estimated 3,000,000 people."

—Ed Guerrero

"A favorite and effective [publicity] stunt to whip up excitement was to have a troop of horsemen dressed up in the white sheets of the Ku Klux Klan ride through towns on their hooded horses in advance of showings of the film."

—Bosley Crowther

What was an unexpected by-product of World War I?

An unusual and unexpected result of World War I was the dissemination of African-American music abroad, particularly by Lieutenant James Reese Europe's "Hellfighters" military band. Europe (1881–1919) had organized the Clef Club in 1910, a conglomerate of black musicians in New York that soon dominated professional musical engagements and private parties. Clef Club musicians presented in 1912 an innovative and highly successful symphony of "Negro music" at Carnegie Hall, and in 1914 Europe's own orchestra was taken up by the fashionable white couple Irene and Vernon Castle. They were popularizing modern social dancing by modifying black dance for white people, making it "respectable." That same year Europe's orchestra became the first black orchestral group to record.

While this was all prior to the full emergence of jazz and the introduction of real black dancing in the 1920s, it did mark a vitally important transition in popular music. It also set the stage for the appearance of more authentic African-American rhythms during the Jazz Age.

During World War I, Europe led a military band that was part of the 15th Regiment of the New York National Guard, which became the 369th Infantry Regiment of the American Expeditionary Force. The 369th were racially segregated African-

American troops who spent 191 days under fire, never yielded a foot of ground, and were awarded France's highest military award, the Croix de Guerre.

Their band was a sensation, playing syncopated music in a black style for both American soldiers and French audiences. Europe had to rehearse his band, not to improve their playing, but to prevent them from incorporating too much of the new African-American style. Once, when French army musicians tried unsuccessfully to copy the Hellfighters' orchestrations, French band members actually went over to examine the black Americans' instruments in order to discover the secret of the unique new sound.

In the spring of 1919, at the end of the war, a million people lined Fifth Avenue to welcome home the victorious 15th Regiment. Led by Europe's Hellfighters band, with Guillard Thompson out in front as drum major, the triumphant troops marched smartly up Manhattan toward Harlem. When they reached 130th Street, however, the military music stopped, the soldiers spread out from their closed ranks, and the Hellfighters band broke into an exuberant "Here Comes My Daddy!" The last mile of the victory march was a homecoming only Harlem could give its own.

If you want to know more:

Reid Badger. *A Life in Ragtime: A Biography of James Reese Europe.* New York: Oxford University Press, 1995.

"Lieutenant Europe, I want you to organize for me the best damn brass band in the United States Army."
—Colonel William Hayword

"Everywhere we gave a concert, it was a riot."
—James Reese Europe

"[James Reese Europe] was just something that had to happen in America. He was at a point in time when all the roots and forces of Negro music merged and gained its widest expression."

—Eubie Blake

CHAPTER 4

∾

From the Harlem Renaissance to the *Brown* Decision, 1920–1954

What was the Harlem Renaissance?

Who was the major black entertainer of the 1920s?

What was special about *Shuffle Along*?

What is the best book to come out of the Harlem Renaissance?

Who are some of the other writers of the Harlem Renaissance?

What was the high point of the Jazz Age?

What were the Negro leagues?

Who was the most promising writer of the Harlem Renaissance?

What is the most important date in jazz history?

Who was the Empress of the Blues?

What African-American master sculptor began and ended her career as a housemaid?

What is *God's Trombones*?

Who was the most popular male blues recording artist of the 1920s?

What was the largest mass movement among African Americans?

Who was the Poet Laureate of Harlem?

Who is the Father of Black History?

Who collected books by and about African Americans?

What blues singer made a pact with the Devil?

What sport became a symbolic arena for black-white rivalry?

Who were the Scottsboro Boys?

Who was the greatest American cartoonist?

Who transformed the image of the mature black woman?

What is black gospel music?

What movie is alleged to have ruined attempts for a federal antilynching law?

Who was the first African American to win an Academy Award?

Who received mail addressed to "God, Harlem USA"?

Who was the Schoolmaster of the Civil Rights Movement?

What was the Tuskegee Syphilis Study?

~

What was the Harlem Renaissance?

The Harlem Renaissance was a period of extraordinary creativity among African-American writers, artists, musicians, and actors. But the Harlem Renaissance has many anomalies. First of all, it was not, strictly speaking, a *renaissance* at all—it was less a rebirth of African-American culture than it was an efflorescence. Second, it did not take place exclusively in Harlem: black culture flourished in many other areas. It was centered in Harlem, though, and one reason was because the publishing industry was and is located in New York, and the Renaissance is now chiefly thought of as a literary movement.

There was no agreement on just what time period the Harlem Renaissance covered, though it certainly centered in the 1920s. Perhaps it began with **Claude McKay**'s militant poem published in the *Liberator* in 1919 in response to the brutal race riots that had swept the country:

> If we must die, let it not be like hogs
> Hunted and penned in an inglorious spot,
>
> . . . .
> If we must die, O let us nobly die,
>
> . . . .
> Like men we'll face the murderous, cowardly pack
> Pressed to the wall, dying, but fighting back!

The poem certainly announced a new, self-confident black militancy, partly a result of the black participation in World War I, a war whose propaganda slogan was "Make the world safe for democracy." Those who fought for that ideal with great courage were not about to be content with less than democracy at home. It is not accidental that **Marcus Garvey**'s nationalistic Universal Negro Improvement Association came into being during the same decade, though politics is often divorced from the Harlem Renaissance in discussions of the history of the period.

If it is uncertain when the Renaissance began, it is even less clear when it ended. In many ways, everything was over in 1929, when the stock market crash and the onslaught of the Great Depression threw Harlem and other black communities into a degree of poverty that was best described in the grim, realistic proletarian novels of the 1930s. But **Zora Neale Hurston** published well into the '30s, as did **Langston Hughes,** so perhaps the Renaissance continued beyond the end of the Jazz Age.

Reference to the Jazz Age reminds us that it was also no accident that the great African-American blues singers and jazz bands flourished during this same period. It would be just as much a mistake to ignore black music during the Harlem Renaissance as to ignore politics, though both of these are seldom dealt with in connection with the literary movement of the period.

The writers were certainly extraordinary: **Countee Cullen, Langston Hughes, James Weldon Johnson, Nella Larson, Jean Toomer, Wallace Thurman, Jessie Faucet.** And the artists are also strong: **Aaron Douglas, Richmond Barthe, Augusta Savage.** African-American performers dominated Broadway during the Roaring Twenties, with memorable singing and dancing shows that made a low-down black dance called the Charleston the physical movement that symbolized the decade, and with shows like *Shuffle Along, Runnin' Wild, Hot Chocolates,* and *Blackbirds.*

The term *Harlem Renaissance* itself is a relatively modern one. Apparently, it was first used extensively in Melvin Tolson's master's thesis at Columbia University in 1940. During the 1920s what was happening was generally referred to as the New Negro Movement. In many ways that is a more instructive name. African Americans of the 1920s were in fact new: new in assurance and confidence, new in affirming their African heritage, new in exhibiting to the world their creative genius in poetry, prose, dance, song, and painting. It was an electric era.

If you want to know more:

Nathan Huggins, *Harlem Renaissance*. New York: Oxford University Press, 1971.

> "Our poets have now stopped speaking for the Negro—they speak as Negroes. Where formerly they spoke to others and tried to interpret, they now speak to their own and try to express."
>
> —Alain Locke,
> first African-American Rhodes scholar

> "In flavor of language, flow of phrase, accent of rhythm in prose, verse and music, color and tone of imagery, idiom and timbre of emotion and symbolism, it is the ambition and promise of Negro artists to make a distinctive contribution."
>
> —Alain Locke

> "Subtly the conditions that are molding a New Negro are molding a new American attitude."
>
> —Alain Locke

> "Negro life is seizing upon its first chances of group expression and self-determination."
>
> —Alain Locke

Who was the major black entertainer of the 1920s?

Florence Mills was undoubtedly the most popular African-American entertainer of the 1920s, the decade that combined the Jazz Age, the Roaring Twenties, and the Harlem Renaissance. Although little remembered today, Mills was beloved in Harlem because, despite her influential fame, she never forgot her origins. She was also the first great crossover artist since **Aida Overton Walker,** bringing African-American singing and dancing to white audiences.

Mills was born in Washington, D.C., on January 25, 1896, to John and Nellie Simons Winfrey, who had left Lynchburg, Virginia, because of the economic depression in the tobacco industry, in which they both worked. At the time, Washington was the largest black city in America, and one that retained some rights and opportunities for people of color because the government was controlled by Republicans. But Mills' illiterate parents were unskilled and merely part of a large influx of black people moving from country to city and from South to North, looking for work. Mills' father was an often unemployed laborer, and her mother took in laundry, including that of a whorehouse.

Mills, however, as "Baby Florence," found a way out of the wretched life of Washington's poverty-stricken Goat Alley. A precocious singer and dancer, she appeared at local amateur shows when she was as young as three years old. At age seven she was an extra in the visiting Williams and Walker show *Sons of Ham,* where the great Aida Walker taught Mills her own hit song "Miss Hannah from Savannah," and more important, served as a role model to the little girl. The next year Mills went on the road full-time as a "pickaninny," a stereotypical cute African-American child, in a white vaudeville act. In a few years she and her sisters organized their own song-and-dance team, playing the East Coast black vaudeville houses.

Exhausted by the grueling life of black vaudeville, Mills landed in Chicago just before World War I, when its South Side was jammed with black immigrants and was jamming with music and nightlife. She went to work at the Panama Cafe, a scandalous cabaret in the honky-tonk and red-light district, famous as the place to go for sexual liaisons across the color line. With Ada "Bricktop" Smith and Cora Green, Mills sang in the Panama Trio, with the legendary **Tony Jackson** on piano, the only piano player **Jelly Roll Morton** admitted was better than he was.

When the Chicago police closed the Panama after a fatal shooting, Mills went back into vaudeville. She was working in New York when Gertrude Saunders left the black hit *Shuffle Along,* and Mills was hired to replace her as the ingenue. *Shuffle Along* presented Mills to a national audience and made her famous. With her curious, high-pitched, bird voice, her intricate and fast dancing, the bronze-colored, hundred-pound, twenty-six-year-old Mills was something new on the American stage: a singer who could bring real black style to popular songs, and real black rhythm to dance steps.

Despite her new popularity, however, race remained the major factor in Mills' life. Irving Berlin said if he could find a white woman who could put over a song as she did, he would be inspired to write a hit a week. Lew Leslie's remodeled night-spot over the Winter Garden theater was renamed The Plantation, and featured Mills singing, but the decor included such stereotypic images as an imitation log cabin and a chandelier in the form of a watermelon.

The nightclub show was easily adapted for Broadway, and Leslie's *Plantation Revue* opened at the Forty-eighth Street Theatre on July 22, 1922. The critics loved Mills' verve and vitality, the breathtaking dancing of the black cast, and the authenticity of real African-American singing and dancing. The success of *Plantation Revue* was still not enough to bring Mills into the all-white American show business establishment, but Sir Charles B. Cochran brought her and the revue to London's Pavilion in the spring of 1923.

There were several significant consequences to Mills' London appearance. She instantly became so personally popular that audiences applauded her before each number, a tribute, Cochran said, he had never seen given any other performer. More important, the impact of African-American song and dance on British intellectuals was dramatic. Critics said that Mills' performance, along with those of her fellow African Americans, was art, even high art, and not mere entertainment. Constant Lambert, for example, musical director of Sadler's Wells Ballet was profoundly inspired by Mills and began adapting jazz rhythms to his work.

Returning to New York, Mills appeared, despite the white cast's opposition, in the *Greenwich Village Follies*. Then came an extraordinary break: Florenz Ziegfeld offered her a lead role in his Follies, the acme of American show business, where she would be the only black performer, and only the second in history, **Bert Williams** having died in 1922. She rejected Ziegfeld's offer. Mills did want to break Broadway's racial restrictions, but she also wanted the world to see black entertainment not simply in one person, but in the fullness of an entire cast and production.

Mills' response, therefore, was to create a show as lavish as a Ziegfeld production—but with an all-black cast. The *Amsterdam News* responded: "Loyalty of Florence Mills to the race against temptation to become a renowned star of an Anglo-Saxon musical extravaganza has saved for the stage and the race what promises to be one of the most distinctive forms of American entertainment ever created—an All Colored revue."

Mills' first step toward her goal was *From Dixie to Broadway,* which opened at the Broadhurst in New York in the fall of 1924 and was the first black musical comedy in the heart of the theater district. Here she sang "I'm a Little Blackbird Looking for a Bluebird," which became her trademark. The white critics were enchanted, calling her "a slender streak of genius," "an artist in jazz," "an exotic done in brass." After the show's road tour, Mills broke another racial barrier. On June 27, 1924, she became the first black woman actually to headline at the Palace, the nation's premier variety theater.

Mills next devoted herself to creating her major all-black revue. It was *Blackbirds of 1926* and opened at the Alhambra Theatre in Harlem. After a stint in Paris, it moved to London, where it ran for 276 performances before moving to the provinces. Mills and *Blackbirds* were extraordinary hits. She became to London what **Josephine Baker** was to Paris. The Prince of Wales saw *Blackbirds* a score of times, and Mills is likely to have had a romantic affair with his handsome brother, Prince George. During her stay she also partook of the sophisticated London and Oxford life of Britain's "Bright Young Things."

Mills' health broke from overwork, and she returned to the

States for an apparently routine appendectomy. She died unexpectedly on November 1, 1927. She was thirty-one years old.
Harlem gave their beloved Florence a dramatic funeral: a choir
of 600, an orchestra of 200, a congregation of 5,000 in Mother
African Methodist Episcopal Zion Church on 137th Street, and
a reverent crowd of 150,000 in the streets. The public tributes
were lavish. *The New York Times* praised "the slim dancer who
paved the way." One London newspaper with unintentional
irony noted that if Mills had been a white woman she would
have been regarded as one of the greatest artists of her time.
George Jean Nathan called her "America's foremost feminine
player."

Mills saw her work as a crusade for racial justice, and she
believed that every white person who saw and appreciated her
performance was a friend won for the race. She created a major
revue composed of authentic African-American song and
dance. The black theater critic Theophilus Lewis said that Florence Mills "always regarded herself as our envoy to the world at
large and she was probably the best one we ever had."

If you want to know more:

Richard Newman. "Florence Mills," in *Notable Black American
   Women,* Jessie Carney Smith, ed. Detroit: Gale Research,
   1992, pp. 752–756.

"Over home I belong to a society for the betterment of
the race to which I am proud to belong."
                                  —Florence Mills, London, 1927

"She was an admirable artist, always true to herself,
proud of the true Negro origins of her art."
                                  —Arnold Haskell

"Florence Mills, bravest and finest of her craft, is dancing before God."
                                  —*Crisis,* December 1927

What was special about *Shuffle Along*?

Shuffle Along was the all-black musical revue that opened in New York at Daly's Sixty-third Street Music Hall, a dilapidated recital auditorium between Central Park West and Broadway, on May 21, 1921. Observers like **James Weldon Johnson** called it "epoch-making." **Arna Bontemps** said it was the "overture to an era of hope." J. A. Jackson wrote that it was "a rainbow of hope and encouragement." Langston Hughes even claimed *Shuffle Along* marked the beginning of the Harlem Renaissance, saying the show "gave a scintillating send-off to that Negro vogue in Manhattan . . . that spread to books, African sculpture, music, and dance."

What was *Shuffle Along* and why was it so important? Its lyrics and music were by **Noble Sissle** and **Eubie Blake,** with its script by Aubrey Lyles and Flornoy Miller, a blackface comedy team who had worked together since their student days at Fisk University. Lottie Gee and Gertrude Saunders were the lead singers till Saunders was replaced as ingenue by **Florence Mills.** Verna Arvey, William Grant Still's wife, called *Shuffle Along* a "preparatory school for colored artists," and she was quite right. A great many people who became well known started their careers in *Shuffle Along,* including Josephine Baker, **William Grant Still,** Catherina Jarboro, **Hall Johnson,** Mae Barnes, **Paul Robeson,** and **Fredi Washington.**

The plot was thin, but there was one. Steve Jenkins and Sam Peck (the prototypes for *Amos 'n' Andy,* by the way) were played by Miller and Lyles. They own a grocery store in a small town where they both run for mayor against a reform candidate. Each steals from the store to finance his campaign, and each hires the same detective to investigate the other. After a series of comic misadventures the reform mayor wins and runs them both out of town.

In fact, there was nothing new about *Shuffle Along.* Its songs and dances had been standard fare for years on the colored vaudeville circuit playing to black audiences. Miller and Lyles' plot was taken from two old plays, *Mayor of Dixie* and *Who's Stealing?* What was new was the audience. White people had never before seen real African-American entertainers and entertainment. They were dazzled by the zesty syncopated music, and even more so by the swinging rhythm of the practiced but free and wild dancing.

Shuffle Along was the first black show of note in New York since Bert Williams' *Mr. Lode of Koal* in 1909. It was marked by several firsts. One was that the chorus girls, with daringly new bobbed hair, were scantily dressed, just like the white chorines of the *Follies* and the *Vanities*. This is more significant than it appears since, given white prejudice, fantasies, and ambivalence about black sexuality, there was no prior assurance that white audiences would permit provocatively dressed black women on a public stage. They did, and song writer Andy Razaf memorialized the moment in doggerel:

> Dusky maidens, snappy and cutieful,
> All in costumes, gorgeously beautiful.

Sissle and Blake's songs for *Shuffle Along* were a collection of winners: "I'm Simply Full of Jazz," "Love Will Find a Way," "I'm Craving for that Kind of Love," and the most long-lasting, "I'm Just Wild About Harry," which resurfaced in 1948 as the campaign song for the election of President Harry S Truman. The songs introduced a black jazz style to Broadway shows. Historian Robert Kimball claims that one need only listen to popular music before and after *Shuffle Along* to hear the difference *Shuffle Along* made.

But it was the show's dancing that made an even greater impact and had an even longer-lasting effect. The *Shuffle Along* chorus line, standing close together and moving with precision and yet carefree frenzy, electrified white audiences. The chorus started the popularity of real tap dancing, replacing the familiar old buck-and-wing routine. The chorines' lively, pulsating vitality led Marshall Stearns as a historian of dance to say that dancing in American musical comedy "finally took wing" with *Shuffle Along*.

The show was so successful it ran for 504 performances, and grossed $1.5 million in two years. Traffic in front of the theater was so heavy it forced the New York Police Department to turn Sixty-third Street into a one-way street. *Shuffle Along* legitimized the black musical as genre and set a standard for the numerous imitators that appeared throughout the decade of the 1920s. None approached its success or influence, but there were so many hopeful rivals that a popular song of the day was entitled "Broadway's Getting Darker Every Year."

Langston Hughes was probably right to say that the lively show made white people more open and sympathetic to the coming "Negro vogue." The social historians are probably correct that middle-class white people reacting against American puritanism and Victorianism needed to learn how to loosen up and move, and *Shuffle Along* showed them how. Nathan Huggins is probably correct, also, that the show continued the "corrupt tradition" of minstrelsy. The *Chicago Defender* agreed, arguing that songs like "Sing Me to Sleep, Dear Mammy" were "concessions enough" to white expectations of what a black musical ought to be.

But there is something more. Despite the continuing elements of minstrelsy, *Shuffle Along* made it possible, for the first time since the 1890s, for people of color to present real African-American song, dance, humor, and style to a broad American audience, first on Sixty-third Street and from there to the whole country. In a review, Claude McKay argued that blacks could "lift clowning to artistry" and so redeem it. Black artists were changed as a result of *Shuffle Along*, able to earn money and recognition by performing elements of their own cultural tradition. And white America was changed and enriched by having unique black culture performed on Broadway.

According to music historian Eileen Southern, *Shuffle Along* was "a Harlem folk show with no concessions to white taste or theatrical cliches." It transformed American musical theater, and it opened a door by which American vernacular culture began to be transformed as well.

If you want to know more:

Robert Kimball and William Bolcom. *Reminiscing with Sissle and Blake.* New York: Viking Press, 1973.

> "If Negroes can lift clowning to artistry, they can thumb their noses at superior people who rate them as a clowning race."
>
> —Claude McKay

> "Musical comedy took on a new and rhythmic life, and chorus girls began learning to dance to jazz."
>
> —Marshall and Jean Stearns

> "The conventions of *Shuffle Along* are those of Broadway, but the voice is nevertheless indubitably Africa expatriate."
>
> —Claude McKay

> "After years of imitation, New York is now learning just what color of blue is the real Negro blues song."
>
> —unsourced review

What is the best book to come out of the Harlem Renaissance?

Critics generally agree that the best book to come out of the Harlem Renaissance was Jean Toomer's *Cane,* published in 1923. Toomer (1894–1967) was a fair-complexioned black man, the grandson on his mother's side of Pinckney B. S. Pinchback, who briefly served as U.S. senator from Louisiana during Reconstruction and was a mainstay of Washington's blue-veined African-American aristocracy. Toomer grew up in that elite Washington environment, attended the famous M Street High School, and tried several colleges briefly.

A decisive experience for Toomer was a trip South in 1921. He experienced the beauty and power of rural black people and their folk culture, and wrote a series of poems, stories, and prose-poem combinations he put together to produce *Cane*. *Cane* is a lyrical, impressionistic collage, avant-garde and rich with symbolism. It explores the black experience in white America and the ever present question of African-American identity. The book is at its most powerful when it looks at the lives of racially oppressed and sexually exploited black women.

Cane is a creative masterpiece, and it is ironic that Toomer, a Washington sophisticate, had to go to rural Georgia and witness the dignity of the black people there to understand that the true realization of identity comes from self-affirmation. While this insight illuminates *Cane*, it had less effect on Toomer himself. He finally decided he had no Negro blood and that he was a member of a new "American" race. Toomer drifted off to become a disciple of the Russian mystic George Gurdjieff and his Institute for the Harmonious Development of Man. He continued to write, but not with his early power, and his later manuscripts remain unpublished.

If you want to know more:

Nellie McKay. *Jean Toomer: Artist.* Chapel Hill, N.C.: University of North Carolina Press, 1984.

"*Cane* is a book of gold and bronze, of dusk and flame, of ecstasy and pain, and Jean Toomer is a bright morning star of the race of literature."
—William Stanley Braithwaite

Who are some of the other writers of the Harlem Renaissance?

Alain Locke called the Harlem Renaissance "a fresh spiritual and cultural focusing" within which "Negro life is seizing upon its first chances of group expression and self-determination." That "focusing" included a great deal of creative writing: publishers were looking for black material, and for a time it seemed everybody in Harlem was working on a depiction of the black experience, including Arna Bontemps, **Walter White,** Bruce Nugent, Jean Toomer, **W. E. B. DuBois, Jessie Faucet, Nella Larson,** and George Schuyler. Many Harlem Renaissance writers remain little known today.

One underappreciated author is **Wallace Thurman** (1902–1934), a cynical, critical, dark-complexioned bohemian who came to New York from Salt Lake City. He was a journalist and editor by trade who worked for both black and white publications and ghostwrote for the popular magazine *True Story*. One of the leaders of the New Negro Movement's radical younger circle, he edited *Fire!!*, the avant-garde aesthetic manifesto. Not only was Thurman the *Fire!!* editor, but he also paid the printing bill, since he was the only antiestablishment rebel with a steady job. Only one issue ever appeared.

Thurman wrote *Negro Life in New York's Harlem,* an insider's exposé published in 1928 as a Haldeman-Julius Little Blue Book selling for 5 cents. He married Louise Thompson, also a political radical, that same year. Their marriage did not last, probably because Thurman was gay. The next year he produced his first novel, *The Blacker the Berry,* about an African-American woman who, like himself, experienced color prejudice from lighter-skinned blacks. The title was an ironic twist on the folk saying "The blacker the berry, the sweeter the juice."

Thurman next wrote a parody of the Harlem Renaissance, a novel called *Infants of the Spring,* published in 1932. It is clever satire and the characters are easily identifiable: Sweetie May Carr is Zora Neale Hurston, Tony Crews is Langston Hughes,

DeWitt Clinton is **Countee Cullen,** Dr. Parkes is Alain Locke, Dr. Manfred Trout is Rudolph Fisher, and Raymond Taylor is Thurman himself. It is interesting to read this now to get a sense of how a participant viewed life among Harlem's literary set.

Thurman was personally unable to meet his own high artistic standards, and he believed the same was true for the other New Negro writers, with the possible exception of Jean Toomer. He turned to nonracial themes and with Abraham L. Furman, a white man, coauthored a novel called *The Intern* (1932), a hospital exposé which was not well received by the critics.

Thurman then went to Hollywood, where he wrote scenarios for low-budget B pictures like *High School Girl* and *Tomorrow's Children.* The latter is of some interest because it dealt with eugenics sterilization, a taboo subject. He continued his bohemian, self-destructive ways, particularly excessive drinking, and died at the age of thirty two of tuberculosis in City Hospital on New York's Welfare Island, the very institution, ironically, he had used as the symbol of disillusionment in *The Intern.*

Another unappreciated and underrated New Negro was **Rudolph "Bud" Fisher** (1897-1934), a wit and intellectual, scientist and novelist, who published simultaneously in the *Atlantic Monthly* and the *Journal of Infectious Diseases.* Born in Washington, D.C., Fisher graduated with a Phi Beta Kappa key from Brown University, then from Howard University Medical School, and became an X-ray specialist in New York as well as an active participant in the Harlem Renaissance.

Fisher's first book was *The Walls of Jericho* (1928), a satirical novel of black Harlem life that humanized its characters by avoiding most of the racial stereotypes usually perpetuated by black and white writers alike. The novel cleverly dissects African-American class strata (with some bias against the bourgeoisie) in a love story about a piano mover and a kitchen mechanic (black slang of the day for a housemaid). The description of the General Improvement Association's costume ball is a funny takeoff on the pretentious parties of the NAACP.

Fisher's *Conjure Man Dies: A Mystery Tale of Dark Harlem* (1932) is considered the first detective story by an African

American. The heroes Dr. John Archer and Detective Perry Dart (archer and dart!) solve the Harlem murder of an African conjurer, and Fisher foreshadows **Chester Himes** as an author of Harlem murder mysteries. Fisher led an active and productive life, but he died young of exposure to radiation—just a few days after Thurman's death during Christmas Week 1934. Their deaths, especially so close together, were sobering to the survivors of the Harlem Renaissance, who were already laboring under the grim realities of the Depression during the bleak 1930s. There are no biographies or complete collections of either Fisher's or Thurman's work.

If you want to know more:

David Levering Lewis. *When Harlem Was in Vogue.* New York: Alfred A. Knopf, 1981.

"[Thurman] was a strangely brilliant black boy, who had read everything, and whose critical mind could find something wrong with everything he read."

　　　　　　　　　　　　　　　　　　—Langston Hughes

"In Harlem, black was white. You had rights that could not be denied you; you had privileges, protected by law. And you had money. Everybody in Harlem had money. It was a land of plenty."

　　　　　　　　　　　　　　　　　　—Rudolph Fisher

"The Negro and all things negroid had become a fad, and Harlem had become a shrine to which feverish pilgrimages were in order. . . . Seventh Avenue was the gorge into which Harlem cliff dwellers crowded to promenade. It was heavy laden, full of life and color, vibrant and leisurely."

　　　　　　　　　　　　　　　　　　—Wallace Thurman

What was the high point of the Jazz Age?

She was not particularly talented either as a singer or dancer, but Josephine Baker was an entertainer with enormous personal vitality and an unparalleled stage presence. She used both boldly in the mid-1920s to enthrall Paris, where she became an international celebrity overnight and remained one all her life. Even in death Baker continues to be an icon of popular culture. In her exuberant semi-nude dancing, Parisians chose to see an erotic savage who fulfilled their fantasies of primitive African sexuality—a black Venus who symbolized for whites the wild freedom of the Jazz Age. If Baker participated in this racism, she maintained her own independence and redeemed herself later in her career by becoming a prominent spokesperson against racial discrimination and for racial justice.

Josephine McDonald was born June 3, 1906, in St. Louis, Missouri, the daughter of Carrie McDonald, a twenty-one-year-old domestic, and Eddie Carson, a flashy ragtime drummer. They were not married. She grew up in a neighborhood marked by poverty, alcoholism, illness, and violence. One of her earliest memories was of the East St. Louis race riot in the summer of 1917, with its brutal murders of African Americans by frenzied whites.

At the age of eight, Baker went out to work; and by age thirteen, she was married to Willie Wells. The stage became first a psychological, then a physical, escape when she joined the otherwise forgettable Jones Family Band and went on the road. She parlayed this modest job into a better one as a dresser with the Dixie Steppers, a vaudeville troupe traveling on the black Theatre Owners Booking Association circuit, and headed, reportedly, by the great blues singer **Clara "Queen of the Moaners" Smith.**

Baker's dream was Broadway, and she joined other black performers auditioning for Noble Sissle and Eubie Blake's *Shuffle Along,* the sizzling 1921 revue that brought African-American song and dance back to the New York stage. She was rejected because she was under the sixteen-year-old minimum age, though she had recently remarried, this time to a Pullman porter named Will Baker, whose name she kept.

Al Mayer, the manager of *Shuffle Along,* did hire Baker the next year for one of the show's traveling companies. She was a hit as end girl on the chorus line, clowning and mugging in a black vaudeville comedy tradition begun by Billy King. Sissle and Blake picked Baker out of the chorus and wrote her into their new revue, *In Bamville,* which became *Chocolate Dandies* and premiered in 1924. The show was unable to capitalize on the success of *Shuffle Along,* but Baker was well received, and she went on to the *Plantation Club,* where **Ethel Waters** was the summer substitute for Florence Mills.

Carolyn Dudley, a wealthy American white woman, hit upon the idea of taking a group of "authentic" Negro vaudeville entertainers to Paris, and she hired Baker after Ethel Waters turned her down. In *La Revue Nègre,* on October 2, 1925, at the Théâtre des Champs-Elysées, a supple, naked Baker, paired with Joe Alex, did a frenzied and highly sexual "Dance of the Savages," wearing only a flamingo feather between her thighs.

A titillated Paris responded instantaneously to a new spin on sex, and Baker became an instant sensation among the stylesetters and pathbreakers. She was engulfed by adoring fans, photographers, courtiers, lovers, pleasure seekers, celebrity chasers, journalists, and various other hangers-on. Baker may have been young and unsophisticated, but she was smart, ambitious, and self-centered, and she not only knew a good thing when she saw one, but knew how to keep it going.

Baker's great moment as Creole Goddess was her unforgettable performance at La Folie du Jour, where she descended onto the stage in an egg-shaped golden cage. She emerged wearing only three gold bracelets and sixteen bananas decorated with rhinestones, and proceeded to dance a wild and frantic Charleston. This may well have been the high point of the Jazz Age.

Josephine Baker, perceived as an exotic jungle animal, was transformed, however, into La Bakaire, the commercial property, by Pepito Abatino, a Sicilian stonemason posing and passing as a titled Italian count. A world-class gigolo, Abatino taught

Baker how to talk, eat, and dress, as well as how to dance real dance steps instead of just shaking her derriere. He managed her contracts, appearances, publicity, and money, of which there was now a great deal. He also brought paternalistic stability to her chaotic and undisciplined life, and their marriage brought her constant and indiscriminate sexual activity under some control.

As Pygmalion, Abatino was a hard taskmaster and a brilliant promoter. He may have originally intended to use Baker for his own ends, but at some point he fell under her power: the tables turned and she became the dominant and dominating one. A few years later he died, heartbroken and alone, in South America. Baker then lived the fast life of an international celebrity: performances, travel, commercial endorsements, parties, and countless affairs with the rich and famous, both men and women.

Over the years, Baker's voice matured somewhat, and her stage presence continued to exude charismatic energy. She became more serious, more politically conscious, and began to criticize American racism. She worked for the Free French during World War II and was awarded a medal of the Resistance from the de Gaulle government. She adopted a "Rainbow Tribe" of children of different races as emblematic of the harmonious world she envisioned. Baker never had the child of her own she wanted. She had an abortion at age thirteen, and she almost died following a pregnancy years later. The father of her stillborn child was probably the Pasha of Marrakesh. Baker died in Paris on April 12, 1975, and was honored with a state funeral.

If you want to know more:

Jean-Claude Baker and Chris Chase. *Josephine: The Hungry Heart.* New York: Random House, 1993.

"[Baker achieved] a silent declaration of love by a single forward movement of her belly, with her arms raised above her head, and the quiver of her entire rear."

—Pierre de Regnier

"We were horrified at how disgusting Josie was behaving in front of this French audience, doing her nigger routine. She had no self-respect, no shame in front of those crackers and would you believe, they loved her."

—Lydia Jones

"A violinist has his violin, a painter his palette. All I had was myself."

—Josephine Baker

What were the Negro leagues?

The Negro leagues were American baseball leagues consisting solely of black teams and players. They were created out of necessity, since African Americans were excluded from the existing mainstream leagues because of race. The first all-black baseball teams existed as early as the late 1860s, around the same time the then all-white National Association of Base Ball Players (NABBP) was organized. The few black players on white teams had to suffer humiliation from racist members of both the opposing team and their own—including the refusal of some of their white teammates even to play—and ugly remarks from the bleachers. The NABBP wasted no time in making a policy to bar all blacks from participating in the game. By 1887, the color line kept all black athletes from playing in organized baseball.

In response, the black baseball hero **Andrew "Rube" Foster** created the Negro National League. He was himself an excellent athlete, and his nickname was bestowed after he outpitched the famous white pitcher George "Rube" Waddell. But

Foster was also a shrewd player. He is credited with inventing the infamous bunt-and-run play, and he insisted that team players play the game using their minds as well as their physical skills. His sharp business sense led him to bring together the other owners of successful black ball clubs in Kansas City in 1920. Together, these men wrote their own constitution and established the Negro National League (NNL).

There were eight clubs in the NNL, with teams based in Chicago, Dayton, Detroit, Indianapolis, and St. Louis. Foster owned the Chicago American Giants. All the teams were owned by blacks except for the Kansas City Monarchs, owned by a white man, J. L. Wilkinson. The NNL was fairly successful in the beginning, with a consistent attendance record and a yearly income of $200,000 in 1923. Because of the success, an Eastern Colored League (ECL) was organized in 1924, also loyally supported by African-American fans.

The Negro leagues suffered from problems caused both by internal tension and the outside pressure of racism. Sometimes these problems brought the leagues close to termination. In 1924 the NNL and the predominantly white-owned ECL declared war on each other because the ECL began to raid the NNL of their best players, enticing them with higher wages. Also, the leagues had a problem with acquiring umpires. Many black players and coaches resented the presence of white umpires, and blacks were not allowed to umpire.

The most frustrating problem for the leagues was the inconsistency and unpredictability of game schedules. Few black teams owned their own ballparks, so club owners were forced to cooperate with white businessmen in order to have a "home" ballpark. Black clubs in this predicament had to make sure their games were played when the white team based in the park was on the road. Also, if weather or a no-show canceled a game, it was virtually impossible to reschedule. As a result, some teams played substantially fewer games than others, which caused a great deal of tension between both teams and leagues.

In 1930, Rube Foster, recognized as the Father of Black Baseball, died. With his absence, the leagues disbanded, and the Great Depression tightened its economic grip around the already suffering black teams. But the emergence of independent teams kept black baseball alive during the Depression and produced some of the greatest ballplayers ever. They included **Leroy "Satchel" Paige,** who played successfully against white peers to sellout crowds.

Gus Greenlee, a black Pittsburgh numbers czar, established in 1933 the second Negro National League. He developed the idea of the East-West All-Star Game, which became black baseball's biggest feature. Black newspapers polled their readers to determine which players would participate in the game, both starters and backup players. Each year hundreds of thousands of fans voted for their favorite players, and tens of thousands traveled to Chicago, where the All-Star Game was always held, to attend the biggest event of the year. The Negro League World Series was not so successful, because fans could not afford to support best-out-of-seven or best-out-of-nine series and they could not attend series with no central, predictable locations. But African Americans from all over the country made it an August tradition to head out to Comiskey Park to watch their favorite players featured in the All-Star Game.

By the 1940s, the Negro leagues' popularity increased immeasurably. Regular-season contests attracted great numbers of fans, both black and white. Also, the Negro leagues' annual East-West All-Star Game outdrew its all-white equivalent by at least twenty thousand fans. Satchel Paige, **Josh Gibson, Roy Campanella, James "Cool Papa" Bell,** and **Ted "Double-Duty" Radcliffe** were the superstars who entertained baseball fans throughout the decade. The black baseball clubs also developed what is known as "tricky baseball," which included creative ways of scoring runs through base-stealing, the bunt-and-run, the run-and-hit, special do-or-die sacrifice plays, and other heart-stopping stratagems.

During this popular upsurge, the country's mood toward integrating mainstream baseball began to soften. World War II highlighted America's own system of racial segregation, and integrationists began to put pressure on the NABBP. In 1944, Kenesaw Mountain Landis, the commissioner of baseball, died at seventy-eight, leaving a void for leadership that was filled by

Albert B. "Happy" Chandler, a cautious, but comparatively sympathetic, supporter of integration. Brooklyn Dodgers president Branch Rickey helped to bring newcomer **John Roosevelt "Jackie" Robinson** into mainstream organized baseball.

Rickey was impressed with Robinson's superb playing skills, but he chose Robinson because he was a twenty-six-year-old army lieutenant who was an All-American at UCLA and a socially conscious human being with wit and wisdom. Together they practiced how to avoid and handle all types of racist scenarios that they knew would happen once Robinson took the field. In 1946, when he became part of the white International League, Robinson not only withstood being kicked, spiked, thrown at, and cursed, but prevailed with a league-leading .349 batting average and 113 runs batted in. In 1947, Jackie Robinson integrated the Brooklyn Dodgers.

Integrating the white leagues was a painfully slow process. **Larry Doby**, Dan Bankhead, Roy Campanella, Don Newcomb, Satchel Paige, and **Willie Mays** joined Robinson in the mainstream leagues. They did not begin a rush of black players to join the majors, but every year a few more clubs would sign one or two black players. It was not until 1959 that the last of the major leagues' teams had integrated its roster.

Integration had exhausted the Negro leagues of many of their star athletes. Interest in Negro league baseball began seriously to wane. Some historians reflect that integration ultimately came about for financial considerations for the mainstream white leagues as well as a testimony for civil rights. The final East-West All-Star Game for the declining Negro leagues was held in 1963 in Kansas City, where Rube Foster had organized the first black professional baseball league.

If you want to know more:

David Craft. *The Negro Leagues.* New York: Crescent Books, 1993.

"Back then any proud black man courageous enough to take his position on the baseball diamond quickly realized it was seventeen men against one."

—David Craft

"If a black boy can make it on Okinawa and Guadalcanal, hell, he can make it in baseball."

—A. B. "Happy" Chandler

"I've tried [working at] a lot of things in the off-season, but the only thing I really know is baseball."

—Hank Aaron

Who was the most promising writer of the Harlem Renaissance?

No one showed more promise at the beginning of the Harlem Renaissance than the poet Countee Cullen (1903–1946), but his serious work ended as the decade did, and the last fifteen years of his life saw no real fulfillment of the great expectations the world had for him. "I Have a Rendezvous with Life" was the poem Cullen composed while still a student at DeWitt Clinton High School in New York. It was thought of so highly that it started him on his way early. But Cullen's view of the proper direction for black letters did not prevail, and his rendezvous did not finally and fully take place.

Little is known of Cullen's background, parentage, or childhood. He was born May 30, 1903, probably in Louisville, Kentucky. At early adolescence he was adopted by one of Harlem's leading ministers, the Reverend Frederick Asbury Cullen, of Salem Methodist Church, and his wife. The senior Cullen was politically active and an officer of the NAACP, but he was conventional and conservative religiously, and Countee Cullen found it hard to construct his own self, particularly in resolving the conflict between Christianity and what he called "pagan tendencies."

After earning a bachelor's degree at New York University,

Cullen went to Harvard for an M.A. While there, at the young age of twenty-two, he published his first book of verse, *Color*. It is also probably his best book, another indication that his early flowering was not to last or mature. Cullen quickly published more books of poems: *The Ballad of the Brown Girl* in 1927, *Copper Sun* in 1927, *The Black Christ* in 1932. He was universally recognized and praised, and he collected prizes and awards: the Spingarn Medal of the NAACP, a Harmon Foundation award, and a Guggenheim grant.

After a stint at *Opportunity* magazine, Cullen taught French and English at Frederick Douglass Junior High School in New York. He continued to write: children's stories, a book about his cat, and a novel, *One Way to Heaven*. The novel is now pretty much forgotten, but it is, in fact, not a bad picture of Harlem life during the Renaissance, and not a bad story of the unlikely romance of a Harlem domestic and her con artist lover. He worked, too, on adapting Arna Bontemps' novel *St. Louis Woman* into a Broadway show that would have starred **Lena Horne,** but **Walter White** and the NAACP undermined the project, believing it degrading to black people.

The social event of the decade, if not beyond, was Cullen's marriage on April 9, 1928, to Nina Yolande Du Bois, the daughter of **W. E. B. Du Bois,** who saw the wedding as emblematic of the best and the brightest of the country's African-American youth. Unfortunately, the newlyweds had some immediate and fundamental problems, not least of which was the fact that Cullen was gay. Countee Cullen sailed for Paris on his honeymoon not with his bride, but with the handsome Harold Jackman, Harlem bon vivant and best man at the famous wedding. Cullen and Du Bois were divorced in 1930, and he later married Ida Mae Roberson, presumably happily.

Cullen's poetic style was conventional (his literary model was John Keats), and he was too classical and Romantic to be sympathetic to the black folk style that informed the writing of Langston Hughes and Zora Neale Hurston. Cullen is famous for saying to Hughes that he wanted to be a poet, not a black poet. In that sense, he personified the African-American struggle for freedom of choice in artistic experience; he did not use or celebrate, as Hughes and Hurston did, the unique folk motifs that have helped make their work endure.

Despite Cullen's formal poetic sensibilities, black themes do run through his work. Several of his lines and phrases are so familiar they have entered the language:

> One three centuries removed
> From the scenes his father loved,
> Spicy grove, cinnamon tree,
> What is Africa to me?

And perhaps the most poignant and touching:

> Yet do I marvel at this curious thing
> To make a poet black and bid him sing!

If you want to know more:

Countee P. Cullen. *On These I Stand: An Anthology of the Best Poems of Countee Cullen.* New York: Harper & Bros., 1947.

> She even thinks that up in heaven
> Her class lies late and snores
> While poor black cherubs rise at seven
> To do celestial chores.
> —Countee Cullen

> And you and I, shall we lie still,
> John Keats, while Beauty summons us?
> —Countee Cullen

> I am for sleeping and forgetting
> All that has gone before;
> I am for lying still and letting
> Who will beat at my door;
> I would my life's cold sun were setting
> To rise for me no more.
> —Countee Cullen

What is the most important date in jazz history?

The most important date in the history of jazz may well be July 8, 1922. That's when **Louis Armstrong** arrived in Chicago from New Orleans responding to the invitation of his mentor, **Joseph "King" Oliver,** to play second cornet in Oliver's Creole Jazz band, then playing at Lincoln Gardens Cafe, owned by Al Capone on Chicago's South Side. Jazz began as a local New Orleans phenomenon, but the closing of the city's red-light district by the U.S. Navy during World War I forced musicians out of New Orleans. They followed the migration of many black people who had either given up hope of being able to survive in a segregated and persistently hostile South, or who went North for the good jobs created by the war, or both.

In any event, a thriving African-American community, fed daily by the influx of black migrants, blossomed in wide-open Chicago, enough to support a collection of clubs, dance halls, and bordellos, and the musicians who played in them. Armstrong was literally a genius, not only the greatest name in jazz, but perhaps the world's most creative and influential musician in the twentieth century. In 1922, though, he was twenty-one years old, unknown except to New Orleans musicians, and an unsophisticated youth. By bringing him out of New Orleans and to Chicago, Oliver was unknowingly introducing Armstrong to the wider world, and the wider world to him. American music was changed forever.

Louis Armstrong was born August 4, 1901 (not July 4, 1900, as many sources have it), in a shack off Jane Alley, an area known as The Battlefield, one of the poorest and most vice- and violence-soaked neighborhoods in the country, let alone New Orleans. His unmarried parents were fifteen-year-old Mary Albert, known as Mary-anne, a washerwoman and part-time prostitute, and William Armstrong, a laborer in a turpentine factory who left at Louis' birth for another woman. Armstrong was raised by his father's mother, but he did live as a child with his mother when she moved to Liberty and Perdito streets, a neighborhood where the lower-class black prostitutes worked.

On January 1, 1913, Armstrong contributed to the local celebration of the New Year by shooting off a pistol at the corner of Perdito and Rampart streets. He was arrested and sent to the Colored Waif's Home, where he learned to play the cornet and was assigned a place in the home's brass band. As James Lincoln Collier says, "the band undoubtedly had a certain vitality and rhythmic courage." Back on the street, Armstrong got a job delivering coal. Too young to be allowed in Pete Lala's Cabaret, where the hot jazz bands played, he was happy to deliver coal to nearby prostitutes' cribs, where he could stop and listen to the music when the women weren't working.

After a stint singing and playing in the streets, Armstrong by 1917 was well enough known and a talented enough player to sit in for Oliver in **Edward "Kid" Ory's** band. Beginning in 1918, Armstrong played with Fate Marable's Jaz-E-Saz Band on the Mississippi River paddleboat *Dixie Belle,* where he learned how to read music and how to tailor his playing for white audiences. He married Daisy Parker, an illiterate prostitute, but his life changed forever when Oliver's call came, summoning him to Chicago.

King Oliver knew that Armstrong was a superb musician, but it was Lil Hardin, the band's pianist, who recognized his real potential. She had been a music student at Fisk University and had begun her own career demonstrating sheet music at the Jones Music Store in Chicago. In 1918, she was asked to fill in on piano with Lawrence Duhe's jazz band. She asked for a copy of the music, and was politely told that they didn't have any music and never used any. She then asked what key the first number would be in, and reported, "I must have been speaking another language because the leader said, 'When you hear two knocks just start playing.' "

Perhaps it was Hardin's dual experience as a trained musician and a member of one of the best of the new hot bands that led her to see beyond the surface of the unsophisticated Armstrong, with his box-shaped suit and country-style haircut. At any rate, she took him in hand, helped him develop self-confidence, taught him how to dress and act in the big city, persuaded him to leave Oliver and move out more on his own, and became his second wife. Armstrong's career began its ascent. He became one of the most popular American entertainers, as well as a pioneering genius of jazz.

A master at improvisation, Armstrong played with an ever-present handkerchief, not merely to wipe away perspiration, but to cover and hide his finger work. He was called Pops, or Satchmo, an abbreviation for "Satchelmouth." His range, body, power, tone, timing, inventiveness, and depth of emotion and feeling were unsurpassed and can only be called stunning. As **Duke Ellington** said, "The guys never heard anything else like it." Nor has anyone else.

Jazz rose to a creative peak in the middle of the 1920s, thanks in substantial measure to Louis Armstrong. Among the classics recorded during this period are King Oliver's band in 1923 with "Dippermouth Blues," "Mabel's Dream," and "Froggy Moore." Armstrong and his Hot Five in 1926 recorded "Heebie Jeebies," "Cornet Chop Suey," and "Muskrat Ramble." There were later sessions like "Struttin' with Some Barbeque," "Hotter Than That," and "West End Blues."

Finally, Armstrong played and sang two of the music forms that gave rise to jazz—hymns like "Just a Closer Walk with Thee" and blues like "St. Louis Blues"—and the popular songs that followed: "Hello Dolly," (when he displaced the Beatles on the charts), "Mack the Knife," "Blueberry Hill," and "What a Wonderful World." With jazz, African Americans created a major art form and shaped the culture of the white majority. No single person was more central to that creation or that influence than Louis Armstrong. He died in New York on July 6, 1971.

If you want to know more:

Gary Giddins. *Satchmo*. New York: Doubleday, 1988.

"Go on Louis; we'll meet some day."
                    —Champion Jack Dupree, at Armstrong's death

"I loved and respected Louis Armstrong. He was born poor, died rich, and never hurt anybody along the way."
                    —Duke Ellington

"You know you can't play anything on the horn that Louis hasn't played—I mean even modern."
                    —Miles Davis

"What did we contribute to the world? We contributed Louis Armstrong."
                    —Tony Bennett

"Armstrong is the Prometheus of the blues idiom, and through him the United States exercised its impact on twentieth-century esthetics."
                    —Wynton Marsalis

Who was the Empress of the Blues?

Bessie Smith was undoubtedly the greatest woman singer of the blues. Patrick O'Connor, while he was editor of *Opera News*, said he believed Smith was, in fact, the most important musical voice of the twentieth century. It was she who took the rural folk blues songs of black Southern common people, added a vaudeville tinge, and elevated this music to a unique and unparalleled level of artistry. She was accorded the title "Empress of the Blues" during her lifetime, and while other queens have come and gone, Smith's exclusive claim to the superior status has never been in doubt.

Bessie Smith was a dark-complexioned, tall, large-framed woman, weighing over two hundred pounds, with a rich, reso-

nant contralto voice, and a dignified stage presence powerful
enough to transform audiences. Born in Chattanooga, Tennessee, perhaps on April 15, 1894 in extreme poverty, her father,
William, was a laborer and part-time Baptist preacher who died
young, as did her mother, Laura. Bessie and her surviving sib-
lings were raised by an older sister, Viola, who took in laundry
to support the family in a one-room shack on Charles Street.

Smith sang and danced for change in the streets of black
Chattanooga, but her brother Clarence found a way out of the
Smiths' desperate situation via a job in show business. When
she was about fourteen, Bessie too found this path and joined
Moses Stoke's traveling show as a dancer, reportedly in a troupe
that included Ma Rainey, the "Mother of the Blues," who may
well have influenced Smith's style. With the "81" Theatre in
Atlanta as a headquarters, Smith sang, danced, and entertained
with various troupes, such as Pete Wesley's Florida Blossoms, in
black tent shows and vaudeville houses throughout the South,
along the Eastern Seaboard, and in the Midwest. Inspired by
World War I she put on a routine called "Liberty Belles," but
the chorus line women were too dark and too heavyset for most
African-American theater managers, although audiences loved
them.

With the unexpected success of Mamie Smith's "Crazy
Blues," the first commercial recording of blues sung by a black
woman, record companies quickly began looking for other singers for the newly discovered African-American "race records"
market. Smith was auditioned by the leading companies and rejected by them all. They found her voice too "rough," her accent too pronounced, and her personality too crude and
unsophisticated. Thomas Edison's personal evaluation in his
"Talent Audition File" was "NG" (no good). Smith even reportedly offended the man at Pace Records when she stopped
her accompanist at the beginning of the trial session with,
"Hold it! I gotta spit."

After initially turning her down, Columbia recorded Bessie
Smith on February 6, 1923, at its Columbus Circle studio in New
York. Accompanied by Clarence Williams on piano, she sang an
Alberta Hunter and Lovie Austin number, "Downhearted

Blues," along with "Gulf Coast Blues." Frank Walker, the white head of Columbia's race records division, said she was scared, and she does sound a bit uncertain, but the pure voice is unmistakable, alive with feeling. Bessie Smith had experienced personally and deeply the despair and hope of the blues. Three minutes and twenty-five seconds of "Downhearted Blues" sold an unbelievable three-quarters of a million copies in the first six months. Smith was paid $125 outright with no royalties.

What made Bessie Smith so immensely popular—and what soon propelled her to become, at $2,000 a week, the highest-paid black entertainer in the country—was not only her innate talent and her special feeling for the blues, but the fact that thousands of African Americans transposed from the rural South to the urban North immediately recognized her "down home" speech, sounds, and sentiments, and were hungry for the flavor of the world they had left behind. Smith made a total of 159 three-minute sides for Columbia Records. In 1929 she starred in an unforgettable seventeen-minute film, a melodrama about an unfaithful lover, in which she is backed by James P. Johnson leading Fletcher Henderson's band, and the Hall Johnson Choir. She was spectacular.

After an early and unsuccessful marriage to Earl Love, Smith in 1923 married Jack Gee, a virtually illiterate Philadelphia night watchman who claimed to be a policeman. He tried to manage Smith's career, but primarily he lived lavishly off her earnings. Bessie Smith was a strong, energetic, tough-talking, hard-drinking, gambling, carousing, and volatile woman. She was bisexual and had a series of affairs while married to Gee. Their marriage soon deteriorated, especially when Smith discovered he was funneling some of her money to his girlfriend, the slender, light-skinned actress Gertrude Saunders. They ended up in violent wild physical brawls in which Smith gave as good as she got.

Over the years, Smith was backed by a number of the most important names in jazz, including Don Redmon and Zutty Singleton, but perhaps her most memorable performances were with a twenty-four-year-old Louis Armstrong on muted cornet. When they did **W. C. Handy**'s "St. Louis Blues" in one take, the greatest talents in world music not only converged, but combined to make one of the most extraordinary recordings ever. Smith left a treasury of songs: "Back Water Blues," "Nobody Knows You When You're Down and Out," "Aggravatin' Papa," "Empty Bed Blues," "Gimme a Pigfoot," "Cake Walking Babies from Home," "Nobody in Town Can Bake a Sweet Jelly Roll Like Mine," "Ticket Agent, Ease Your Window Down," and "I'm Wild About That Thing," to list only some of the better-known sides.

Smith's career began to skid in the 1930s, partly because of the economic devastation of the Great Depression, and partly because the tastes of Northern audiences had become more sophisticated and they were no longer so attracted to the down-home style. She cut her last records on November 24, 1935, at the Columbia studio at 55 Fifth Avenue in New York. Three days later a new young singer came into the same studio for her first record date. This was **Billie Holiday,** who was deeply influenced by Bessie Smith, as were **Mahalia Jackson** and **Aretha Franklin.** A torch was being passed.

In the 1930s, though, Smith's personal life became a bit happier and less explosive when she teamed up with Richard Morgan, an easygoing Chicago bootlegger who was **Lionel Hampton**'s uncle. Her happiness was short-lived, however. They were driving one night on the way to a show date in Mississippi when their car hit a truck parked on the narrow road. Smith's arm was virtually severed, and she died of shock, blood loss, and internal injuries in Ward 1 of the Afro-American Hospital, 615 Sunflower Drive, Clarksdale, Mississippi, on September 26, 1937 at 11:30 a.m. There is no truth to the rumor that she was first denied treatment at a white hospital.

There was a large funeral in Philadelphia, but relatives squabbling over money let her lay in an unmarked grave until 1970, when Juanita Green and Janice Joplin paid for a tombstone. The inscription reads, "The greatest blues singer in the world will never stop singing." In the 1940s, music historian Rudi Blesh planned a biography, but Smith's husband Jack Gee held out for an unreasonable payment, the project was dropped, and the trunk containing Smith's photographs and personal effects was lost.

Smith is now no longer remembered at all as a dancer, and it is little known that she composed both the music and the words to many of her most impressive songs. She was barely literate, so she had to hear lyrics and memorize them even for recording sessions. She didn't like white people and she didn't like fair-skinned blacks either, preferring dark-complexioned colleagues, lovers, and even audiences. Smith is remembered as a drunken brawler, and she was often too drunk to perform, but she was generous to her friends, and in her raw honesty there is always a total authenticity. Carl Van Vechten (whom she disliked as a condescending white liberal), wrote, "It was the real thing: a wonderful heart cut open with a knife until it was exposed for all to see." She might have been the star of John Hammond's Carnegie Hall concert of December 23, 1938, "From Spirituals to Swing: An Evening of American Negro Music," but the historic evening was dedicated to her memory instead.

If you want to know more:

Chris Albertson. *Bessie.* New York: Stein and Day, 1972.

> "I've got the world in a jug
> The stopper's in my hand."
> —Bessie Smith, "Downhearted Blues"

> "They'd just never heard anything like that before."
> —Sidney Bechet

> "My mama says I'm reckless,
> My daddy says I'm wild,
> I ain't good lookin,'
> But I'm somebody's angel child."
> —Bessie Smith

"Bessie's shouting brought worship wherever she worked."

—Ethel Waters

"And Freedom had a name. It was called the blues."
—Walter Mosley

What African-American master sculptor began and ended her career as a housemaid?

Nancy Elizabeth Prophet, whom W. E. B. Du Bois called "our greatest Negro sculptor," began her life working as a housemaid in Providence, Rhode Island, and ended her days in the same city and in the same job, despite international recognition of her artistic genius. She was born March 19, 1890, in Warwick, Rhode Island, the daughter of Rosa Walker and William H. Prophet. One of her grandmothers was a Narragansett Indian who had bought her African-American husband out of slavery. Both of Prophet's parents were laborers, and as a young woman she worked as a domestic in the fashionable white homes on Providence's East Side.

In 1914 Prophet attended the Rhode Island School of Design, where she studied drawing and painting as well as sculpture. She entered her work in a Newport, Rhode Island, exhibition, where it was accepted—if she would agree not to attend the opening reception. She refused. Accepted at the École Nationale des Beaux-Arts, Prophet went to Paris in 1922, where she collapsed for two months from hunger and nervous exhaustion. She faced starvation, and although she claimed lack of food made her mind clearer, she was reduced to stealing from a dog's dish. She was admitted to the American Hospital with malnutrition, but when the doctors there saw her wasted body, they insisted she was addicted to drugs.

Through all her poverty and suffering, Prophet continued to work, creating life-sized busts in metal, stone, and wood. Their titles reflect her mental state: "Discontent," "Silence," "Bitter Laughter." Her work was known and praised by Du Bois, **Henry O. Tanner,** and Countee Cullen, but she was her own most severe critic and she destroyed any piece that did not meet her own rigid standards. After she began to be recognized and exhibited, she won prizes in both France and America.

In 1934 Prophet was hired to teach at Spelman College, the black women's college in Atlanta, and later at Atlanta University. She grew increasingly eccentric and reclusive, and both her name and reputation faded. In the mid-1940s she returned to Providence and was forced to resume work as a live-in maid. She died there in 1960, alone, unknown, forgotten, and poor. One of her employers provided the money for her funeral.

Prophet's reputation has revived, but only ten pieces of her sculpture are known to survive. Another twenty-five, known from photographs or descriptions, have been lost, have deteriorated under improper care, or perhaps were destroyed by her. Du Bois described her aptly in the *Crisis* in 1932: "Elizabeth Prophet never whined or made excuses for herself. She worked. She never submitted to patronage, cringed to the great or begged to the small. She worked."

If you want to know more:

Blossom S. Kirschenbaum. "Nancy Elizabeth Prophet, Sculptor." SAGE 4 (Spring 1987), 45–52.

> "I remember . . . how my arms felt as I swung them up to put on a piece of clay. . . . I was conscious of a great rhythm."
>
> —Nancy Elizabeth Prophet, *Diary*

> "Cutting stone. How I love it working alone. I feel so much in contact with myself."
>
> —Nancy Elizabeth Prophet, *Diary*, December 22, 1925

"The true work of art is a creation not of the hands but of the mind and soul of the artist."

—Nancy Elizabeth Prophet, *Diary*, February 18, 1929

"Starvation."

—Nancy Elizabeth Prophet, *Diary*, March 10, 1929

What is *God's Trombones*?

The trombone is the wind instrument supposedly most capable of expressing the same range of emotions as the human voice. For this reason, James Weldon Johnson, poet, diplomat, novelist, NAACP officer, and musician, used *God's Trombones: Seven Negro Sermons in Verse* as the title of a book he first published in 1927.

Johnson's intent in composing these poems was to preserve the dying folk art of what he called "the old time Negro preacher." He remembered the particular style and phrasing from his own childhood in Jacksonville, Florida, but he was really moved one night in Kansas City, when he was in a black church to make an NAACP speech. He listened to the rhythmic oratory of a minister who preached a common-property sermon that covered the span from creation to the final judgment. Johnson began taking notes.

Johnson was careful not to write in dialect, which he felt was capable of communicating only pathos or humor, but he was most eager to represent the unique black sermonic language that expressed the distinctive racial spirit and flavor from within, and which was, in his view, "a fusion of Negro idiom with Bible English." Johnson's sermon-poems are "The Creation," "The Prodigal Son," "Go Down Death—A Funeral Sermon," "Noah Built the Ark," "The Crucifixion," "Let My People Go," and "The Judgment Day." Sterling Brown said of Johnson's sermon-poems, "Material which is usually made ludicrous is invested with dignity and power."

In Johnson's imagery, there is dignity and power indeed. There is Noah and his folks, gathered in the old ark as it begins to ride and rock, sailing a sea without a shore. There is the Prodigal Son running with the hot-mouthed, jasmine-smelling, scarlet-dressed, sweet-sinning women of Babylon—with brass bands and string bands playing. There is God telling Death to go down to Savannah, Georgia, to bring the tired Sister Caroline to Him, while we weep not, for she is not dead but resting in the bosom of Jesus. Of everything he wrote, *God's Trombones* was Johnson's favorite, so much so that when he died, he was buried holding a copy of it in his hand.

If you want to know more:

James Weldon Johnson. *God's Trombones: Seven Negro Sermons in Verse.* New York: Penguin, 1990.

> "Listen!—Listen!
> All you sons of Pharaoh.
> Who do you think can hold God's people
> When the Lord God himself has said
> Let my people go?"
> —James Weldon Johnson

> "Sinner, oh, sinner,
> Where will you stand
> On that great day when God's a-going to
> Rain down fire?"
> —James Weldon Johnson

Who was the most popular male blues recording artist of the 1920s?

The greatest of the early country blues singers was **"Blind Lemon" Jefferson,** the most popular male blues recording artist during the 1920s, when the blues first came to national attention. With something over a million record sales, Jefferson brought the authentic rural blues of East Texas to a national black audience, many of whom had moved North and wanted to hear the sounds of home.

In spite of Jefferson's popularity and influence, very little is known about his life. Supposedly he was born July 11, 1897, in Freestone County, near Coachman, Texas, to a sharecropper, Alec Jefferson, and his wife, Classie Banks Jefferson. The date is highly speculative, and Jefferson may well have been born a decade or so earlier. It is also not known whether he was born blind or lost his sight in childhood. There are stories about his uncanny ability to differentiate the value of paper money, find his way, and even tell how much liquor had been drunk from a bottle, but these are probably apocryphal.

His parents were reportedly members of Shiloh Baptist Church in Kirwin, Texas, and Jefferson was said to have sung there. In fact, his first published record was "I Want to Be Like Jesus in My Heart," which he recorded under the name of Deacon L. J. Bates.

What is known is that very early Jefferson began to play and sing for money on street corners, in honky-tonks and whorehouses, and at county suppers and picnics. He became an itinerant musician, walking the roads and riding the freight trains from one red-light district to another around the South. He was often in Memphis, but Dallas became something of a headquarters for him, especially its Deep Ellum black neighborhood, where he stood on the corner of Elm Street and Central Avenue, playing and singing for coins with a tin cup attached to his guitar. His high-pitched, even shrill, tenor voice may actually have evolved as he struggled to make himself heard above the noise of the street and traffic.

Jefferson was a thickset, stocky man who liked to gamble and who was said to be a bootlegger on the side. As a popular singer, he never wanted for female companionship. He was said to have married a woman named Roberta, by whom he had a son named Miles, but this is unconfirmed. Jefferson made his first records in Chicago in 1925. He went on to make one hundred recordings, forty-three of which were issued, all but one by Paramount. Among the best and best known are "Matchbox Blues" and "Long Lonesome Blues." Many of his songs were overtly sexual, like "Black Snake Moan," "Bed Springs Blues," and "Yo Yo Blues." Jefferson is said to have coined the phrase *rock and roll*, a sexual euphemism, and to have been the first to record "Careless Love."

The details of Jefferson's death are as obscure as those of his life. He supposedly froze to death in a Chicago blizzard in December 1929, but it may well have been on March 30, 1930. His body was returned to Texas, and he was buried in the Negro Cemetery in Wortham. The list of country blues singers who were influenced by Blind Lemon Jefferson is in fact a roster of the most important male performers since Jefferson's own times: **Big Bill Broonzy, B. B. King, Leadbelly, Muddy Waters, Robert Johnson, Charley Patton, T-Bone Walker,** and **Lightnin' Hopkins.**

If you want to know more:

Bob Groom. *Blind Lemon Jefferson*. N.P.: Blues World, 1970.

> "Well, the blues come to Texas
> Loping like a mule.
> You take a high brown woman
> Man, she's hard to fool."
> —"Long Lonesome Blues"

> "I'm sitting here wonderin' will a matchbox hold my clothes
> I ain't got too many matches but I got so far to go."
> —"Matchbox Blues"

> "I've got a high brown and she's long and tall
> Lord, Lord, Lord, she'll make a panther squall."
> —"Black Snake Moan"

What was the largest mass movement among African Americans?

Apart from the Baptist Church, the popular movement that attracted African Americans in the largest numbers was **Marcus Garvey**'s Universal Negro Improvement Association, which flourished during the 1920s. Garvey and the UNIA were Africanist, prideful, nationalistic, militant, even separatist, and, as their success testified, they spoke to a deep level of racial consciousness within the black community, a level obviously not addressed by the establishment and integrationist African-American organizations and their leaders.

Garvey was born August 17, 1887, in St. Ann's Bay, Jamaica, of undiluted African ancestry. His father claimed descent from Maroons, those escaped slaves who built communities in the inaccessible interior of the island. Garvey was educated locally. He worked as a printer in his native country, and also worked on a plantation in Costa Rica and for a newspaper in Panama. In London he came under the influence of Duse Mohammed Ali, an Egyptian, who celebrated African history, and Garvey wrote for his paper, the *Africa Times and Orient Review*.

Garvey's experience of the unjust treatment of black workers and his acquaintance with African independence movements, combined with his reading of **Booker T. Washington**'s inspirational story of self-reliance, *Up from Slavery*, created a defining sense of racial awareness and a desire for worldwide black liberation from white domination. "I asked," Garvey said, "where is the black man's government . . . ?"

With Washington's Tuskegee Institute as a model, Garvey came to the States in 1916 and set out to build a program of racial redemption. He was an eloquent orator, and his message resonated with working-class black people, including returned soldiers who had become enlightened by seeing how differently blacks were treated in Europe. They were disgusted that their participation in World War I on behalf of democracy did not mean an end to segregation and the badge of inferiority at home. Also, African-American civilians had moved North in considerable numbers to take advantage of wartime industrial employment: living in the North and getting higher salaries raised expectations white America had no intentions of fulfilling.

"Up, you mighty race," Garvey said. "You can accomplish what you will!" It was a powerful and inspiring message. Garvey drew a picture of a people who had once been great and who could be great again. He told how many millions of the world's population were people of color. He relished the cultural and material richness of Africa. "Africa for the Africans," he said, and added meaningfully, "at home and abroad." Garvey's movement was "Back to Africa"—physically for some, psychologically for all.

Garvey began a newspaper, the *Negro World*, to express his views. Some of the best talent of the day, such as Claude McKay and William Ferris, wrote for it, and it circulated widely. Banned by the European colonial authorities in Africa, the *Negro World* was smuggled into the continent's ports by African-American sailors, and its message was so engaging it was in some places literally drummed into the interior. In America, Garvey staged colorful parades, proclaimed himself Provisional President of Africa, and created a uniformed army and a corps of Black Cross nurses.

Perhaps Garvey's most dramatic move was the founding of the Black Star Line. These were to be steamships sailing between Africa and the United States, carrying black people home to populate prosperous settlements in the motherland and bringing materials and products back for sale. The Black Star Line cost a fortune and was a total commercial and financial disaster. But the very daring of the concept inspired black people around the world to believe that a black person could undertake large-scale enterprises, whose scope had been thought to be the exclusive province of whites.

Garvey's chauvinism appealed especially to West Indians, to working-class African Americans, and to others who were simply disillusioned with the unfilled promises of American democracy. The UNIA had thousands of members in hundreds of cities, and there were branches around the world. Garvey also made enemies: the liberal integrationists deplored his separatist rhetoric, and thought him a buffoon because of his fancy uniforms and royal court. A "Garvey Must Go" campaign on the part of the African-American elite, including W. E. B. Du Bois, resulted in Garvey's framed arrest and conviction on a charge of mail fraud. He went to Atlanta Penitentiary and was deported in 1927.

With poor management and without Garvey's leadership—and under the pressures of the Great Depression—the movement dramatically declined. Garvey died in London, June 10, 1940, almost forgotten. He had made connections with the white racist groups because they were also for black separatism, and this alienated many of his followers. His rise to influence, however, showed how powerful to the black masses were the appeals of pride and self-reliance. Kwame Nkrumah of Ghana and other African leaders admitted their debt to him in the struggle for African independence. And an immigrant Vietnamese dishwasher in Harlem named Ho Chi Minh heard Garvey speaking on the corner of 135th Street and Lenox Avenue. He was so inspired he decided to return home to help free his own people from colonialism.

If you want to know more:

Robert A. Hill and Barbara Bair. *Marcus Garvey: Life and Lessons.* Berkeley, Ca.: University of California Press, 1987.

"Stand on your own two feet and fight like hell for your place in the world."

—Amy Jacques Garvey

"I asked, 'Where is the black man's government? Where is his kingdom? Where is his president, his country and his ambassador, his army, his navy, his men of big affairs?' I could not find them, and then I declared, 'I will help make them.' "

—Marcus Garvey

"How dare anyone tell us that Africa cannot be redeemed, when we have 400,000,000 men and women with warm blood coursing through their veins?"

—Marcus Garvey

"The only protection against injustice in man is power—physical, financial, and scientific."

—Marcus Garvey

"We have gradually won our way back into the confidence of the God of Africa, and he shall speak with the voice of thunder, that shall shake the pillars of a corrupt and unjust world, and once more restore Ethiopia to her ancient glory."

—Marcus Garvey

"Black men, you were once great; you shall be great again. Lose not courage, lose not faith, go forward. The thing to do is to get organized; keep separated and you will be exploited, you will be robbed. You will be killed. Get organized and you will compel the world to respect you."

—Marcus Garvey

Who was the Poet Laureate of Harlem?

A product of the Harlem Renaissance and one of the most popular African-American writers ever, Langston Hughes (1902–1967) has been called "The Poet Laureate of Harlem." He was certainly known and beloved by all the residents of Harlem, and he was perhaps the first black American to earn a living, albeit a precarious one, by his writing. Over the years Hughes turned out volumes of essays, autobiography, fiction, plays, children's books, short stories, and anthologies, but he was always primarily a poet.

Langston Hughes was born February 1, 1902, in Joplin, Missouri, related to black political leader **John Mercer Langston,** and to Lewis Leary, who was shot and killed while taking the federal arsenal at Harpers Ferry with John Brown. Hughes was alienated from his father, a black man who had deep feelings of racial self-hatred. On his way to visit his father in Mexico while still a teenager, Hughes composed what became perhaps his best-known poem, "I've Known Rivers." He wrote of the Euphrates, the Congo, the Nile, and the Mississippi, the great waterways along which Africans and people of African descent have lived their lives over the centuries.

Like much of Hughes' writing, this poem is deceptively complex. Meaning in his poems is concealed more than it is revealed, and so his poems become metaphors for his own life. He, too, was complex, but appeared simple. He protected himself psychologically behind masks, and facades; he evaded and dissimulated, and he concealed his vulnerability behind a genial and complaisant exterior. It is hard to know who the real person was. Hughes was probably homosexual, though he appeared asexual. He was more politically radical than he let on, particularly when it became dangerous to be identified as any kind of leftist.

Hughes' genius—and his contribution—lay in his identification with working-class black people. His respect for and love of their music and speech made them the basis for his writing. In his poetry Hughes combined black speech, the blues form, dance rhythms, and the flavor of both church services and jook joints. Unlike Countee Cullen and others who aspired to write in traditional and classical European forms, Hughes enthusiastically took elements of African-American vernacular, which became the ingredients of as well as the inspiration for his work.

The result was that Hughes became one of the first writers to express true black consciousness, to interpret to people of color the unacknowledged beauty within themselves, and to raise racial folk forms to literary art for the world to see. Hughes saw the incredible creative power of African-American speech, music, and style, and out of them he constructed an African-American aesthetic that has not yet been equaled.

Through a lifetime of personal rejections and rebuffs, Hughes learned to live on the life-affirming creativity of the black masses. Whatever disappointments he encountered elsewhere, he had a home: there was always, in his words, "the undertow of black music with its rhythms that never betray you, its strengths like the beat of a human heart. Hughes never wavered in his identification with "my people." "I don't study the black man," he wrote. "I feel him."

Hughes spent most of his life living on the margins, traveling cheaply, staying with friends, giving endless readings of his work for small fees to black schools and African-American organizations. He defended the uniqueness of black folk culture in an important essay, "The Negro Artist and the Racial Mountain," in which he spoke to both black and white critics who thought he was only writing trash picked up from the gutter: "Let the blare of Negro jazz bands and the bellowing voice of Bessie Smith singing Blues penetrate the closed ears of the colored near-intellectuals until they listen and perhaps understand."

If you want to know more:

Arnold Rampersad, *The Life of Langston Hughes.* 2 vols. New York: Oxford University Press, 1986.

"I am the black girl who crossed the dark sea
Carrying in my body the seed of the Free."

—Langston Hughes

"When Susanna Jones wears red
A queen from some time-dead Egyptian night
Walks once again.
Blow trumpets, Jesus!"

—Langston Hughes

"The night is beautiful
So the faces of my people."

—Langston Hughes

Who is the Father of Black History?

Carter G. Woodson, who began adult life as a coal miner in West Virginia, is called the "Father of Black History" because he initiated publications and organizations to take seriously the investigation of the African-American experience. He founded the Association for the Study of Negro Life and History in 1915; *The Journal of Negro History* in 1916; Associated Publishers, to produce books on African-American life, in 1921; and, in 1926, Negro History Week, which has now become Black History Month.

Born December 19, 1875, in Virginia, to parents who had been slaves, Woodson attended Berea College, the University of Chicago, and Harvard University. At the latter institution he received in 1912 a Ph D in history, the second African American, after W. E. B. Du Bois, to do so. His major professor, Edward Channing, believed blacks had no history, which may have influenced Woodson's decision to devote his life to eliminating ignorance, correcting the historical records of its racist bias, and promoting accurate black history.

Persistently rejected by philanthropists and foundations, Woodson worked sixteen to eighteen hours a day doing research, writing, editing, administering, publishing, lecturing, and promoting. He turned his own modest salary back to the association to help support it. He produced articles, books, reviews, and a major text book in 1922, *The Negro in Our History*. He pioneered in the use of census data, and wrote widely on the social history of African Americans, and, perhaps more than any other scholar, established that black people were major participants in American history. He was particularly interested in documenting the African-American story, and *The Journal of Negro History* regularly included primary source materials as well as articles and essays.

Woodson was not an easy man to like or to get along with. He was a person of independence, strong views, and incorruptible integrity, so much so that he was seen as difficult, uncompromising, demanding, adversarial, and stubborn. He never married, and only **Mary McLeod Bethune** dared address him by his first name. Woodson worked to popularize black history, believing that African Americans needed the self-esteem that came from having a usable past. He disliked the pretensions of the black bourgeoisie, but was too sophisticated himself to approve of jazz or ecstatic religion or other manifestations of black working-class culture. He became more politically radical as he got older, perhaps because he saw that education and enlightenment were not changing the world of or for black people, as quickly as he had once hoped.

Woodson died in Washington, D.C., on April 3, 1950.

If you want to know more:

Jacqueline Goggin. *Carter G. Woodson: A Life in Black History*. Baton Rouge, La.: Louisiana State University Press, 1993.

"My experience has very much diminished my faith in the veracity of History; it has convinced me that many of the most important facts are concealed; some of the most important characters but imperfectly known; many false facts imposed on historians and the world; and many empty characters displayed in great pomp. All this, I am sure, will happen in our American history."

—John Adams, July 24, 1789

"We should emphasize not Negro History, but the Negro in history. What we need is not a history of selected races or nations, but the history of the world, void of national bias, race, hate, and religious prejudice."

—Carter G. Woodson

Who collected books by and about African Americans?

One of the primary imperatives of African-American intellectuals has always been the preservation of African and African-American heritage. This has meant establishing the existence of this heritage, disseminating it, and correcting the historical record where it has been corrupted by Eurocentric commentators. Probably no one has carried out these tasks more effectively than **Arthur Alfonso Schomburg** (1874–1938), who forced the reconsideration of African-American history and culture by amassing a huge collection of books, manuscripts, pamphlets, prints, and other artwork by and about people of African descent.

Schomburg was born in San Juan, Puerto Rico, on January 24, 1874. His mother was a black laundress from the Virgin Islands, and his father was a German merchant. Schomburg received some education in Puerto Rico, where he reported he was told by a grade school teacher, in response to his question, that black people had no history, a statement Schomburg spent virtually his entire life successfully disproving.

Schomburg emigrated in 1891 to the United States, where he worked in a lawyer's office, was active in the Porto Rico Revolutionary Party, and began to write articles. In 1906 he went to work for Bankers Trust Company, where he became head of the mail room. He was an active Prince Hall Mason; in 1911 he and John Edward "Bruce Grit" Bruce founded the Negro Society for Historical Research; and in 1922 Schomburg was elected president of the American Negro Academy.

Long before the founding of the Negro Society for Historical Research, Schomburg had begun his life's work of collecting Afro-Americana. Schomburg collected broadly and was, perhaps because of his Puerto Rican origin, especially interested in Afro-Spanish material. He had manuscripts in the hands of **Phillis Wheatley** and **Lemuel Haynes,** and rare books by Juan Latino and **Olaudah Equiano.** Today these kinds of artifact are virtually nonexistent, and prohibitively expensive if and when they do turn up. Schomburg collected at a time when few bibliophiles, book dealers, or institutions were interested in black culture, so he was able to find the works and pay very little for them.

Meanwhile, as Harlem was changing into a black neighborhood, the New York Public Library, which had a commitment to serving the reading needs of immigrant groups as they moved into various sections of the city, also began collecting black material at the 135th Street Branch. The artistic and literary nature of the Harlem Renaissance, with its African influences and its positive self-consciousness, led to an exploration of the black past and created a new stature for African-American culture and history.

At the urging of the Urban League, the Carnegie Corporation purchased for $10,000 Schomburg's massive collection of Afro-Americana, then the largest in private hands, and gave it to the library. This formed the core of what became in time the Schomburg Center for Research in Black Culture, now the world's leading institution for research in the field. After Schomburg had served for two years as librarian at Fisk University, another Carnegie grant made it possible for him to become curator of his own collection. He held that position at his death, in New York, on June 10, 1938.

Thanks to Arthur A. Schomburg's passion for discovering the past, thousands of books, prints, and manuscripts that might have been lost forever have been preserved to tell their story.

If you want to know more:

Elinor Des Verney Sinnette. *Arthur Alfonso Schomburg: Black Bibliophile and Collector.* Detroit: Wayne State University Press, 1989.

"The African American must remake his past in order to make his future."

—Arthur A. Schomburg

"Though it is orthodox to think of America as the one country where it is unnecessary to have a past, what is a luxury for the nation as a whole becomes a prime social necessity for the Negro."

—Arthur A. Schomburg

What blues singer made a pact with the Devil?

Robert Johnson was perhaps the finest performer of Mississippi Delta self-accompanied blues. He started out with what appeared to be a minimum of musical talent, but then he mysteriously disappeared for a while, and returned a fully accomplished guitarist and singer. The transformation was so startling that people said he must have made a pact with the Devil, a notion Johnson not only did not deny, but one which makes some appearance in his songs, and is a possibility not inconsistent with his personality.

In fact, there was an almost eerie quality to Robert Johnson. He was a shy man, but just beneath the surface there was intense personal pain, an emotion with an ominous side, a kind of dangerous desperation. He was born May 8, 1911, in Hazelwood, Mississippi, the illegitimate son of Julia Dodds and Noah Johnson. He lived with several families under several names and took Johnson as a surname when he discovered who his real father was.

Musically, Johnson was influenced by Charley Patton and Son House, but he was himself a brilliant guitarist and vocalist who influenced everyone who came after him. In a falsetto voice he created lyrics or added to common lyrics his own sense of fate, hopelessness, and risk. He was a real itinerant, turning up unexpectedly here and there across the Delta, and rambling across the South to Memphis and St. Louis. Johnson was an intense person, and the energy that did not go into his music was directed toward women. He married as an adolescent, but his wife died in childbirth at age sixteen. His shyness combined with the aura of reckless danger that surrounded him seems to have made him almost irresistible to women. He would simply approach a woman at a dance hall and quietly say, "Can I stay with you?" The answer was almost always affirmative.

In 1936 Johnson cut sixteen sides in San Antonio for the American Record Company, and the next year he recorded again in a Dallas warehouse. He turned out songs as fresh and powerful now as the moment they were recorded: "Terraplane Blues," "Come On in My Kitchen," "Hell Hound on My Trail." These are blues songs without an underlying sense of hope, and they are infused with real despair:

> I have a bird to whistle
> And I have a bird to sing
> I got a woman that I'm loving
> Boy but she don't mean a thing.

Don Law, the white man who managed the San Antonio recording session, recalls sending Johnson off for the night before he was to record, but of having his dinner interrupted by a call from the police. Johnson had been arrested, beaten up, and put in jail. Law bailed him out and sent him to a colored rooming house with 45 cents for breakfast. Later that night there was another phone call, this time from Johnson himself. "I'm lonesome," was all he said. "What do you mean, you're lonesome?" Law asked. "Well," Johnson said shyly, "there's a lady here. She wants 50 cents and I lacks a nickel."

Johnson was pleased with his recordings and reportedly gave copies to a number of women by whom he had children. Don Law remembered Johnson's hands, the most beautiful he had ever seen, he said, and large enough to do physical things with a guitar other men couldn't do. Johnson's last days are not well documented. He died August 16, 1938, in Greenwood, Mississippi, probably killed by poison administered by a jealous husband. His reputation was known and maintained by a few fans until Columbia reissued his complete recordings on CD and tape in 1990, after which they won a Grammy Award and sold 500,000 copies.

If you want to know more:

Peter Guralnick. *Searching for Robert Johnson.* New York: E. P. Dutton, 1989.

> "You may bury my body
> Down by the highway side
> So my old evil spirit
> Can get a Greyhound bus and ride."
>
> "Me and the Devil Blues"

> "I got up this morning
> The blues walking like a man
> Worried blues
> Give me your right hand."
>
> "Preachin' Blues"

> "I'm going to write a letter
> Telephone every town I know
> If I can't find her in West Selma
> She must be in East Monroe I know."
>
> "I Believe I'll Dust My Broom"

> "And death could not ever ease his kinda pain."
>
> —Walter Mosley

What sport became a symbolic arena for black-white rivalry?

Until recent years, boxing was one of the few sports in which African Americans had comparatively equal access along with whites. Black men were traditionally skilled fighters, perhaps because slave owners often set up bouts between slaves, usually for gambling purposes, just as they did with fighting dogs and gamecocks. Perhaps black excellence came from the fact that the openness of boxing as a route to money or even manumission created a real incentive to succeed.

The one-on-one nature of boxing as well as its use of both physical and mental abilities soon made the sport a symbolic testing place for representatives of the white and black races. The racial pride of both groups was at issue here, but behind that was the white claim to racial superiority. The ring therefore became a metaphorical arena as well as a physical one, where whites believed they could demonstrate and maintain their superiority, and blacks believed that, if given a fair chance, they could prove that they were at least equal.

The very first American heavyweight title contender was, in fact, an African American, Tom Molineaux. He had been a slave in Virginia, but won his freedom in a match with another slave, and moved to England. In 1810 at Copthall Common, England, Molineaux fought the English champion, Tom Cribb. Molineaux knocked Cribb down in the twenty-eighth round, but the referee gave Cribb extra minutes to revive. Cribb won the fight in the forty-third round, but it had taken an unfair advantage to do it.

The nation's first African-American champion was Joe Gans of Baltimore, Maryland, who took the world lightweight title in 1901, and the world welterweight title in 1906. He retook his lightweight title the same year, winning on a foul, but the reaction to his win was violence against black people all over the country. These random attacks were the first time a black boxing victory resulted in white fury, but not the last. A pattern was set for prizefighting to become the preeminent national event where an athletic contest turned into a titanic racial rivalry.

It took African Americans some time since Tom Molineaux in 1810 to have another chance at the heavyweight championship. There were many qualified black fighters, but none was permitted to contend for the title. White resistance was personified by the statement of heavyweight champion John L. Sullivan around the turn of the present century who said, "I will not fight a negro. I never have, and I never shall." **John Arthur "Jack" Johnson,** an extraordinarily able black fighter from Galveston, Texas, with a string of wins, let it be known he wanted a crack at the title in 1903, but Jim Jeffries, the reigning champion declared, "I will not fight a negro! If I am defeated, the championship will go to a white man, for I will not fight a colored man."

Johnson continued to win bouts and agitate for a chance at the crown. Eventually, it went to Tommy Burns, a Canadian, who finally gave in and agreed to fight in Sydney, Australia, on December 26, 1908. Johnson destroyed Burns, the fight was stopped in round fourteen, and Jack Johnson became the first black world heavyweight champion. The racially charged nature of his victory meant that the black community was overjoyed and the white community incensed. Many whites were so angry they declared the need for a "Great White Hope" to bring down the black titleholder.

Retired champion Jim Jeffries answered the call with, "I realize full well what depends on me. . . . That portion of the white race that has been looking to me to defend its athletic superiority may feel assured that I am fit to do my very best." African Americans were just as conscious of what was at risk. One black newspaper, the *Chicago Defender,* declared, "The future welfare of his [Johnson's] people forms a part of the stake."

The match was set for July 4, 1910, in San Francisco, and was at the time the most lucrative deal in sports history: Jeffries and Johnson each were to receive over $100,000. Over thirty thousand people jammed an arena designed for half that number. Johnson wore an American flag attached to his navy blue shorts. The two fighters did not exchange the customary handshake. Johnson was in control from the first round, as an outclassed Jeffries clinched, spit blood, and received one brutal uppercut after another, each accompanied by Johnson's laugh.

In the fifteenth round Johnson delivered a series of hard, decisive blows, and Jeffries' seconds threw in the towel. A black man had defeated the Great White Hope. Enraged white people from Georgia to Nebraska demanded revenge: thirteen African Americans were murdered and hundreds more were injured. Johnson himself was harassed for the rest of his life, largely because he married white women and lived a flamboyant lifestyle. The white public could scarcely stand a black man who, they believed, flaunted his prowess and his success. Jack Johnson died in an automobile accident on June 10, 1946. **Arthur Ashe** called him "the most significant black athlete in history."

If you want to know more:

Jack Johnson. *Jack Johnson Is a Dandy: An Autobiography.* New York: New American Library, 1969.

> "Hardly a blow had been struck when I knew that I was [Jeffries'] master. From the start the fight was mine. . . . The 'white hope' had failed, and as far as the championship was concerned it was just where it was before . . . except that I had established my rightful claim to it beyond all possible dispute."
>
> —Jack Johnson

Who were the Scottsboro Boys?

On March 25, 1931, near Lookout Mountain, Tennessee, a fight broke out in a boxcar on a freight train running from Chattanooga to Memphis. The nation was well into its most serious economic depression, and thousands of homeless and out-of-work hobos all over the country rode the rails looking for work or just staying on the move. The fight was between a group of young white men and young black men. The blacks won and threw the whites off the train. Local law enforcement was informed and the train was stopped at the Paint Rock, Alabama, depot.

Two young white women were also riding the boxcars: Ruby

Bates, aged seventeen, and Victoria Price, twenty-one. They were prostitutes who had been in trouble with the law and were afraid of incurring new charges. Bates had once been arrested for "hugging a Negro." Apparently, they were asked if the black men had "bothered" them, and Price stated they had been repeatedly raped. Nine young black men, aged thirteen to eighteen, were quickly rounded up from various sections of the train, and taken to the jail at Scottsboro, Alabama, the nearby Jackson County seat. Word of the incident spread, a lynch mob immediately gathered, and the young men were saved from almost certain murder by the protective pressure of 120 National Guardsmen. The nine became known as the Scottsboro Boys, partly because they were teenagers, but mainly because the white South always referred to black males of all ages as "boys" as a mark of disrespect and means of control.

In less than two weeks, the youths had been tried and sentenced to death for rape. These young men were poor, uneducated, and unemployed; one was nearly blind, and another seriously ill with syphilis. Most were strangers to each other before their arrest. Virtually no defense was made at their trial. Bates and Price showed no physical signs of rape. Many white Southerners wanted them lynched, while the more fair-minded believed that the very fact that there was a trial testified to the workability and validity of the Southern legal system, despite an automatic assumption of guilt. It was all so patently unjust, however, that two groups came to the young men's side, the International Labor Defense (ILD) and the National Association for the Advancement of Colored People (NAACP).

The two organizations could not have been more different, and they symbolized basic differences in thinking about how to approach the problems of American racism and injustice. The ILD was essentially a white Communist body, and its critics believed it was using the Scottsboro case as a radical device to influence the masses. The NAACP was essentially black and reformist, fearful of losing its respectability, and opposed to public protest, which it felt was counterproductive. **Walter White** of the NAACP thought the ILD really wanted the Scottsboro defendants dead so it could display murdered martyrs.

The ILD thought the NAACP's moderate reformism merely delayed the inevitable revolution of the people.

The ILD took over the defense, partly because it was an active, aggressive, and well-financed organization, partly because it won the confidence of the defendants and their mothers, partly because of the NAACP's foot-dragging and timidity. The ILD secured Samuel Liebowitz of New York, probably the best criminal lawyer in the country, as the youths' defender. Despite brilliant legal work on his part, however, he and his clients were defeated in and by the Southern courts. Many observers in fact called the trial a "legal lynching." Liebowitz was shocked at the blatant racism of the system, and sympathetic whites in the North became aware of deep-seated institutionalized Southern bigotry. The cases were appealed and retried.

Scottsboro became a national cause. Ruby Bates recanted her story and joined the defense. The Supreme Court intervened because there had not been a black on an Alabama jury roll since Reconstruction. In 1935, a new defense committee was formed under the leadership of Allan Knight Chalmers, the minister of Broadway Tabernacle, an old white abolitionist church in New York. Through it all, the defendants stayed in jail, often mercilessly beaten, constantly mistreated, and denied even their basic rights as prisoners. President Franklin Delano Roosevelt intervened behind the scenes politically. Chalmers finally arranged with Alabama Governor Bibb Graves a secret deal for the defendants' pardon, but Graves reneged at the last minute.

What happened to the Scottsboro Boys? In 1937 the charge against Olen Montgomery was dropped. He got a job as a laborer, working six days a week from 4:30 a.m. till 8:30 p.m. for $7.50. Clarence Norris was paroled in 1944 and pardoned in 1976 by Governor George Wallace. Haywood Patterson escaped in 1948 to Detroit, and Michigan refused to extradite him. Ozie Powell was paroled in 1946. Charges against Willie Roberson were dropped in 1937. Charlie Weems was paroled in 1943. Charges against Eugene Williams were dropped in 1937. Andy Wright was paroled in 1944, and the charges against Roy Wright were dropped in 1937.

What was Scottsboro about? It was really about racism and

how racism dehumanizes both blacks and whites alike. It was about a criminal justice system based on bigotry rather than even elementary fairness. It was about the split between moderates and radicals with regard to how to change America. Mostly, however, Scottsboro seems to support **James Baldwin**'s notion that racism is basically about sex, especially white fantasies about black sexuality, fantasies held by white men and women alike. In one of the trials, one of the prosecution lawyers said if the Scottsboro youths were freed, every white woman in the South would have to wear a revolver "to protect the sacred parts of her body."

If you want to know more:

James Goodman. *Stories of Scottsboro: The Rape Case That Shocked 1930's America and Revived the Struggle for Equality.* New York: Pantheon Books, 1944.

"I'm just being held here because I'm a Nigger."
—Olen Montgomery

"I ain't got justice here."
—Andy Wright

"It seems as though I have been here for century on century."
—Andy Wright

"Stand up for your rights, even if it kills you. That's all that life consists of."
—Clarence Norris

"We have been sentenced to die for something we ain't never done. Us poor boys been sentenced to burn up on the electric chair for the reason that we is workers—and the color of our skin is black."
—the Scottsboro Boys

Who was the greatest American cartoonist?

George Herriman, who drew the daily and Sunday comic strip *Krazy Kat* for thirty years through the 1920s and '30s, is considered by many to be the greatest American cartoonist. His work was characterized by stong lines, a subtle Chaplinesque wit, surrealistic Arizona desert settings, clever word spellings, and an ironic story line which he repeated daily.

The strip's chief character was Krazy Kat, an androgynous feline who was sentimentally in love with Ignatz, a married male mouse. Ignatz despised Krazy, and demonstrated his contempt by managing to hit him/her in the head every day with a brick. Krazy, however, was descended from Kleopatra Kat, an Egyptian in whose culture the tossed brick was not a weapon, but the bearer of a love note. Krazy, therefore, was foolishly enraptured by the regular assault, misreading Ignatz's disgust as romantic affection. The plot was complicated by Officer B. Pupp, a dog policeman who was in love with Krazy and who unsuccessfully attempted, in moralistic but soft-hearted ways, to protect him/her from the mouse's daily missile.

George Herriman was born August 22, 1880, at 348 Villere Street in New Orleans. His family soon moved to Los Angeles, where his father worked as a baker, tailor, and barber. In his early twenties, Herriman sold some cartoons in New York and was handpicked by William Randolph Hearst for his *New York Evening Journal.* On July 26, 1910, as part of another cartoon strip, he first drew a cat beaned by a brick-wielding mouse. On October 28, 1913, *Krazy Kat* became a regular feature, and the strip continued until Herriman's death on June 25, 1944.

It was not known during his lifetime that George Herriman was African American. He never mentioned his racial background, and he was known to his colleagues as "The Greek," a comment on his indeterminate ancestry. He constantly wore a Stetson hat, indoors and out, which hid his dark, curly hair. At his death, his daughter told the press he had been born in France, which she may well have believed. Herriman's birth certificate, however, identified him as "colored," and his parents and grandparents were all listed in the 1880 census as mulattos, New Orleans Creoles.

Herriman's was a classic case of "passing," that is, moving across the color line from black to white by someone light-skinned enough to conceal his African heritage and be taken for Caucasian. The reasons for passing are largely economic and psychological. Economic opportunities have always been, and continue to be, many times greater for nonblacks. And the daily psychological stress of surviving the humiliation and discrimination of racism is a constant burden. The fact that passing can even take place at all also points to the irrationality of America's legal definitions and social practices concerning race.

It would be interesting but speculative to wonder if Krazy Kat's indeterminate identity was some psychic reflection of Herriman's own neutral state. Also, as a young man he drew a short-lived strip called *Musical Mose* which featured a black musician who disguised himself every day in a different ethnic identity, but was always found out and beaten up. It is equally interesting to wonder if Herriman had chosen to go through life as an African American, whether he would have been allowed to become America's greatest cartoonist.

If you want to know more:

Frederick McDonnell, Karen O'Connell, and Georgia Riley de Havenon. *Krazy Kat: The Comic Art of George Herriman.* New York: Harry N. Abrams, 1986.

"When I first met Bill [de Kooning], I remember he and Edwin Denby would wait for the newspapers to come out and latch on to the latest *Krazy Kat* cartoon."
—Elaine de Kooning

"[He] has invented in his comic strip, *Krazy Kat,* a nonsense creation which, for humor and originality is comparable only to *Alice in Wonderland.*"

—*Vanity Fair*

" 'Brick,' Officer, 'Brick'; what brick?"

—Ignatz Mouse

Who transformed the image of the mature black woman?

Mature black women have been traditionally portrayed in popular American culture as Aunt Jemima, the pancake cook; or the quintessential Mammy of *Gone With the Wind,* as played by **Hattie McDaniel**; or Beulah, the TV maid. These are really all the same image: a rotund domestic servant, sometimes sassy, always subservient, sometimes accompanied by a shiftless black man who is discovered being fed in the kitchen. Above all, this person is perceived as self-sacrificially loyal to her white masters, who shake their heads affectionately and pretend she rules them and their households.

This deeply ingrained portrait was effectively challenged on the stage and in films by Ethel Waters, an actress who created a new image: the strong, matriarchal, nurturing earth mother.

Waters herself had a difficult life. She was conceived when her eleven-year-old mother, Louise Anderson, was held down by an older sister, Viola, while John Wesley Waters, a white pianist, raped her. Waters was born on October 31, sometime in the late 1890s or perhaps in 1900, in Chester, Pennsylvania. She was raised by her grandmother, Sally Anderson, who was a live-in domestic servant, and the model for Waters' later dramatic portrayal of the warm, stable, centered, older black woman. Like her contemporaries Florence Mills and Josephine Baker, Waters grew up in a dirt-poor, crime-saturated, vice-ridden neighborhood where survival itself was a major miracle.

But also like Mills and Baker, Waters could sing and dance, and this was her ticket out of the ghetto, as it was theirs. She began her career as a teenager, singing "When You're a Long, Long Way from Home" in Jack's Rathskeller in Philadelphia. It was not long before Waters, billed as "Sweet Mama String-bean," built a reputation as a hot shimmy dancer, standing with her arms outstretched, shaking her tall lanky body, and singing bawdy songs in East Coast black clubs, tent shows, and vaude-ville houses. Her specialty was raunchy double (or even triple) entendre songs like "Shake That Thing," "Take Your Black Bottom Outside," "I'm Coming Virginia," and "My Handyman Ain't Handy No More."

Waters began to refine her singing, probably for the benefit of the wealthy white clientele of the Plantation Club over the Winter Garden Theatre on Broadway, where she was the sum-mer replacement for Florence Mills in 1924. Her singing evolved from the rough urban blues of Ma Rainey and Bessie Smith to a smoother, better articulated, more sophisticated style. In so doing, Waters made black singing understandable and accessible to mainstream, that is, white audiences. She es-sentially legitimized the genre of popular songs sung by black women, and she made possible the modern cabaret-type per-formances of Billie Holiday and **Sarah Vaughan,** who followed her. Waters thus played a major role in the transformation of vocal performance, just as she did of African-American women's imagery.

Waters is no longer chiefly remembered either as a singer or dancer. Her first stage appearances and films, however, were simply continuations of her vaudeville performances, both in content and presentation: *Africana* (1927), Lew Leslie's *Black-birds of 1930: Glorifying the American Negro* (1930), and *Rhapsody in Black* (1931). Real change began when Irving Berlin heard Waters sing "Stormy Weather" backed by Duke Ellington at the Cotton Club, and signed her for *As Thousands Cheer* (1934). Here she sang more serious numbers: "Harlem on My Mind," "Heat Wave," and "Supper Time." Her success catapulted her to a salary of $1,000 a week, making her the highest-paid woman on Broadway.

Waters' acting career began in earnest with her role as Hagar in DuBose Heyward's *Mamba's Daughters* in 1939 with **Fredi Washington.** She went on to play Petunia opposite Dooley Wilson in *Cabin in the Sky,* as well as in the subsequent film treatment with Eddie "Rochester" Anderson. Waters insisted on interpreting the role her way, and, against considerable opposition, portrayed Petunia as a dignified woman of profound religious commitment, instead of a humorous caricature of "primitive" black religion as defined by white writers.

Waters went on to the role of Granny in *Pinky* (1949) with Jeanne Crain, for which she received an Oscar nomination as Best Supporting Actress. But Waters' greatest role was undoubtedly as Berneice in *Member of the Wedding* by Carson McCullers in 1950. It ran for 501 performances on Broadway and was a well-received 1952 film. It was here more than in any other vehicle that Waters transformed the vernacular image of black woman from Mammy to Earth Mother.

Waters' personal life was neither happy nor successful, and she was known to be jealous and competitive, egotistic, and given to temper tantrums. In 1957 she first attended a Billy Graham evangelistic crusade meeting in Madison Square Garden in New York. She joined the choir and virtually began a new career, participating in religious revivals and church services, and singing her theme song, "His Eye Is on the Sparrow." Waters died in California on September 1, 1977.

If you want to know more:

Ethel Waters with Charles Samuels. *His Eye Is on the Sparrow: An Autobiography.* Garden City, N.Y.: Doubleday, 1951.

"I was a tough child. I was too large and too poor to fit, and I fought back."

—Ethel Waters

"When I was a honky-tonk entertainer, I used to work from nine until unconscious. I was just a young girl, and when I tried to sing anything but the double-meaning songs, they'd say, 'Oh, my God, Ethel, get hot!' "

—Ethel Waters

What is black gospel music?

Listen to **Mahalia Jackson** sing "Amazing Grace." Listen to **Rahsaan Roland Kirk** play "The Old Rugged Cross." Listen to **Aretha Franklin**'s spectacular performance of "Yield Not to Temptation." If you have also heard these songs as they are traditionally played and sung in white evangelical churches, you know that when black people sing them something radically and excitingly different happens.

Add to this transformation of white music the songs and styles that come directly from the black experience—Bessie Griffin's mother moaning, "When you see me crying / Lord, Lord, Lord / It ain't nuthin' but my trainfare home"—and you have the "gospel sound" proclaiming both "good news and bad times." As **James Baldwin** said, "There is no music like that music, no drama like the saints rejoicing, the sinners moaning, the tambourines racing, and all those voices coming together and crying holy unto the Lord."

One of the early formative giants of gospel was Arizona Dranes, a blind and impoverished Texas pianist and singer who recorded in the late 1920s. A sanctified member of the Church of God in Christ, her fast piano-playing combined white march music and African rhythms with a sporting-house ragtime beat. Her singing of songs like "Lamb's Blood Has Washed Me Clean" approached ecstatic frenzy.

The great catalyst of black gospel music was **Thomas A. "Georgia Tom" Dorsey,** a musical genius who wed black and white evangelistic music to the blues. He was the piano accompanist to both Ma Rainey and Bessie Smith, and the composer of the blues classic "It's Tight Like That" recorded with Tampa Red. Converted in Chicago's Pilgrim Baptist Church, Dorsey went on to create another masterpiece, "Precious Lord, Take My Hand." As Anthony Heilbut points out, Dorsey is a living link between the old blues singer Blind Lemon Jefferson and modern popular music.

Like jazz, black gospel entered the musical mainstream when whites adapted and popularized it. But the genealogy is clear. Elvis Presley heard and was influenced by black gospel at the East Trigg Baptist Church in Memphis, where the great **Queen C.** (for Queen Candace of Ethiopia) **Anderson** was the leading soloist, and whose pastor, **W. Herbert Brewster,** wrote "Move On Up a Little Higher." Presley sold a million records of Dorsey's "Peace in the Valley," but the full story of popular music's roots in black gospel is yet to be written.

There are familiar names in black gospel music: James Cleveland, Sister Rosetta Tharp, the Five Blind Boys, Willie Mae Rose Smith, the Dixie Hummingbirds, Clara Ward. But there are many other important artists less well known: Robert Anderson, Alex Bradford, Roberta Martin, Sallie Martin. There are great songs: "Stand By Me," "Old Ship of Zion," "How I Got Over," "Ain't No Grave Can Hold My Body Down," Dorothy Love Coates' "My Soul's on Fire and the World Can't Harm Me." Despite commercialization and acculturation, the black Protestant folk church continues to produce songs and singers that carry this vital and animated culture.

If you want to know more:

Anthony Heilbut. *The Gospel Sound: Good News and Bad Times.* New York: Limelight Editions, 1985.

"Let Jesus fix it for you,
He knows just what to do.
Whenever you pray
Let him have his way,
And he will fix it for you."
—Charles Albert Tindley

"Something within me
That holdeth the reins;
Something within me
That banishes pain;
Something within me
I cannot explain.
All that I know,
There is something within."
—Lucie E. Campbell

What movie is alleged to have ruined attempts for a federal antilynching law?

Walter White of the National Association for the Advancement of Colored People said that the immense popularity of David O. Selznick's 1939 classic film *Gone with the Wind* effectively ended any hopes for getting antilynching legislation through the U.S. Congress. Whether or not he was right, it is certainly true that the movie demonstrated the power of the medium to shape popular thinking. *Gone with the Wind* dramatized the story of the Civil War and Reconstruction and, like its predecessor *The Birth of a Nation,* portrayed as truth the myths which glorified the racist Confederacy and demeaned African Americans.

According to *Gone with the Wind,* slaves were treated kindly, black people were unfit for freedom, and ignoble Yankees and uppity free blacks subjected a noble but prostrate South to the indignities of "black rule"—indignities which justified the restoration by murder and violence of unchallenged white male supremacy. The Confederate States of America may, technically, have lost the war, but these two films guaranteed that the South was the victor in the ideological explanation and interpretation of what had happened.

Like *Birth of a Nation*, *Gone with the Wind* was based on a popular novel. The author was Margaret Mitchell, an Atlanta, Georgia, debutante who privately collected pornography and spent a year at Smith College in Massachusetts. At Smith, she became enraged at finding one of the school's few black students in her history class, and she successfully demanded to be transferred to another section. Mitchell spoke of her kindly attitude to individual black people, and she was hurt, surprised, and perplexed by the social criticisms of her novel and the movie based on it.

Also like *Birth of a Nation*, *Gone with the Wind* was an epic production taking years to film, costing a fortune, and running extra long. A total of 474,538 feet of film was shot, edited down finally to 20,300 feet, making a movie that ran for three hours and forty minutes. It premiered December 15, 1939, in the racially segregated Fox Theater in Atlanta, which meant the black actors were prohibited from attending. Georgia proclaimed a state holiday for the opening.

Several of *Gone with the Wind*'s African-American performers were so good that they were able to transform their roles beyond the racist stereotypes. This was especially true of Hattie McDaniel, who played Mammy. She was the first black actor to win an Academy Award, voted Best Supporting Actress. Butterfly McQueen was brilliant as Prissy, who "didn't know nuthin' 'bout birthin' no babies," but she performed so well she was forever after identified with the role and permanently typecast as a feather-brained servant. McQueen refused to keep playing the same part, and as a result, her professional career was ruined. She was reduced to working as a clerk in Macy's and as a dishwasher. Other notable black performers were Oscar Polk as Pork, Everett Brown, who played Big Sam, and, surprisingly, Eddie "Rochester" Anderson, who was Uncle Peter, but behind so much makeup no one recognized him.

If you want to know more:

Ed Guerrero. *Framing Blackness: The African American Image in Film.* Philadelphia: Temple University Press, 1993.

> "[*Gone with the Wind*] has been seen by an audience of more than 230 million, [and it has been] dubbed in five languages and sub-titled in 30 more. Since June 5, 1987, it has played every day at Ted Turner's CNN Cinema 6 in Atlanta."
>
> —Michael Blowen

> "In American book sales, Margaret Mitchell's *Gone with the Wind* is second only to the Bible. It has sold more than 25 million copies and continues to be popular.
>
> —Michael Blowen

Who was the first African American to win an Academy Award?

Hattie McDaniel was a self-assured, outspoken, formidable woman who insisted on infusing with dignity the countless servant, cook, and domestic roles she played on radio and in films. As Mammy in *Gone with the Wind* she won a Best Supporting Actress Oscar in 1939, the first African American to receive an Academy Award.

McDaniel was born June 10, 1895, in Wichita, Kansas, which meant she had to learn a black Southern accent for her film roles, although she refused to use one in her *Beulah* radio show. Her parents were former slaves and her family became entertainers. McDaniel began an early career in minstrelsy and vaudeville, singing on Denver radio station KOA with George Morrison and the Melody Hounds, and singing blues songs on the Theatre Owners Booking Association (TOBA) black vaudeville circuit, including songs she composed herself.

Because Hollywood refused to give African Americans serious film parts, McDaniel, along with Louise Beavers and others, perfected the Mammy/maid role. She was criticized by the NAACP for helping perpetuate negative black stereotypes, but McDaniel replied that she'd rather *play* a maid than *be* one. Ironically, the sassy integrity and egalitarian stance with which McDaniel imbued her servant roles helped to alter the racial climate and enlarge the opportunities for African Americans in movies.

McDaniel paid a price for her success. David O. Selznick, the producer of *Gone with the Wind,* refused to allow McDaniel—or other black members of the cast—to attend the film's premiere in Atlanta in December 1939. She died on October 26, 1952, at the Motion Picture Country Home and Hospital in Woodland Hills, California.

If you want to know more:

Carlton Jackson. *Hattie: The Life of Hattie McDaniel.* Lanham, Md.: Madison Books, 1990.

"I did what I had to do."

—Hattie McDaniel

Who received mail addressed to "God, Harlem USA"?

One of the by-products of the Great Migration, with its relocation of hundreds of thousands of African Americans to Northern cities, was the rise of many new religious movements. They were often led by charismatic figures such as Prophet James F. Jones in Detroit, Mother Rosa Horn in Harlem, Noble Drew Ali in Newark, Sweet Daddy Grace, who had churches along the Eastern Seaboard, Elder Solomon Lightfoot Michaux in Washington, D.C., and perhaps the best known of all, **Father Divine** in New York and Philadelphia. Sociologists tend to interpret these new groups, with their crowd psychology, magnetic leaders, and ecstatic worship, as popular responses to the problems and stresses of urban dislocation.

According to his biographer, Jill Watts, Father Divine was born George Baker in 1879 in Rockville, Maryland, a poor black community composed mainly of former slaves and their families. His father, also named George Baker, was a day laborer, and his mother, the former Nancy Smith, a domestic. Around the age of twenty, Baker left home for Baltimore, where he worked as a gardener and became active in a Baptist church.

Baker took a number of trips South as an itinerant preacher, and in 1906 was present at the Azusa Street Revival in Los Angeles, where modern-day Pentecostalism was born. Self-educated, he explored and accepted New Thought, a religious philosophy that claimed unlimited power for the human mind, since it is a reflection of the divine mind. Positive thinking, Baker came to believe, could result in physical health and worldly success as well as religious salvation.

By 1919, Baker, who now called himself Father Divine, had gathered a small group of followers and relocated to the all-white community of Sayville, Long Island, New York, where he implemented his new faith. The group lived cooperatively, pooling their financial resources from their jobs as laborers and domestics, and establishing an economic pattern Divine expanded to considerable collective wealth as the movement grew.

Father Divine came to national attention because of a remark he probably didn't make. He was arrested, tried, and convicted of being a "public nuisance" on the complaint of Sayville white people. Shortly after Divine's sentencing, Lewis J. Smith, the trial judge, suddenly and unexpectedly dropped dead of a heart attack. According to a popular story, Divine, when informed, said, "I know. I hated to do it." What we know he did say is that Judge Smith undoubtedly killed himself by negative thinking.

The movement, now called the Peace Mission Movement, became so large that Divine moved to Harlem. Father Divine was perceived by his many followers as God incarnate, and the community gathered around him was understood to be heaven on earth. Male and female followers lived separately, and sex of any kind was strictly forbidden as inappropriate to life in the Kingdom. During the Great Depression of the 1930s the movement established employment agencies and small businesses, acquired property for cooperative housing, kept or took thousands of people off the welfare rolls, and became famous for providing inexpensive dining rooms for the needy.

There was a small but significant number of white adherents, and the movement strongly supported black rights, including the "Don't buy where you can't work" campaign, confirming Divine's role as an early civil rights leader, as Robert Weisbrot has pointed out. In 1936 Divine entered politics with his Righteous Government Platform and hopes of establishing a third party, but the effort did not succeed.

As an adherent of New Thought, Divine understood full well the power of language and the power of mind, especially the ability of language to define reality, and the power of mind to effect—if not actually create—reality by imagining it. In this context, the interracial Peace Mission Movement eliminated the distinction of race by eliminating the vocabulary that made racial distinctions possible. The words *Negro, colored,* and *black,* for example, were simply expunged. People of different colors were referred to as "light-complected" or "dark-complected," merely value-free and nonprejudicial descriptive terms. Father Divine himself claimed to have become personally raceless by transcending race.

The center of Peace Mission worship was the nightly eucharistic banquet. Father presided over a luxuriously appointed table where scores of courses passed under his blessing. Participants and guests were seated by race, alternately black and white, a practice called "enacting the bill," that is, making the U.S. Constitution's Bill of Rights real, and defying segregation laws and social custom by practicing racial integration.

Banquets went on for hours, punctuated by exuberant singing and testifying, and culminating in an address by Father. The banquet was the movement's Holy Communion, a joyous celebration made possible because the Kingdom had come and

God was physically present in the flesh in the midst of his people. The banquet demonstrated, also, material well-being in the midst of economic depression, and the ability of Father and his followers to achieve abundance. Religiously, the marriage supper of the Lamb prophesied and promised by scripture took place every night.

On April 26, 1949, Father married Edna Rose Ritching, a twenty-one-year-old white Canadian follower. She was a member of the Rosebuds, an interracial women's singing group who dressed in red, white, and blue uniforms symbolizing patriotic loyalty to the raceless Constitution, but with red blazers adorned with an added V for virtue. The marriage was spiritual in character, and the new Mother Divine as a spotless virgin bride represented the union of God with his church, especially its interracial and international nature.

Father Divine died in Philadelphia on September 10, 1965, and Mother Divine continues to preside over what is now a dwindling and geriatric organization. She correctly compares the Peace Missiion with the Shakers, who were also celibate, but she continues faithfully to represent Father Divine and God "tangibilated," to borrow one of his many creative uses of language. Once dismissed as a joke, Father Divine is increasingly perceived as a serious and pioneering civil rights advocate and one of the most interesting and effective modern African-American religious leaders.

If you want to know more:

Jill M. Watts. *God, Harlem U.S.A.: The Father Divine Story.* Berkeley, Ca.: University of California Press, 1992

"Condescendingly I came as an existing spirit unembodied, until condescendingly inputing Myself in a Bodily form in the likeness of men I come, that I might speak to them in their own language, coming to a country that is supposed to be the Country of the Free."

—Father Divine

"Marcus Garvey was a phenomenon but he was not half way to Divine. Garvey made God black, and the Devil white. That was revolutionary in an age of Nordic gospel. But Father Divine has not simply made God black; he had made a black man God."

—William Pickins

"Peace, it's wonderful! Aren't you glad?"

—Father Divine

"So glad we don't have to
Die to travel
At the light-rate speed
To reach GOD
So far up in the sky!"

—"We Don't Have to Die."
a Peace Mission song to the tune
of "Tiptoe Through the Tulips"

Who was the Schoolmaster of the Civil Rights Movement?

Benjamin Mays was teacher, role model, and inspiration for many of the people who participated actively in the Civil Rights Movement. Coretta Scott King told him in 1981, "Most of the black leadership in our country during the last forty years has in some way been inspired by you. . . . Martin Luther King, Jr. called you his spiritual mentor."

Born August 1, 1895, Benjamin Mays hardly exaggerated when he claimed he came out of his mother's womb kicking against segregation and discrimination. In fact, his earliest memory was of a white lynch mob in Greenwood County, South Carolina, in 1898. He never forgot it, and his whole life was lived in response to it. The title he chose for his autobiography, *Born to Rebel*, reveals the spirit of a man who managed to free himself from the prison of racism by a combination of remarkable personal fearlessness and a deep passion for education.

Mays' story is the account of daily black life in the South after whites brought a violent end to Reconstruction and before the Civil Rights Movement established black freedom. The brutality of racism can scarcely be imagined by those who did not live through it. It was a total social, economic, and cultural system bent on maintaining white supremacy through everything from the dishonest exploitation of tenant farmers (like Mays' family) to the constant psychological humiliation of Jim Crow. There was no recourse in the courts, the ballot, the federal government, the churches, the press, or anywhere else.

The year Mays started school, Greenwood County expended $6.29 annually for the education of each white child, and 23 cents for each black child. He cleaned outhouses for $6.00 a month to pay his tuition at Orangeburg State College's high school, from which he graduated at the age of twenty-one. He was fifty-two years old (and had earned a Ph.D. from the University of Chicago) before he was allowed to vote.

While there was virtually no escape from racism, there were survival techniques. Mays studied "Agricultural Latin," the school's device for bringing liberal arts into a vocational curriculum. More than once, he came close to being mobbed for insisting on his rights. He found ways to maintain his integrity: he walked up flights of stairs to avoid segregated elevators; blacks were allowed only on elevators designed for freight.

Mays reported on one aspect of Southern racism that is still little discussed: sexuality. He was taught to avoid white women totally, since the slightest hint of impropriety—as defined by the women—could mean lynching. At the same time, black women were entirely at the mercy of white men. Black fathers often refused to permit their daughters to work for white farmers, go anywhere unless they were accompanied by a brother, or work in white homes under any circumstances.

Given this background, Mays' career is all the more remarkable: Baptist pastor; executive secretary of the Tampa Urban League; dean of the School of Religion at Howard University; vice president of the National Council of Churches; president of the Atlanta School Board; and the position he held for twenty-seven years and for which he is best known, president of Morehouse College in Atlanta.

Mays was a liberal in religion, a gentleman who always put personal integrity first, a teacher who never compromised high standards, an administrator who believed a college's primary task is to build character. There is no way of counting the people for whom Benjamin Mays was a role model. And it is no mystery why he was called the "Schoolmaster of the Civil Rights Movement."

If you want to know more:

Benjamin E. Mays. *Born to Rebel.* Athens, Ga.: University of Georgia Press, 1987.

"The people in the church did not contribute one dime to help me with my education. But they gave me something far more valuable. They gave me encouragement."

—Benjamin E. Mays

"The tragedy of life does not lie in not reaching your goal. The tragedy lies in having no goal to reach."
—Benjamin E. Mays

"It isn't how long one lives, but how well. Jesus died at 33; Joan of Arc at 19; Byron and Burns at 33; Marlowe

at 29; Shelley at 30; Dunbar before 35 . . . and Martin
Luther King, Jr., at 39."
> —Benjamin E. Mays, in a eulogy at
> Martin Luther King, Jr.'s funeral,
> Ebenezer Baptist Church,
> Atlanta, Georgia, April 9, 1968

"Every person is born into the world to do something
unique and something distinctive, and if he or she does
not do it, it will never be done."
> —Benjamin E. Mays

What was the Tuskegee Syphilis Study?

In 1932 the United States Public Health Service (USPHS)
began a scientific investigation in the area of Tuskegee, Alabama, the seat of Macon County and the site of Booker T.
Washington's Tuskegee Institute and a large U.S. veterans' hospital. Located thirty miles east of Montgomery, Macon County
in 1930 had a total population of 27,000 people, 82 percent of
whom were black, largely illiterate, and extremely poor cotton
sharecroppers.

The USPHS project was a study of 399 African-American
men in the tertiary, that is, the third (and final) stage of syphilis, as well as of another 201 men who were free of the disease
as a control group. The method of the study was to leave the
syphilis intentionally untreated, and the purpose was to observe
its natural course until death. The white medical doctors initiat-
ing the study apparently believed syphilis among blacks was essentially a "different disease" than among whites, that African
Americans were inherently promiscuous sexually, and that these
men were too poor and ignorant to seek treatment even if they
understood they were infected.

The men selected had had no previous treatment, so they
provided a unique opportunity for a "study in nature," as opposed to an experiment strictly defined, according to Dr. Talia-

ferro Clark, chief of the USPHS Venereal Disease Division. Numerous tests and examinations were conducted on the subjects over the course of forty years, including clinical exams, blood tests, and autopsies of those who died. The men were told they were receiving free "treatment" from the government, and their participation was encouraged with placebos, free meals, transportation, and, most effectively, payment of $50 for burial expenses.

In order to keep the participants from receiving medical treatment, local black doctors were instructed not to treat them, as was the Alabama Health Department, as well as draft boards during World War II. Thirteen articles in standard medical journals appeared on the study from 1936 until 1973. The phrase "untreated syphilis in the male Negro" appeared in nine titles, so the medical world was not unaware of the nature of the study. Findings included the facts that untreated syphilis increased cardiovascular disease, that it reduced life expectancy by 20 percent, and that it was directly responsible for 30 percent of the deaths of those autopsied.

Although the study was no secret, the public first became aware of it in 1972 with an Associated Press news story. The U.S. Department of Health, Education, and Welfare then stopped the project among the seventy-four participants who were still living. An investigating panel set up by HEW reported in 1973 that the study was "ethically unjustified" because no informed consent had been received from the men, and because nonintervention was particularly inappropriate after the discovery of penicillin in the 1950s.

It was estimated that some number between twenty-eight and one hundred of the subjects had died as the direct result of advanced syphilitic lesions.

If you want to know more:

James H. Jones, *Bad Blood: The Tuskegee Syphilis Experiment,* new ed. New York: Free Press, 1993.

"There was no racial side to this. It just happened to be a black community."

—Dr. J. R. Heller

"The Tuskegee Study reveals the persistence of beliefs within the medical profession about the nature of blacks, sex, and disease—beliefs that had tragic repercussions long after the alleged 'scientific' bases were known to be incorrect."

—Allan M. Brandt

"Remember this is your last chance for special free treatment."

—notice to subjects from the
Macon County Health Department

"Any questions can be handled by saying these people were at the point that therapy would no longer help them."

—U.S. Center for Disease Control

CHAPTER 5

~

From the Freedom
Movement to the Second
Renaissance, 1954–1995

What was the *Brown* decision?

Elvis Presley credited what African-American performer as his musical mentor?

What was the Freedom Movement?

What is black blood?

What are freedom songs?

Who is the best-known African-American painter?

Who overcame a withered leg to become an Olympic champion?

Whom did Ossie Davis call "our own black shining prince"?

Who was the first African-American artist to have his work acquired by the Museum of Modern Art?

What African-American athlete excelled in a traditionally white sport?

Who was denied admission to law school both because she was black and a woman?

What is Hampton's *Throne*?

What was the Motown sound?

What African-American writer and intellectual was also a spokesperson for the Civil Rights Movement?

Who was the first African American to serve on the Supreme Court?

Who is the Queen of Soul?

What African American was a leading literary critic?

Was Cleopatra black?

Who is the first African American to win the Nobel Prize in literature?

∽

What was the *Brown* Decision?

America's legal policy on racial segregation in the twentieth century was set in 1896, with the Supreme Court's *Plessy* v. *Ferguson* decision, which institutionalized the formula of "separate but equal" in public institutions and facilities. One of the most important areas it controlled was public education. The law legally excluded African Americans from white schools in states with Jim Crow laws on the books, that is, the Southern states, where nearly 90 percent of all black people lived.

"Separate but equal" was, in fact, a sham, since public facilities were always racially segregated, but almost never equal in any way. In education, for example, in 1900, $15.41 a year was spent in this country on every white child in the public schools, but only $1.50 on every black child. By 1940, nothing had improved: $49.30 was spent on every white child, and $4.50 on every black.

In the face of such obvious inequities, several private charitable philanthropies came to the aid of black public schools in the South, notably the Slater, Jeanes, and Rosenwald funds. In 1900 there were 92 public high schools for African Americans throughout the South, and by 1950 these had increased to 2,500. However, the level of education and the opportunities for it were still poor: in 1930, as many as 230 Southern counties had no public high schools for black students at all. Even so, blacks struggled on their own for education with measurable success; only 5 percent of blacks were literate at Emancipation in 1864, but by 1950, fully 90 percent could read and write.

The National Association for the Advancement of Colored People, the major organization working on behalf of black people's rights, realized that the guaranteed "equality" of *Plessy* v. *Ferguson* was universally violated, and they considered bringing legal action in every school district in the South in order to force compliance with the law. If this had been done, the NAACP would certainly have won every case, but the fact that such an enterprise would drain so much time, energy, and money made it almost impossible to contemplate.

The prospects for legal action improved during the 1930s, however, because of President Franklin D. Roosevelt and the New Deal. Roosevelt was not particularly committed to black people or civil rights, but he was highly interested in appointing judges ideologically sympathetic to him and his program to the courts, especially since early New Deal legislation was declared unconstitutional by the conservative Supreme Court. The appointment of Democratic liberals throughout the legal system meant that there were now—unintentionally—people on the bench not unsympathetic to black claims for more equal treatment.

The NAACP was working on inequities in higher education, because the disparities there were clear, dramatic, and demonstrable in court. One of the most important cases involved a qualified Missouri resident named Lloyd Gaines, who graduated from Lincoln University (in Missouri) in 1935 and wanted to go to law school. The state of Missouri had a law school for state residents as part of the state university, but no black students were allowed in the university. Supported by the NAACP, Gaines sued for admission. He lost. When the case finally came to the Supreme Court, it ruled that Missouri must either admit Gaines to its law school, or, following *Plessy*, construct a separate but equal law school for him. Astonishingly, Missouri opted for the latter.

While the case was moving slowly through the courts, Gaines attended law school at the University of Michigan, but he mysteriously disappeared, perhaps murdered because he dared defy the segregation system. In any event, the Gaines case warned publicly supported schools that they could be forced to take seriously the "equal" clause of *Plessy* v. *Ferguson* and provide adequate facilities, one way or another, for African-American citizens.

This, and other legal victories, convinced the NAACP, however, that the construction of a whole educational system for black people on a par with the existing ones for whites could never really be achieved. They also realized that the creation of any part of such a system served, in fact, to strengthen racial segregation. As a result, the NAACP decided to abandon its policy of working to get "separate but equal" legally enforced, and, determined instead, to challenge the entire Jim Crow structure itself.

A number of legal cases dealing with segregated education then began to work their way through the courts. The Supreme Court's decision was read on May 17, 1954, at 12:52 P.M. by Chief Justice Earl Warren, ironically an Eisenhower appointee to the Court. In *Brown* v. *Board of Education of Topeka*, the Court's unanimous ruling overturned Plessy: "We conclude that in the field of public education the doctrine of 'separate but equal' has no place. Separate educational facilities are inherently unequal."

The landmark case took its name from Linda Brown, a black child in Topeka, Kansas, whose father, Oliver, a welder on the Santa Fe Railroad, tried unsuccessfully to register her for third grade at a white school closer to her home than the black elementary school she was required by law to attend. The case was part of a class action suit organized by the NAACP. The real point was not that blacks wanted to go to school with whites, but that they wanted access to quality education.

The Supreme Court's decision was not based on whether the "tangible" factors in the Court's dual education system were equal or not, but on the belief that segregation itself is a badge of inferiority and that a Jim Crow system as such "deprive[s] the children of the minority of equal educational opportunities," which they are guaranteed by the Fourteenth Amendment. The effect of *Brown* was nothing less than the elimination of the legal basis for the whole system of American apartheid, and the requirement that it be dismantled.

If you want to know more:

C. J. Russo, et al. *"Brown* v. *Board of Education* at 40: A Legal History of Equal Educational Opportunities in America." *Journal of Negro Education* (Summer 1994).

"The *Brown* case was so important because it precluded states from having their racism legitimized under the law."

—A. Leon Higginbotham

"If you look at the Civil Rights Act, the Voting Rights Act, Fair Housing, etc., all are rooted in *Brown*'s delegitimation of racism."

—A. Leon Higginbotham

"For all men of good will 17 May 1954 marked a joyous end to the long night of enforced segregation."

—Martin Luther King, Jr.

"No where [did] it say that segregated schools are also damaging to white children."

—Na'im Akbar

"This is a great day for the Negro. This is democracy's finest hour."

—Adam Clayton Powell, Jr.

"Less than four years after my birth, something happened that would indelibly mark me and my peers for life."

—Henry Louis Gates, Jr.

Elvis Presley credited what African-American performer as his musical mentor?

Elvis Presley, an unknown nineteen-year-old white truck driver for the Crown Electric Company in Memphis, Tennessee, changed American—and the world's—music decisively and forever on July 5, 1954. That day, in Sam Phillips' tiny Sun Records studio at 706 Union Avenue, Presley recorded African-American artist **Arthur Crudup**'s "That's All Right, Mama," and Presley's electric combination of black blues with white country established a new genre called rock 'n' roll.

Phillips founded Sun in order to record African-American performers because he believed black musicians and music had retained their originality and authenticity in the face of the stultifying commercialism of white popular music by a cautious and greedy industry. Peter Guralnick, Presley's biographer, thinks both Phillips and Presley had an intuitive sense that an important musical crossover was coming, as well as an instinctual feel for what the new sound might be like. Of course it couldn't be defined; it was a sound no one had ever heard.

On that decisive July 5, Presley was working with two other white musicians, Bill Black on bass and Scotty Moore on guitar, both from the Starlight Wranglers. Presley tried repeatedly without success to sing a ballad that would make a usable record. They took a break and began "fooling around," as someone afterwards remembered, with "That's All Right, Mama," a black blues song to which Presley gave a country beat. Sam Phillips suddenly realized he was hearing something different.

Phillips had once predicted, "If I could find a white man who had the Negro sound and the Negro feel, I could make a billion dollars." Presley's spontaneous version of "That's All Right, Mama" had all the energy, freshness, and vitality Phillips had been listening for. He heard, as an article in the *Memphis Press-Scimitar* soon described it, "a white man's voice singing Negro rhythm with a rural flavor."

Presley always freely acknowledged his serious debt to black music, including gospel from the Reverend **W. Herbert Brewster**'s East Trigg Baptist Church, which he heard broadcast live on Sunday nights on Memphis station WHBQ. In fact, Presley and his first girlfriend, Dixie Locke, sometimes attended East Trigg on Sunday evenings, sneaking out of their own Assembly of God services. **Queen C. Anderson** was a featured singer at East Trigg, along with the Brewsteraires, and W. Herbert Brewster himself had written "Move On Up a Little Higher," sung by **Mahalia Jackson**, and "How I Got Over," featured by Clara Ward.

The song that initiated rock 'n' roll though, "That's All Right, Mama," was composed, performed, and recorded by Arthur "Big Boy" Crudup, a Delta blues singer born August 25, 1905, in Forest, Mississippi. He was raised by his father, an unmarried farm laborer. Crudup as a child taught himself to play the guitar, and he sang in gospel choirs and quartets in local churches. His nickname came from his weight, which was over two hundred pounds, and his height, which was over six feet.

He worked as a field laborer, he played and sang in Mississippi juke joints, and he became a bootlegger in Silver City. In 1939 he rode the rails to Chicago, where poverty forced him to live under the Thirty-ninth Street El.

Largely underrated as a singer, Crudup performed raw country blues, but he became better known as a highly talented songwriter, and he was one of the first country blues artists to use an electric guitar. In Chicago he sang with the Harmonizing Four, a gospel quartet, and he cut his first records on the Blackbird label in the early 1940s. Like many other country blues singers, he also broadcast on *King Biscuit Time* over station KFFA, Helena, Arkansas.

Crudup's signature song, "Mean Old Frisco," was apparently the first Chicago blues song recorded using an amplified guitar. On September 1, 1941, he cut his own composition, "If I Get Lucky," with the now-familiar opening lines:

> That's all right, Mama,
> That's all right for you.
> Treat me lowdown and dirty
> Any old way you do.

Presley referred often to the influence of **B. B. King** and other black singers on his own style, and he even said he was trying to carry on their music. His strongest statement, however, was reported in the *Charlotte Observer* on June 27, 1956. Presley was being publicly criticized for the allegedly bad influence of his music and style, and in a lengthy statement, he defended himself by crediting Arthur Crudup as his model:

> The colored folk been singing it and playing it just like I'm doin' now, man, for more years than I know. They played it like that in the shanties and in their juke joints, and nobody paid it no mind 'til I goosed it up. I got it from them. Down in Tupelo, Mississippi, I used to hear old Arthur Crudup bang his box the way I do now, and I said if I ever get to the place where I could feel all old Arthur felt, I'd be a music man like nobody ever saw.

Arthur Crudup had sold his songs outright for small fees, so he never earned royalties from Presley's success with his music. He died March 28, 1974, in Nassawados, Virginia.

If you want to know more:

Peter Guralnick. *Last Train to Memphis: The Rise of Elvis Presley.* Boston: Little, Brown, 1994.

> "I was born poor, I lived poor, and I'm going to die poor."
>
> —Arthur Crudup
>
> "The elements weren't new and they had been put together before. . . . The proportions were new, though: the tempos were all-out fast and the tone was flat-out insolent. To some, rock-and-roll was as threatening as Communism or desegregation."
>
> —Margo Jefferson
>
> "There was just no reference point in the culture to compare it."
>
> —Roy Orbison
>
> "[Presley] got voluptuous phrasing and ecstatic self-confidence from gospel. He got wit and menace from blues, and from what we now call gay theatrics (Liberace, Little Richard, Jackie Wilson), he got glamour and self-parody."
>
> —Margo Jefferson

What was the Freedom Movement?

The *Brown* decision of 1954 sent an electrifying message across America. The physically and psychologically oppressive structure of racial segregation had at last been undermined by the Supreme Court of the United States. It had, in effect, overturned the *Plessy* v. *Ferguson* decision of 1896 which legalized "separate but equal." While *Brown* spoke specifically to discriminatory public education, it was not hard to see that despite its firm establishment in law and custom throughout the South, the whole Jim Crow structure had been dealt a serious blow. What would happen next?

The spark appeared at first as only a minor incident. In Montgomery, Alabama, on December 1, 1955, **Rosa McCauley Parks,** a black forty-two-year-old seamstress who earned 75 cents an hour working in a downtown department store, was arrested for refusing to obey the driver's order to give up her seat to a white man on a segregated city bus. Bus drivers in Alabama had police power. Blacks had to get on the bus at the front door, pay their fares, then get off and walk to the back door, get on again, and sit in the Jim Crow section in the rear. There were no black bus drivers. More than one black Montgomery passenger had been shot and killed by drivers for challenging the system.

Mrs. Parks' action, dramatic as it was, was not entirely spontaneous. She was an officer of the local NAACP, a member of the branch led by E. D. Nixon, a militant member of the Brotherhood of Sleeping Car Porters, who had actually been looking for a way to confront the city's segregated public transportation. Also, Parks had recently attended the Highlander Folk School in Monteagle, Tennessee, a liberal, prolabor center that fostered breaking down the color line and encouraged social action. With Parks' arrest, the black community organized a boycott of the bus company and established the Montgomery Improvement Association (MIA) to negotiate their modest requests for decent treatment.

Meeting in churches, the association set up emergency car pools, and, despite harassment and legal assault, made the boycott effective. It was not easy. Black women working as domestics had to walk miles to white neighborhoods, since the police managed to inhibit the car pools by making arrests for minor or trumped-up traffic violations. After 381 days, however, the

U.S. Supreme Court declared Montgomery's segregated public transportation system unconstitutional. Rosa Parks had lost her department-store job, but the black people of Montgomery won an astonishing victory. Through their unity, organization, perseverance, and courage they successfully defied and defeated not only a three-hundred-your-old practice, but one of the foundations of the entire racist social structure.

The MIA elected **Martin Luther King, Jr.,** its president. He was the young minister of the Dexter Avenue Baptist Church, and had recently returned South to a pastorate after earning a Ph.D. at Boston University. Born January 15, 1929, at 401 Auburn Avenue in Atlanta, he was the son of Martin Luther King, Sr., and Alberta Williams King, both solidly middle-class members of a family of Baptist preachers. King attended Morehouse College and Crozer Theological Seminary where he showed no particular promise of leadership.

But in the Montgomery boycott, King combined the rhetoric of righteousness and American democracy with Baptist eloquence and a Gandhian philosophy of nonviolent passive resistance. He emerged as a national symbol and spokesperson of a vital new civil rights movement. King was at first a highly reluctant reformer who sought to avoid both leadership and responsibility. But after his house was bombed by segregationists on January 30, 1956, he sat up alone, wrestling with the question of what he should do. During the night, in his "kitchen experience," King felt a divine assurance overcoming his own weakness, and he discovered as existentially real, personal, and vital the religious faith that had surrounded him all his life and which he had always taken completely for granted, even into the ministry.

The Montgomery boycott was one of the first expressions of a great grass-roots freedom movement, the likes of which the country had never seen before, and it began to spread across the South. In 1959 King organized the Southern Christian Leadership Conference (SCLC), a group of ministers, to lead and coordinate protest. It, in fact, often came to the support of spontaneous local demonstrations already under way. Personally, King began an exhausting schedule of public speaking and fund-raising on behalf of the cause. In retrospect, because of King's Nobel Peace Prize and the national holiday in his memory, as well as the romanticizing of him and the Civil Rights Movement, it is sometimes forgotten that the white South stiffened in violent resistance to integration, that most Northern whites merely watched from the sidelines, and that King himself was so hated in some quarters he was known as "Marxist Lucifer Coon."

Black people, despite all the opposition, however, sensed freedom in the air and began to make things happen. In February 1956, Autherine Lucy won a three-year court battle for admission to the University of Alabama as a graduate student in library science. In September 1957, black students seeking to integrate Central High School in Little Rock, Arkansas, were met by a defiant Governor Orval Faubus and a resistant white mob. Racist whites were emboldened by the "Southern Manifesto," a document signed by many members of the U.S. House and Senate which suggested that the Supreme Court's ruling on desegregation need not necessarily be obeyed. A reluctant President Dwight D. Eisenhower finally sent 1,000 men of the 101st Airborne Division to Little Rock to protect the half-dozen black children trying to go to school at Central High.

The Civil Rights Movement both speeded up and spread outward on February 1, 1960, when four black students at North Carolina Agricultural and Technical College "sat in" at the Greensboro, North Carolina, F. W. Woolworth Company lunch counter to protest the store's policy of refusing to serve African Americans. They were joined by hundreds, then thousands, of students in one hundred and fifty cities who were soon filling up Southern jails while singing songs about freedom. In April, the Student Nonviolent Coordinating Committee (SNCC, pronounced *snick*) was organized under such leaders as Robert Moses and Marion Barry to encourage the new student activism.

In September 1962 there was a crisis at the University of Mississippi in Oxford when James Meredith, the first African-American student admitted to Ole Miss, tried to attend classes despite student and public opposition. President John F. Kennedy, at least as cautious and uncommitted as President Eisenhower, and even more politically calculating (although he owed his 1960 election to the black vote), was finally forced to send in protective and peace-keeping federal officers.

In the spring of the next year, 1963, the whole country watched, with horror, television coverage of antisegregation marches in Birmingham, Alabama. Commissioner of Public Safety Eugene "Bull" Connor set police dogs and turned fire hoses (so forceful they took the bark off trees) on peacefully demonstrating black children. Arrested, Martin Luther King used his time in prison to write the "Letter from Birmingham Jail," his most eloquent articulation of the nature and purpose of the Movement and a defense of its methods.

Those who survived the streets of Birmingham could take credit for the Civil Rights Bill passed by Congress in July, because the rightness of their cause and their courage in fighting for it inspired the nation to push the Congress to act. At the March on Washington in August, a coalition of civil rights organizations and spokespersons sought to keep the momentum going and press the Movement further. It was here that King gave his "I Have a Dream" speech, a dramatic summary of his idealistic integrationist position.

Black people were paying a high price, however, in their struggle to move the South to obey the law of the land and desegregate. There are documented cases of thirty-two African Americans and nine whites who were murdered between 1955 and King's assassination in 1968, deaths that all can be directly attributed to participation in the Freedom Movement. The first was that of the Reverend George Lee, gunned down on May 7, 1955, in Belzoni, Mississippi, for organizing blacks to register to vote. Lee and his friend Gus Courts had started a local NAACP chapter and persuaded ninety other people to get on the voting list. Lee's murder, accompanied by a coroner's jury ruling that the death was of "unknown cause," forced eighty-nine to withdraw. "Now there's one person registered," Courts said. "Me." When he was shot and wounded, however, he too gave up and moved his family from Belzoni to Chicago.

Perhaps the best-known victim was **Medgar Evers,** field secretary of the Mississippi NAACP, who was shot and killed in his driveway in Jackson on June 12, 1963. This was the same night that President Kennedy, yielding to pressure, called the civil rights struggle a "moral" issue, the first time an American president had categorized the movement in terms of right and wrong. Perhaps the most poignant murders took place three months later on Sunday, September 15, 1963, at 10:22 A.M., when the Sixteenth Street Baptist Church in Birmingham was bombed. Four little girls attending Sunday school were killed instantly: Addie Mae Collins, Denise McNair, Carole Robertson, and Cynthia Wesley. Dr. King preached their joint funeral service.

In an important sense, the Civil Rights Movement ended the next year with the march from Selma to Montgomery, Alabama, on behalf of voting rights. Demonstrators started out on March 7, 1965, from Brown Chapel AME Church, but at the Edmund Pettus Bridge they were attacked and viciously beaten by mounted policemen. Again the whole country saw it on television, and, like Birmingham, the determination of black people to secure their rights despite the crude violence of the white South resulted in Congress passing the Voting Rights Act of 1965. An accompanying reason, of course, was that President Lyndon Johnson, unlike Kennedy, was more supportive of the Movement and had clout with Congress. Joe Smitherman, the sympathetic white mayor of Selma, said, "Of all the things that have happened in our lifetime, this is the single most historic piece of legislation ever passed."

The Civil Rights Movement was essentially about obtaining for African Americans their basic legal rights as citizens, rights that had been established a hundred years earlier in Reconstruction, but were denied by the laws and customs of racial segregation. Segregation kept black people from public schools, public transportation, and public facilities of all kinds, as well as from privately owned places like stores and restaurants theoretically open to the public. Desegregation was, in fact, a great victory, hardly imaginable only a few years before, especially the opening of voter registration rolls.

Enfranchisement meant African Americans could now influence elections in the local districts, cities, towns, counties,

264 EVERYBODY SAY FREEDOM

and states where the issues directly concerning their lives were determined, as well as have a real voice in national politics and national government. As Mayor Smitherman's statement reveals, though, voting was generally perceived as the apogee, the citizen's most crucial right because it was the one by which all other rights could be achieved, expressed, and protected. With the accomplishment of voting rights, however, the movement suddenly and seriously faltered. What happened?

Politically, it was clear that the parties were not going to adapt themselves to the new African-American situation. While voter registration drives added thousands of new black voters to the rolls, virtually all of them Democrats, white Southerners deserted the party of their fathers in droves to become Republicans. Lyndon Johnson was well aware of this and predicted the Democrats' actual loss of the South when he signed the Voting Rights Act.

In August 1964 the Mississippi Freedom Democratic Party (MFDP), organized by SNCC and led by Fannie Lou Hamer, challenged the regular state organization for seating at the Democratic National Convention in Atlantic City. The regulars hated Johnson as a traitor to the South; they categorically opposed civil rights, and they had no intention of supporting the national ticket. But the national party betrayed their MFDP friends and Johnson sent Walter Mondale and Hubert Humphrey in to rationalize denying them their seats. African Americans learned yet again that their best white liberal friends were not to be trusted.

With virtual achievement of the basic citizenship rights enjoyed by whites, however, it became clear that African Americans continued to suffer from the effects of 350 years of slavery and Jim Crow, even despite the massive migration to the more industrialized North. This meant that desperately needed jobs, health care, housing, and education were not going to come from the newly won freedom to sit in a nonsegregated bus or eat at a Woolworth lunch counter, or even from the freedom to vote. Furthermore, the white majority did not see these areas as rights to which everyone was entitled, but as privileges to be individually earned by wealth or deserved by merit.

While King himself never wavered from his dream of a color-blind, racially integrated society, his thinking nevertheless dramatically evolved and altered. His vision expanded from a local to a regional to a national to an international one. He tried to take the Movement to Chicago but he came up against systemic Northern urban racism and the structural inequalities of power, and quite simply, neither his message nor his methodology had an impact. He saw the nation's involvement in Vietnam as part of America's international capitalist imperialism. He looked over the mountaintop to which he had brought people, and asked himself if what he saw was the kind of society anybody ought to be integrated into.

King, who had trusted white people of good will, trusted the majesty of constitutional law, and trusted the power of the federal government, now saw that these were the very impediments to realization of the deeper and broader conception of justice to which he had come. The Poor People's March was intended not to solicit the government's protective support, but quite literally to shut government down! King thus became a real national threat and was considered by the FBI to be "the most dangerous man in America." He went to Memphis, Tennessee, to march with city sanitation workers who earned so little money they were still eligible for welfare after a week's work. King was shot to death on the balcony of the Lorraine Motel on April 4, 1968.

A prophet rather than a saint, Martin Luther King, Jr., spelled out the moral and policy decisions the country faced, and accurately predicted the right-wing takeover that would follow the nation's wrong ethical choices. But there were real achievements, even beyond desegregation. The number of black elected officials, especially in the South, increased dramatically. The Civil Rights Movement became a model for the Women's Movement. Perhaps most important, the Freedom Movement energized African Americans for the literary, political, artistic, and cultural explosion that created the new black renaissance of the latter part of the century.

If you want to know more:

David J. Garrow. *Bearing the Cross: Martin Luther King, Jr., and the Southern Christian Leadership Conference.* New York: William Morrow, 1986.

> "One day the South will recognize its real heroes."
>
> —Martin Luther King, Jr.
>
> "The people are our teachers."
>
> —Prathia Hall, SNCC
>
> "This is the cross that we must bear for the freedom of our people."
>
> —Martin Luther King, Jr.
>
> "I had no idea that history was being made. I was just tired of giving in."
>
> —Rosa Parks
>
> "The civil rights movement gave me the power to challenge any line that limits me."
>
> —Bernice Johnson Reagon
>
> "If this society fails, I fear that we will learn very shortly that racism is a sickness unto death. . . . In spite of years of national progress, the plight of the poor is worsening."
>
> —Martin Luther King, Jr.

What is black blood?

Actually, there is no such thing as "black blood." The blood of all human beings is interchangeable and the same, except for differences in type (A, B, AB, or O) and Rh factor, neither of which has any connection with race. In America, however, the term "black blood" has generally been used to refer to African and African-American ancestry, probably because to call such a relationship "blood" is to imply a kind of biological difference which is believed to exist scientifically, even though it does not, and which is used to maintain social differences and control.

The systems of slavery and racism in the United States were constructed on "the one-drop rule." This was a shorthand way of saying that any person with "one drop" of "black blood" (that is, anybody with any African or African-American ancestor, however remote) was black, and only black. The reason for this is clear: racial slavery as an economic system and racism as a pseudo-scientific biological system could not tolerate any deviation from the alleged norm of pure whiteness. These interrelated systems required an absolute separation of the two races, and allowed no room for any variations in between the two groups (in their attempt to be logically consistent), unlike the cultures of the Caribbean and Latin America.

This social system was enacted into law in the Southern states. Curiously, however, the definition of African ancestry (one great-grandparent, for example, or one great-great grandparent) varied from state to state, so one could be legally black (and therefore enslaved or subject to Jim Crow laws) in one state but not in another. Under the racist regime in South Africa, Japanese businessmen were legally classified as white because the government was eager for them to come to South Africa under favorable circumstances in order to do business.

Scientific or not, blood has remained a powerful symbol of race. Even though the American Red Cross knew full well that all human blood is the same, it kept blood plasma segregated by race well past World War II. This was a cause for African-American resentment and protest during the war, but to no avail. Not until November 19, 1950, did the Red Cross national board vote to eliminate the racial identity of blood donors. Local blood banks, like the one in Birmingham, Alabama, kept on segregating, nevertheless, claiming they were merely observing the city's Jim Crow laws.

Ironically, it was an African-American scientist and physician who helped make blood banks possible by determining that plasma—blood fluid with the cells and platelets removed—can be preserved and stored for later use. **Dr. Charles R. Drew** (1904–1950) began his research at McGill Medical School in Canada, and continued at Columbia-Presbyterian Hospital in New York. He became director of the Red Cross blood bank in New York City in 1941, and his work saved a great many lives during World War II, particularly of British soldiers. He resigned over the racist policy of segregated blood, and taught at Howard Medical School in Washington until an automobile accident took his life.

Josephine Baker, the great black entertainer, spun out a fantasy about race and blood which was written down by Felix de la Camara and Baker's companion, Count Pepito Abatino. It was published in Paris in 1931 as a novel entitled *Mon sang dans tes veines (My Blood in Your Veins)*. In her improbable story, a white family named Barclay, rich from manufacturing chewing gum, lives on a plantation-like estate near Boston. Their son Fred grows up with a black servant's daughter named Joan. Of course they are ideally suited, but Fred rejects Joan because of her race and becomes engaged to marry a white girl from New Orleans.

Fred is run over by a Rolls-Royce, however, and is carried, about to die, to a doctor's cottage in the woods. Joan appears and gives him a life-saving transfusion, her blood flowing directly from her body into his. She dies, Christ-like, and Fred lives, but now a black-white man because he carries her blood. However sentimental a story, *My Blood in Your Veins* illustrates the power of blood as a metaphor for race as well as the lingering if untrue myth that "black" and "white" people are of biologically significant different types.

If you want to know more:

Richard Hardwick. *Charles Richard Drew, Pioneer in Blood Research.* New York: Scribner, 1967.

"The angel of mercy's got her wings in the mud,
And all because of Negro blood."
> —Langston Hughes, on the Red Cross'
> segregation of blood plasma

"It was the most tremendous lie we had ever told ourselves in the South: that one drop of black blood was
enough to condemn an individual to slavery, which in
turn protected the incredible, invincible, overwhelming
myth amongst us that the crime of miscegenation had
never occurred—that the purity of the two races, but especially the white race, had been preserved, forever
separate, forever untainted."
> —Barbara Chase-Riboud

"[T]he term 'white person' shall apply only to the person who has no trace whatsoever of any blood other
than Caucasian, but persons who have one-sixteenth or
less of the blood of American Indians, and no other
non-Caucasian blood shall be deemed white persons."
> —Virginia statute, 1924

What are freedom songs?

The African-American freedom struggle of the 1960s was a
movement enlivened by music. Freedom songs were a sign of
the movement's vitality, and an indication of its interconnected-
ness with the Afro-Protestant folk church, source of many of its
songs. As in the labor movement of the 1930s, songs from a
people's common culture, often with appropriately adapted lyrics, helped create solidarity among participants, helped express
believers' feelings, and helped communicate their message to
the world.

The best-known freedom song is "We Shall Overcome." It is
an adaptation of "I'll Overcome Someday," an African-Ameri-

can hymn with original verses such as "I'll be like Him" and "I'll wear the crown." The first modern adaptation was sung by striking African-American members of the Food and Tobacco Workers' Union in Charleston, South Carolina, in 1945. Since the 1960s, "We Shall Overcome" has spread across the world to be sung by protesters from South Africa to China.

There is a wonderful specificity and historicity in these songs: many are about real people, real events, and real places. A verse of "Hallelujah, I'm A-Travelin' " reads as follows, "In old Fayette County, set off and remote / The polls are now open for Negroes to vote." "No more Pritchett over me," one of the countless verses of "Oh Freedom," speaks of the brutal Albany, Georgia police chief Laurie Pritchett. From the Hinds County jail came a takeoff on "Frere Jacques": "Are you sleeping, Brother Bob?" referring to the U.S. attorney general at the time, Robert F. Kennedy, who was notoriously inactive on behalf of the Movement.

Among the old familiar songs are "We Shall Not Be Moved," "This Little Light of Mine," "Which Side Are You On?" "I'm on My Way to the Freedom Land." When the Movement went North, the tone of the songs changed, however. As **Stokely Carmichael** said in 1966, "It's time out for singing 'We Shall Overcome.' " It's time to get some Black Power." Songs from Chicago symbolized the change: "Lead Poison on the Wall," and "Burn, Baby, Burn."

The spirit of the early Movement is captured in the song "I Love Everybody" where one of the verses begins, "I love Hoss Manucy." Who was he? Holstead "Hoss" Manucy was the local Ku Klux Klan leader in St. Augustine, Florida. Remembering that line, Dorothy Cotton of the Southern Christian Leadership Council wrote, "Then somebody would always stop, because it was hard to sing, 'I love Hoss Manucy' when he'd just beat us up, to say a little bit about what love really was. He's still a person with some degree of dignity in the sight of God, and we don't have to like him, but we have to love him. He's been damaged too. So we sing it, and the more we sing it, the more we grow in ability to love people who mistreat us so bad."

If you want to know more:

Guy Carawan and Candie Carawan, eds. *Sing for Freedom: The Story of the Civil Rights Movement Through Its Songs.* Bethlehem, Pa.: Sing Out, 1990.

> "The only thing we did wrong
> Stayed in the wilderness a day too long.
> But the one thing we did right
> Was the day we began to fight.
> Keep your eyes on the prize.
> Hold on."
>
> —"Keep Your Eyes on the Prize"

> "You know I would not be Governor Wallace
> I'll tell you the reason why,
> I'd be afraid my Lord might call me
> And I would not be ready to die."
>
> —"Go Tell It on the Mountain"

> "Let's spread the story,
> Let's tell the tale
> Let's tell the world of
> Bull Connor's jail"
>
> —"Birmingham Jail"

Who is the best-known African-American painter?

Romare Bearden is probably the best-known African-American artist. A master in several fields, he became famous for collages in which he arranged bits of photographs and colored paper on flat surfaces along with paint to create strong and evocative images of African-American life. African-American art historian James Porter said Bearden's pieces looked like stained glass, and as visual texts, they rank among the finest work by an American artist.

Bearden was born September 2, 1912, in Charlotte, North Carolina, to Richard and Bessye Johnson Bearden. The family lived in Pittsburgh and in New York, where his mother was New York editor for the *Chicago Defender*, a leading black paper. Their home on 131st Street became a center of interesting people and activities. Bearden displayed talent early and studied at Lincoln and Boston universities and at the Art Students League in New York with the German satirical and social artist George Grosz.

Bearden was influenced, too, by E. Sims Campbell, the black cartoonist, and Bearden even tried his own hand at cartoons for the *Baltimore Afro-American*. He also tried song writing and social casework, and he even played baseball, as a pitcher for a black team, the Boston Tigers. Artistically, he was influenced by the Italian Renaissance, Dutch painters of the seventeenth century, Cubism, and abstract expressionism.

Bearden's work largely celebrates the African-American experience, however, and here one can see the influence of black literature and of jazz and blues. In fact, the closest correspondences exist between Bearden's collages and jazz, connections illuminated by his relationships with African-American intellectuals Albert Murray and **Ralph Ellison**.

Unlike many artists, Bearden received recognition in his own lifetime. There was a major retrospective show at the Museum of Modern Art in New York in 1971, and Bearden received a National Medal of the Arts in 1987. "Art is the soul of a people," he once said, and in his portrayals of a crowded urban black street scene, or a sensuous woman at her languorous bath, or a lush Caribbean island, Bearden articulated that soul. He was a large-framed man, so fair-skinned, Elton Fax said, that Bearden identified himself as African American by choice. A genius with many gifts, that was as true of his work as it was of his person. Romare Bearden died in 1988.

If you want to know more:

Myron Schwartzman. *Romare Bearden: His Life and Art.* New York: Harry N. Abrams, 1990.

> "Black art has always existed. It just hasn't been looked for in the right place."
>
> —Romare Bearden

> "Whatever subject the artist chooses, he must celebrate it in triumph."
>
> —Romare Bearden

> "There are roads out of the secret place within us along which we must all move as we go to touch others."
>
> —Romare Breaden

Who overcame a withered leg to become an Olympic champion?

Wilma Rudolph had double pneumonia and scarlet fever as a four-year-old child and as a result was left with a crippled left leg. She wore braces and corrective shoes for years while her many brothers and sisters massaged her withered leg daily, and her mother took her to Meharry Medical College in Nashville for therapy, a ninety-mile round-trip on a segregated Greyhound bus, every week. These efforts, combined with a strong competitive will to win, led Rudolph to overcome her disadvantages and become an all-star basketball player at sixteen. She was recruited to Tennessee State University by track coach Edward Temple because he recognized her unusual ability and potential.

Rudolph was born June 23, 1940, to Ed and Blanch Rudolph, near Clarksville, Tennessee. She weighed only four and a half pounds at birth. She was the fifth of eight children, and her father had eleven children by another marriage. He was a railroad porter and Blanch Rudolph was a domestic, working as a maid in white people's houses.

Some early defeats and an unwanted pregnancy only increased Rudolph's passion to excel. The high point of her athletic career was the 1960 Rome Olympics, where despite a sprained ankle, she won the 100-meter dash (in 11.0 seconds), the 200-meter dash, and the 400-meter relay. She set world records and became the first American woman to win three Olympic gold medals. There was no money 'for nonprofessional athletes, however, so Rudolph worked as a second-grade teacher, athletic coach, and at several other jobs. Wilma Rudolph died of cancer near Brentwood, Tennessee, on November 12, 1994.

If you want to know more:

Wilma Rudolph. *Wilma.* New York: New American Library, 1977.

> "Do it; don't dream about it."
> —Mrs. Haskins, Wilma Rudolph's fourth-grade teacher
>
> "When I played, I went all out."
> —Wilma Rudolph
>
> "Today I sometimes think about people like Alice Coachman and Mildred McDaniels. Not many people in America today know much about Alice Coachman and Mildred McDaniels, and that's why I think about them. They were black women track stars."
> —Wilma Rudolph

Whom did Ossie Davis call "our own black shining prince"?

The story of **Malcolm X** is now generally well known, both from the best-selling autobiography he told to **Alex Haley,** and from the **Spike Lee** film, which adhered closely to Haley's book. Of course, Malcolm told his story from his own knowledge and his own perspective and then it was filtered through Haley. This means there is still work to do on Malcolm's biography: new information to locate, old errors to correct, and unpublished letters to find and evaluate. Malcolm X is so important that it is imperative to know and understand him as fully and accurately as we can.

Born Malcolm Little on May 19, 1925, in Omaha, Nebraska, his father, Earl, was a preacher and organizer for the Garvey Movement who, Malcolm believed, was murdered by white supremacists. His mother, Louise Langdon Norton, born in Grenada, was unsuccessful in her attempt to hold the family together, and became unstable. In Boston, living with his sister, Malcolm became a small-time hustler and petty criminal. He ended up in prison, where he encountered and was converted to the Honorable Elijah Muhammad's Nation of Islam, an African-American Muslim religious group. He discarded his given surname as the product of dehumanizing slavery, and, like other muslims, took "X" to symbolize the lost identity stolen by the slave system.

Out of prison, Malcolm continued his subservience to Elijah Muhammad, whom he saw as the agent in redeeming his life, a role model, and undoubtedly as some kind of father figure, as well. Malcolm soon became the chief spokesperson for the Nation, and achieved national recognition as a brilliant orator and expositor of militant black nationalism. As such, he stood clearly in the tradition of **Marcus Garvey**'s African Zionism, **Martin R. Delany**'s emigrationism, and the separatism of all those who despaired of people of color ever finding a place in racist America.

In seeking and advocating an alternative life for African Americans, Malcolm stood in sharp contrast to **Martin Luther King, Jr.,** who struggled for black inclusion into a harmonious and racially integrated society. In James Cone's telling phrase, King's hopeful American dream was Malcolm's realized American nightmare.

From his Harlem base, Malcolm built up the Nation organizationally, and articulated a black militancy that frightened many white people, and that many black integrationists also found unpalatable. *The Hate That Hate Begot* was the not unsurprising title of a TV documentary at the time which focused on him and the movement. At the same time, Malcolm was in fact speaking on behalf of a large number of black people, many from the oppressed underclass, who were not benefiting either economically or politically from the Civil Rights Movement. They were paying a high price for living in a racist country, and they identified with Malcolm's daringly outspoken criticisms. He spoke for them.

Malcolm idolized Elijah Muhammad, known within the Nation as the Lamb, until he discovered his saintly leader's marital infidelities and the existence of "divine babies" (eight children by six teenage girls) at the Nation's Chicago headquarters. His disillusionment was deeply wrenching, and he began to separate himself from the Nation. A pilgrimage to Mecca brought Malcolm more in touch with mainstream Islam, gave him a broader worldwide perspective, and led him to meet white people who were not "devils" full of racial prejudice. (Islam has no internal distinctions or discriminations based on race.)

Malcolm was changing intellectually, becoming more Africanist and internationalist, more socialist, Marxist, and aware of worldwide capitalist, colonial imperialism, and more sophisticated in his understanding of the role of race. In short, he was becoming much more dangerous. He was killed by thirteen shots at close range in the Audubon Ballroom in upper Manhattan on February 21, 1965, presumably by either direct or indirect agents of the Honorable Elijah Muhammad. Malcolm left four small daughters and his wife, Betty Shabazz, who was pregnant with twins. At his funeral, Malcolm's friend **Ossie Davis,** the actor, called him "our own black shining prince." The *New York Times,* in contrast, said, "The Apostle of Hate Is Dead."

Both Malcolm's message and his image were kept alive by poor black people who played tapes of his speeches on the streets of urban ghettos. They displayed his icon on posters and T-shirts before it became fashionable for bourgeois people to imitate them. The failures of integration, the abandonment of the cities by government at all levels, the betrayal of the black underclass by everyone, all led to a rejection by many plain people of Martin Luther King's idealistic but ineffectual message of brotherly love, and the elevation of Malcolm to folk hero, the only spokesperson for America's black oppressed and disinherited.

If you want to know more:

The Autobiography of Malcolm X. New York: Grove Press, 1964.

"A man has to act like a brother before you can call him a brother."

—Malcolm X, 1964

"You get freedom by letting your enemy know that you'll do anything to get your freedom; then you'll get it."

—Malcolm X

"Malcolm was a path, a way into ourselves."

—Maya Angelou

"Learn to see, listen, and think for yourself."

—Malcolm X

"Malcolm X is the great puzzle of the civil rights era, perhaps because his achievement—the inner emancipation of black people—was the most important."

—Archie Epps

"America's greatest crime against the black man was not slavery or lynchings, but that he was taught to wear a mask of self-hate and self-doubt."

—Malcolm X

Who was the first African-American artist to have his work acquired by the Museum of Modern Art?

Jacob Lawrence is the leading African-American painter of the last part of the twentieth century. Known especially for the social realism of his style and for several series of paintings on themes in black American history, he became the first African-American artist whose work was acquired by the Museum of Modern Art (MOMA), the country's leading center of contemporary art. In 1942, when Lawrence was only twenty-five years old, MOMA purchased half the panels in his series *The Migration of the Negro*.

Lawrence's migration paintings chronicle the great exodus of Southern blacks from farm to factory, from country to city, and from South to North during the first third of the century, part of which he knew from experience, part of which he researched at the Schomburg Center. In sixty panels Lawrence combined abstraction with social realism to depict crowded waiting rooms, northbound trains, abandoned rural shacks, and crowded city streets. Twenty-six of the paintings were published in the November 1941 issue of *Fortune* magazine. The panels not acquired by MOMA went to the Phillips Collection in Washington, D.C.

Jacob Lawrence was born September 7, 1917, in Atlantic City, New Jersey, the first child of Jacob and Rosealee Armstead Lawrence. As an adolescent he studied under Charles Alston in a Harlem settlement house, and then in the federal government's Civilian Conservation Corps and Works Progress Administration, where he was artistically influenced by cubism and socially influenced by the human suffering of the Great Depression.

In 1941 Lawrence married Gwendolyn Knight, a fellow painter. He taught art at Pratt Institute in New York until 1970, when he joined the faculty of the University of Washington in Seattle, the same year he received the NAACP's Spingarn Medal. Other series of paintings he has created tell the stories of **Toussaint-L'ouverture, John Brown, Frederick Douglass**, and **Harriet Tubman. Henry Louis Gates, Jr.,** was speaking specifically of the *Migration* series, but he might well have been talking about all of Lawrence's work when he wrote, "There is no literary equivalent to Lawrence's visual narratives."

If you want to know more:

Ellen Wheat. *Jacob Lawrence: American Painter*. Seattle: University of Washington Press, 1986.

> "I hope that when my life ends, I would have added a little beauty, perception, and quality for those who follow."
>
> —Jacob Lawrence
>
> "You bring to a painting your own experience."
>
> —Jacob Lawrence
>
> "I use a series form because it lets me tell the story."
>
> —Jacob Lawrence

What African-American athlete excelled in a traditionally white sport?

Tennis has traditionally been a white sport, played by the upper class in their racially restricted country clubs. But **Arthur**

Ashe, an African American, excelled at tennis. In 1975, at the age of thirty-one, Ashe won at Wimbledon, and he went on to become captain of the U.S. Davis Cup team. But Arthur Ashe was not only a superior athlete: he was a respected writer, social critic, and civil rights activist, noted especially for speaking out against South African apartheid and on behalf of Haitian refugees.

Ashe was born July 10, 1943 in Richmond, Virginia, to Arthur Robert Ashe, Sr., a city playground guard, and Mattie Cunningham Ashe, who died when he was six. His father's job gave Ashe access to public athletic facilities, where early on he showed talent for tennis. Richmond's racial segregation, however, prevented him from playing on indoor courts. Instead he was taken under the wing of Dr. Robert Johnson of the American Tennis Association, a black organization; Johnson trained Ashe and served as his mentor during his tennis career. The white U.S. Lawn Tennis Association rejected Ashe's application for a tournament, but by 1965 he was the top collegiate tennis player in the country.

Ashe's principles, his stands for justice and civil rights, made him an inspiration to South African blacks when he played in that country. He was also the first free black man most had ever seen. Even after he contracted AIDS through a blood transfusion, he continued to be active, and was arrested outside the White House in Washington picketing for Haitian refugees. Arther Ashe died in New York on February 6, 1993.

If you want to know more:

Arther Ashe and Arnold Rampersad. *Days of Grace: A Memoir.* New York: Alfred A. Knopf, 1993.

> "You learn about equality in history and civics, but you find out life is not really like that."
>
> —Arthur Ashe

Who was denied admission to law school both because she was black and a woman?

Pauli Murray was denied admission to the University of North Carolina Law School because she was black, and to the Harvard Law School because she was a woman. Her life was spent trying to set right this kind of wrong, not only for herself but for others.

Born in Baltimore, Maryland, on November 20, 1910, Murray was raised by an aunt in Durham, North Carolina. There, surrounded by the racial etiquette of the South, she grew determined to rebel against the restrictions of Jim Crow. She moved to New York, lived with relatives, and was the only African American among 4,000 students at Richmond High School. She graduated from Hunter College in 1933 during the Depression, when sixteen million Americans were unemployed, and she worked with several left-wing and labor organizations before entering Howard University Law School.

Murray was a pioneer several times over. She led Gandhi-inspired direct-action sit-ins in segregated Washington lunchrooms in the 1940s. Her novel *Proud Shoes* was an account of a racially complex family history thirty years before **Alex Haley**'s *Roots*. She seems to be the one who first thought of shifting National Association for the Advancement of Colored People policy from legal cases that sought to enforce the "equal" side of the separate-but-equal law to a direct challenge of segregation itself. Just as opposed to what she called "Jane Crow," Murray used her knowledge of the Fifth and Fourteenth Amendments to help prepare the Equal Rights Amendment and was involved in the formation of the National Organization for Women.

Murray's personal life was precarious. She lived in tiny rooms and suffered from malnutrition. She spent time in jail for challenging segregation. She once crossed the country riding in freight trains. But there were moments of ironic satisfaction. She described presenting the case for Odell Waller, a sharecropper accused of murdering a white man, to a group of poverty-stricken black ministers in a Southern town, and of their slowly approaching her afterwards, one by one, to place on a table worn dollar bills for Waller's defense.

When a group of Howard students was arrested for violating the segregation rule on an interstate bus, she experienced the joyous realization that they had not been charged with disorderly conduct, and that she therefore had a case.

Murray's models were **Eleanor Roosevelt** and **Martin Luther King, Jr.,** but characteristically, not without reservations. Mrs. Roosevelt befriended her despite Murray's tart letters criticizing the president's indifference to racial issues. And she never forgave King for not taking **Rosa Parks** when he went to Stockholm to receive the Nobel Peace Prize. Ironically, Murray found herself at odds with the Black Power activists at Brandeis University, where she was teaching in the mid-1960s. Their macho sexism, militant nationalism, and bad manners ran counter to all her values.

After writing a book of poetry, compiling *States' Laws on Race and Color* for the Women's Division of the Methodist Church, taking a doctorate at Yale Law School, and teaching in Ghana, Pauli Murray at age sixty-three entered General Theological Seminary in New York as a candidate for the ministry in the Episcopal Church. She was a leader in the struggle for women's ordination in that denomination, and in 1977 she was one of the first women, and the first black woman, to be ordained. She celebrated her first Communion in the North Carolina chapel where her grandmother had been baptized a hundred years earlier. She died in Pittsburgh, Pennsylvania, July 8, 1985.

If you want to know more:

Pauli Murray. *Song in a Weary Throat—An American Pilgrimage.* New York: Harper and Row, 1987.

"I entered law school preoccupied with the racial struggle and single-mindedly bent upon becoming a civil rights lawyer, but I graduated an unabashed feminist as well."

—Pauli Murray

What is Hampton's *Throne*?

Founded in 1829, the National Museum of American Art of the Smithsonian Institution in Washington, D.C., did not acquire the work of an African-American artist until 1977, when it permanently installed **James Hampton**'s religious folk structure now known as Hampton's *Throne*. The *Throne* is actually a collection of 180 hand-built objects in three parallel rows, $10^1/_2$ feet tall at the highest point, and occupying a room-sized space of 27 by $14^1/_2$ feet. Viewers coming upon these objects for the first time are dazzled because they are all covered with gold and silver foil.

The purpose or function of Hampton's construction is not entirely clear. Its official title is *The Throne of the Third Heaven of the Nations' Millennium General Assembly*. It appears to be, essentially, a throne and chancel for Jesus Christ's Second Coming. The centerpiece is obviously a throne-like armchair. The millennial hope for an era of peace and justice is part of traditional Christian expectation, and it has obvious political and social implications as well. The addition of the phrase "General Assembly" may mean that the throne room was designed as Christ's seat for some international reign, or it may simply have been an allusion to the United Nations, which came into being during the time of Hampton's work.

One of the more astonishing characteristics of Hampton's collection is that the objects on each side of the throne itself are all perfectly symmetrical. They seem to consist of various altars, seats, lecterns, tables, and so forth. One side apparently represents the Old Testament, and the other side the New. Each piece is highly decorated, usually with large angels' wings. In fact, their wings constitute a major decorative motif.

All the material Hampton used is what art critics call "found objects." That is, they either are themselves or are made from junk and trash: discarded furniture, burnt-out lightbulbs, cardboard cylinders, used jelly glasses, Kraft paper, and so forth. The overall effect is radiant because everything is covered with the shiny foil Hampton reclaimed from cigarette packs and wine bottles. Over the throne is a hand-lettered sign reading "Fear Not."

James P. Hampton was born in Elloree, South Carolina, on April 8, 1909. His father was a poor, part-time gospel singer and Baptist preacher who left his family in order to pursue his itinerant calling. Hampton may have been educated until the tenth grade. He served in the noncombat 385th Aviation Squadron during World War II in Texas, Hawaii, Guam, and Spain. After the war, he worked as a short-order cook until 1946, when he was hired as a janitor in government buildings in Washington. It was at this job that he collected the cast-off material for his massive project.

Hampton rented an unheated garage and worked on his throne for five or six hours every night for years. He was a small shy man who never married (although he unsuccessfully looked for a "holy" woman to aid him in his life's work) and had no friends. He reported that God visited him every night, instructing him on the creation of his project, according to a record Hampton left of his religious experiences. They began with his report of an appearance by Moses in Washington on April 11, 1931.

He had visions also of St. Mary and Adam. Hampton may have been inspired by the Reverend A. J. Tyler of Mount Airy Baptist Church, who was fond of pointing out that Washington, D.C., was known as a city of monuments, but there was no monument in Washington to Jesus. Hampton left another notebook, perhaps of additional religious revelations, perhaps even of more detailed information about the throne and its accoutrements and their uses, but it is written in an unknown language.

Hampton died in 1964. When his sister came to Washington to clear up his effects, she discovered the garage and the *Throne*. By chance, a Washington photographer who hoped to rent the garage arrived at the same time. Except for this coincidence the *Throne* might have been destroyed or lost. Fortunately, its existence became known, and led to the eventual acquisition by the National Museum of American Art.

Art historians speak admiringly of Hampton's imaginative, if eccentric, gifts for improvisation, selection, and design. Beyond these, however, are profound religious sensitivities, his belief that God had a purpose for him, and his own calling to prepare for the millennial age of Christ's divine reign. James Hampton had a mighty vision, and tacked to his bulletin board was the maxim, "Where there is no vision the people perish."

If you want to know more:

Regina A. Perry. *Free Within Ourselves: African-American Artists in the Collection of the National Museum of American Art.* Washington, D.C.: National Museum of American Art, 1992.

"The *Throne* stands as remarkable testimony to [Hampton's] devotion, patience, faith and imagination."
—Lynda Roscoe Hartigan

"[Hampton's *Throne*] may well be the finest work of visionary religious art produced by an American."
—Robert Hughes

What was the Motown sound?

The Motown sound was produced by the most influential record company of the 1960s, Motown, which released 535 singles during that decade, an astonishing 357 of which made the charts. Born in Detroit, Michigan, Motown turned the economically declining Motor City into Hitsville, USA. It created its distinctive sound by blending gritty gospel from the black Baptist tradition with rock 'n' roll, the musical fad of white American teenagers at the time.

With the assistance of the brilliant song-writing team of Eddie Holland, Lamont Dozier, and Brian Holland, Motown created superstars and superhits with regularity. The stars included Stevie Wonder, Diana Ross, the Supremes, Smokey Robinson, the Temptations, the Four Tops, the Jackson Five, Mary Wells, Marvin Gaye, Martha and the Vandellas, and Gladys Knight and the Pips. Among the hits were "Baby Love," "Stop in the Name of Love," "I Heard It Through the Grapevine," "Please Mr. Postman," "I Want You Back," and "Can't Help Myself."

Motown was founded with a $700 investment by Berry Gordy, Jr., born in 1929 to an enterprising Detroit family that had migrated north from Alabama. He became involved in the music business as a songwriter for Jackie Wilson in the late 1950s. With his friend William "Smokey" Robinson, Gordy decided to begin his own record company in a two-story house on West Grand Boulevard. Their first hit, in 1961, was Robinson's "Shop Around," which went to number one on the rhythm and blues chart and number two on the pop chart. By the mid-'60s, they had a $30,000,000 corporation.

Motown became the international center for music that was, as Gordy called it, "the sound of Young America." Its genius was in finding a way to adapt African-American music to make it acceptable to white America, a process that had already brought jazz into the mainstream. As music scholar Nelson George writes, "In the spirit of the Eisenhower era, the major labels dismissed real black music as a curiosity, recording this gutsier style first as 'race music,' then as 'blues,' and by 1960 as 'rhythm and blues,' all on subsidiary lines . . . which were not pushed in the white marketplace." Despite the racism of the industry, rhythm and blues was not only accepted but became phenomenally popular when performed by white singers like

Elvis Presley and Jerry Lee Lewis, who borrowed heavily from the black tradition for their "unique" sound.

Motown was the only successful record company in the '60s that acquired black musical talent and based its identity on rhythm and blues. Its first star was Mary Wells. Perhaps its greatest accomplishment was the group of young women, the Supremes, originally the Primettes, who rivaled the Beatles (who were themselves greatly influenced by Motown) as the most popular musical group in the world, and were without question the biggest-selling female act in the history of recorded music. The original members were Diana Ross, Mary Wilson, and Florence Ballard.

The Motown sound characterized the 1960s, and influenced the popular music that followed. It fueled the myth of the possibilities for success of black capitalism. It so brought African-American music into the mainstream that it was co-opted by the entertainment conglomerates. Its unforgettable sounds can still be heard: every city has a radio station that features the Golden Oldies of the Motown sound.

If you want to know more:

Nelson George. *Where Did Our Love Go? The Rise and Fall of the Motown Sound.* New York: St. Martin's Press, 1985.

"Smokey Robinson is America's greatest living poet."
—Bob Dylan

" 'The Motown sound' . . . had a steady beat, great background harmony parts, horns, catchy lyrics, and a story line that everyone could identify with."
—Martha Reeves

"[The Motown sound] is a combination of rats, roaches, love, and guts."
—Berry Gordy, Jr.

What African-American writer and intellectual was also a spokesperson for the Civil Rights Movement?

James Baldwin was a sensitive, complicated, and tormented intellectual who combined a productive lifetime of writing fiction, essays, and drama with a deep involvement in the Freedom Movement of the 1960s. His writing, influenced by Henry James, struggled, as did Baldwin himself, with the dilemmas of being human. His personal life was often a disaster, but both in life and in writing, he searched for identity and self-esteem. Without them, he believed, real love is not possible. Without love, one cannot recognize the true identities of others, hidden as they are behind cultural myths and social prejudices, particularly racism.

Baldwin was born August 6, 1924, in Harlem Hospital in New York. His biological father was unknown and Baldwin carried with him always the pain of illegitimacy along with the burden of race and the alienation of homosexuality. His ambiguous relationship with his stepfather, a preacher who went insane, affected him deeply, and he found a surrogate father in the African-American painter Beauford Delaney.

Baldwin was a bright child who excelled in school and came under the influence of the writer **Countee Cullen,** who was teaching at Frederick Douglass Junior High School. As an adolescent, Baldwin was drawn to religion, and he became a Pentecostal preacher in the singing, shouting, testifying Mountain Calvary Church of the charismatic Mother Rosa Horn. The spirit and power of the Afro-Protestant folk church stayed with Baldwin always, as did the calling to witness and prophecy, albeit in the more secular context of American racism.

Baldwin went to Paris in 1948, the first of many trips, visits, and residences, as he attempted to escape America for a bohemian life of talk, drink, and gay encounters and affairs. He met Lucien Happersberger, a Swiss, who became not only his lover but a close, lifelong friend. Happersberger was a bisexual, and his promiscuity, combined with the pressures of his wife and children, became, over the years, emblematic of Baldwin's desperate search for a stable relationship. He was unable ever to achieve one, despite an endless series of lovers, many of them exploitative.

In 1957 Baldwin traveled for the first time to the American South. It was during an early phase of the Civil Rights Movement, and Baldwin saw Southern whites trapped in their own mythology, and blacks made heroic by their struggle. He saw, too, the negative effects of racism on the inner lives of black and white people alike, including the white obsession with black sexuality and the profound connection of sexuality with racism and violence.

Baldwin was responsible for one of the more memorable moments of the Civil Rights Movement. He had telegraphed Attorney General Robert F. Kennedy, the president's brother, in May 1963 to criticize the administration for its inaction in the racial crisis in Birmingham, Alabama. Birmingham's brutal sheriff, Eugene "Bull" Connor, had jailed over 2,500 black protesters, including Martin Luther King, Jr., along with a large number of children. In response, Kennedy asked Baldwin to arrange a meeting with some respected and known African-American leaders who could and would articulate for their black expectations. On May 24, in Kennedy's New York apartment, a small group gathered which included **Harry Belafonte, Lena Horne, Lorraine Hansberry, Kenneth Clark** (representing Dr. King), and Jerome Smith, a Freedom Rider who had been severely beaten in the South and who showed Kennedy his scarred back.

The meeting was a disaster. A defensive Kennedy recited statistics about progress, but failed to comprehend what the African Americans were really saying, namely that civil rights were, at heart, a moral issue affecting the very soul of the nation. Kennedy also had no understanding of the terrible realities of racism and said that, as an Irish-American, his family, too, had experienced oppression. Led by Hansberry, the blacks got up and walked out in frustration and despair. The government retaliated by putting Baldwin under FBI surveillance.

Baldwin's own personal experiences as a human being and as a black man in a white society informed his novels and short stories and plays. He also looked at the same realities from the outside when he wrote his powerful essays. Many of his books have become standards, and some are even classics: *Go Tell It on the Mountain, Giovanni's Room, Another Country, The Fire Next Time.* Perhaps more than any other writer, Baldwin communicated something of what it meant to be African American. He died in France in 1987.

If you want to know more:

David Leeming. *James Baldwin: A Biography.* New York: Alfred A. Knopf, 1994.

> "I've been here 350 years but you've never seen me."
> —James Baldwin
>
> "You're only white as long as you think I'm black."
> —James Baldwin
>
> "Do I really want to be integrated into a burning house?"
> —James Baldwin
>
> "Whatever white people do not know about black people reveals, precisely and inexorably, what they do not know about themselves."
> —James Baldwin

Who was the first African American to serve on the Supreme Court?

In 1967, President Lyndon B. Johnson appointed attorney-activist **Thurgood Marshall** to be the first black justice to serve on the U.S. Supreme Court. This historic event was consistent with the legend of Thurgood Marshall who, throughout his legal career made so many strides for African Americans in their struggle for justice that he was nicknamed "Mr. Civil Rights."

Marshall was born in Baltimore, Maryland, in 1908. He received a B.A. from Lincoln University in Pennsylvania in 1930, and graduated at the top of his class at Howard University Law School in 1933. To pay his college tuition, he worked his way through school doing such odd jobs as grocery clerk, dining car waiter, and bellhop, while taking time for the debating team. He became known for his penchant for meticulous research and for his prodigious memory.

After receiving his law degree, Marshall went into private practice in Baltimore. Depression conditions and Marshall's sympathies did not establish a large income, and sometimes it was difficult to earn a living. Marshall quickly became involved in community activities as a way of making his name known to potential clients, but he was more devoted to those activities than other ambitious young lawyers who used the same strategy. The Baltimore branch of the NAACP was revitalized partly because of his efforts. One of his biggest achievements during this time was the case of *Murray* v. *Pearson,* which won the right for blacks to study in the University of Maryland Law School. This case and other desegregation lawsuits that Marshall constructed became a focus for organizational activities.

Soon, Marshall's devotion to the NAACP and the struggle for civil rights began to hurt his private practice. As historian Mark Tushnet notes, "Once Marshall got into a case, he devoted virtually all of his attention to it." Charles Houston, the head of the NAACP's legal counsel and Marshall's former mentor at Howard University, understood the problem and, in 1936, decided to make him officially part of NAACP's legal staff. Marshall became director of the NAACP's new Legal Defense and Education Fund in 1939, and his team of lawyers won twenty-nine out of thirty-two Supreme Court cases.

While working for the NAACP, Marshall won major lawsuits that focused on defeating segregation. In 1938, he prepared the

Supreme Court brief which granted a black student, Lloyd Gaines, the right to enter the University of Missouri Law School. Marshall was also involved in the following victories: *Smith* v. *Allwright*, 1944, ending segregated primaries; *Morgan v. Virginia*, 1946, invalidating state laws segregating interstate passengers; and *Sweatt* v. *Painter*, 1950, resulting in the admission of black law students to the University of Texas. His greatest legal achievement was the *Brown* v. *Board of Education of Topeka* case, argued in 1954, which declared an end to the "separate but equal" system of racial segregation.

With Marshall's efforts of legal victories and community organizing, he faced many life-threatening dangers, including lynching and angry mobs. In 1946, he was recognized for his dedication by being awarded the NAACP's Spingarn Medal for his outstanding achievements in the field of law.

If you want to know more:

Mark Tushnet. *The NAACP's Legal Strategy Against Segregated Education, 1925–1950*. Chapel Hill, N.C.: University of North Carolina Press, 1987.

"In many ways, indeed, Houston's greatest contribution to the litigation campaign crystallized in the person of Thurgood Marshall."

—Mark Tushnet

"[T]he Negro himself will more readily acquiesce in his lot unless he has a legally recognized claim to a better life. I think the segregation decision of 1954 probably did more than anything else to awaken the Negro from his apathy to demanding his right to equality."

—Thurgood Marshall

Who is the Queen of Soul?

The Queen of Soul is indisputably **Aretha Franklin**, an African-American woman who not only sings breathtaking gospel songs and evocative blues, but has influenced, through her style of blended blues and gospel, all of contemporary popular American music. Considered one of the greatest living American musicians, she was born in Memphis, Tennessee, on March 25, 1942, to the Reverend Clarence La Vaughan Franklin and Barbara Siggers Franklin. Her father was a famous gospel preacher and singer, a traveling evangelist with the Clara Ward Singers who commanded up to $4,000 a sermon. He built New Bethel Baptist Church in Detroit, where Aretha grew up, into a mammoth congregation, where he was such a showman and sharp dresser that he was affectionately known as "Black Beauty" and the "Jitterbug Preacher."

Franklin's mother was herself a gospel singer of enough quality to be a favorite of **Mahalia Jackson**'s. For her own reasons, however, she left the family of five children when Aretha was six years old, and died shortly after. Franklin's childhood was unhappy, and she became a shy, moody, unresponsive, deeply wounded woman, showing all the signs of the abuses she suffered.

At the age of eight, Franklin was singing in her father's church choir, and at twelve she soloed in church, for which she was paid $15. At fourteen she made stunning recordings of "Never Grow Old," "Precious Lord, Take My Hand," and "Yield Not to Temptation." Her voice is young here, but unsurpassed in its honesty and full power. Pregnant at fifteen, she dropped out of high school and named the baby for her father. It is exactly Aretha Franklin's pain, however, that comes through in her singing, and makes her the true successor to both **Bessie Smith** and Mahalia Jackson. Before an audience, Franklin loses her inhibitions and shares her own hurt and distress.

Following the example of Sam Cooke, who had left the New Bethel Baptist choir for the commercial world, Franklin in 1960 moved to New York. Columbia Records, under John Hammond, signed a contract with her. Although "Rock-a-bye, My Baby" was well received, she was not a success as a pop singer, probably because Columbia's conventional material and formulaic orchestrations were inappropriate to her unique voice and identity.

In 1966 Franklin moved to Atlantic Records, under producer Jerry Wexler, who understood what was needed: "I took her to church, sat her down at the piano, and let her be herself," he reported. The result was "I Never Loved a Man (The Way I Love You)," an immediate hit that went to the top of *Billboard*'s rhythm and blues chart and crossed over to the popular chart as well. Franklin took five gold records her first year and went on to win over a dozen Grammy Awards. High points in her career include singing a soul version of "The Star-Spangled Banner" at the 1968 Democratic convention, and "Precious Lord, Take My Hand" at the funerals of both Mahalia Jackson and Martin Luther King, Jr.

Franklin has created with feeling and power a series of outstanding recordings both sacred and secular: "Amazing Grace," "Are You Sure?" "Chain of Fools," "(You Make Me Feel Like) A Natural Woman," "What a Friend We Have in Jesus," "How I Got Over," "Think," "Respect." Her style rooted firmly in the black church, Franklin exemplifies African-American soul—and its music.

If you want to know more:

Mark Bego. *Aretha Franklin, the Queen of Soul.* New York: St. Martin's Press, 1989.

"I urged Aretha to be Aretha."

—Jerry Wexler

"What happened to Aretha as a teenager set a pattern of victimization by the men in her life. At the age of fifteen, Aretha Franklin had already earned her right to sing the blues."

—Mark Bego

"It was the ecstatic, soaring spirit of the Baptist and Pentecostal traditions that shaped Miss Franklin's singing style."

—John Rockwell

> "I have to really feel a song before I'll deal with it and just about every song I do is based either on an experience I've had or an experience someone I know has gone through."
>
> —Aretha Franklin

> "I sing to people about what matters. I sing to the realists, people who accept it like it is. I express problems, there are tears when it's sad and smiles when it's happy. It seems simple to me, but to some feelings take courage."
>
> —Aretha Franklin

What African American was a leading literary critic?

Anatole Broyard was born in New Orleans, Louisiana, on July 16, 1920, the son of Anatole and Edna Miller Broyard. His father was a master carpenter in a contracting business with his brothers. A difficult and independent child, Broyard grew up in Brooklyn, New York, where his immediate family had moved, and he attended Brooklyn College and the New School for Social Research. Broyard found a congenial milieu in the iconoclastic life of Greenwich Village, and wrote a memoir of his bohemian existence, published posthumously in 1993 as *Kafka Was the Rage*. He was captain in the U.S. Army during World War II, and claimed he survived the army only by reading Wallace Stevens.

Broyard contributed articles and stories to periodicals like *Partisan Review* and taught creative writing at Columbia and New York universities. He became the daily book review editor of *The New York Times* and then a senior editor of its weekly *Book Review*, where he favored fiction and belles-lettres and manifested what Alfred Kazin called "an addition to literature." Broyard maintained a private interior life and never openly identified with the African-American community. In the July 1950 *Commentary* magazine he wrote an essay entitled "Portrait of the Inauthentic Negro," in which he described a variety of avenues of "escape from the self." He published *Aroused by Books* (1974) and *Men, Women, and Other Anticlimaxes* (1980).

In 1989 Broyard was diagnosed with prostate cancer, a situation which exhilarated him and resulted in his book *Intoxicated by My Illness* (1992). He died in Boston October 11, 1990. As Herbert Gold noted, Anatole Broyard quite literally invented his life as he went along.

If you want to know more:

Anatole Broyard. *Kafka Was the Rage: A Greenwich Village Memoir.* New York: Carol Southern Books, 1993.

"Greenwich Village was Broyard's Walden Pond."

—Arthur Danto

"If it hadn't been for books, we would have been entirely at the mercy of sex."

—Anatole Broyard

Was Cleopatra black?

Afrocentrism is both a scholarly and an ideological movement to establish the proper place of Africa and Africans past and present in world history and culture, a position Afrocentrists believe has been minimized by Eurocentric omissions and distortions of the record. Afrocentrism emphasizes the racial blackness of ancient Egypt, Egypt's high level of civilization, and its determinative influences on classical Greece and Rome. Other major themes include the African presence in pre-

Columbian America, the destruction of African civilization by white colonialism, and the essential unity of all peoples of African descent around the world. It is a serious attempt to establish a contemporary African identity linked with a re-examined African past.

Historically, as Professor Anthony Martin of Wellesley College points out, "black studies" has always been Afrocentric. He means that the intellectual and political black self-consciousness and nationalism which have provided a scattered and oppressed people with meaning and purpose have always focused on Africa as the center both of black origins and of black destiny. Interestingly, African Americans' worldview once identified with the Israelite slaves held in Egyptian bondage; now the worldview of Afrocentrists identifies with the Egyptians!

Contemporary Afrocentrism has many critics. Some simply argue against displacing the traditional Eurocentric view of the Western origins of modern civilization. Others are not willing to accept the extreme claims of some Afrocentrists, such as the biological superiority of melanin or other nonscientific assertions, or any strain of accompanying anti-Semitism. Many critics, too, say an Afrocentric bias is ultimately no different from a Eurocentric one because any "centrism" simply recycles the discredited notions of racial and cultural superiority.

Afrocentrism is the form vernacular black nationalism is taking at the close of the twentieth century, and it has caught the imagination of increasingly large numbers of African-American people. It certainly fills an intellectual and psychological need for people who continue to be excluded from mainstream America. Also, it is clearly a needed corrective, Afrocentrists insist, to racial and cultural twistings of historical interpretation. Like all nationalisms, however, it is in danger of fostering its own myths of superiority, and, like all reductionist analyses, it runs the risk of merely substituting one's own oversimplification for someone else's.

As Professor Wilson J. Moses writes:

I am certain of one thing: Afrocentrism today is a charismatic, not an intellectual movement, it is a born-again true-believer type of enthusiasm similar to creation science, and rationalized with the same sort of evengelical passion, it is not likely to be stopped by intellectual arguments. Afrocentrism is among the masses of the black people and it's very deeply rooted in their consciousness. So I don't think you're ever going to oppose it. It may be wrong, but that's sort of like attacking George Washington and the cherry tree.

If you want to know more:

Molefi Asante. *The Afrocentric Idea*. Philadelphia: Temple University Press, 1987.

"Afrocentricity is simple. If you examine the phenomena concerning African people, you must give them agency. If you don't, you're imposing Eurocentrism on them."

—Molefi Asante

"If Afrocentrism means there is a melanin theory of human behavior and knowledge, or that only black people can think black thoughts, then it's just academic rubbish."

—Henry Louis Gates, Jr.

"We must take Afrocentrism from the sensational newspaper stories and emotional outbursts to a measured deliberation of why America continues to be confounded by race."

—Gerald Early

Who is the first African-American to win the Nobel Prize in literature?

Toni Morrison is the first African American to be awarded the Nobel Prize in literature, and she is one of the finest living

American novelists. She certainly ranks with Hawthorne, Melville, Twain, and Faulkner as one of the premier American writers of all time. She was born Chloe Anthony Wofford in a steel mill town, Lorain, Ohio, on February 18, 1931. Her working-class parents came from sharecropping families in Alabama and Georgia. Her father, a welder in an aircraft factory during World War II, put his signature on every plane on which he'd welded a perfect seam.

Morrison attended Howard, where she acted with the university players, and she took an M.A. in English from Cornell. While living in Syracuse, New York, and working as a textbook editor for a subsidiary of Random House, she began to write fiction. Her novels are *The Bluest Eye* (1970), *Sula* (1973), *Song of Solomon* (1977), *Tar Baby* (1981), *Beloved* (1987), and *Jazz* (1992). *Song of Solomon* was the first black-authored book accepted by the Book-of-the-Month Club since Richard Wright's *Native Son* in 1940.

Morrison rose to become a senior editor at Random House, where she was able to encourage black writers. She became an academic, teaching literature and creative writing at SUNY Albany, and, since 1989, at Princeton. She has received many honors and awards, including the Pulitzer Prize, but the most important international recognition came in 1993 when she was awarded a Nobel Prize in literature, the first African American to be honored with the world's most prestigious literary prize.

Beloved is arguably Morrison's greatest work to date. It is based on the true story of Margaret Garner, a slave in her twenties in the 1850s who escaped from Kentucky to Ohio with her four children. When she was apprehended by slave catchers, she calmly and deliberately killed one of her children rather than allow her to live out her life in the unspeakable horrors and burdens of the slave system. A marvelous storyteller, Morrison uses this event in *Beloved* to transform the black oral tradition into written literature of the highest quality.

With both style and themes that are clearly African American rather than Eurocentric, Morrison in effect creates on paper a powerful and mythic black past. There is no memorial to slaves or to those who lived through slavery, but Morrison celebrates the heroism of ordinary people by constructing a literary monument to the slaves who died as well as to those who survived. *Beloved* stands with *The Scarlet Letter* and *Moby Dick* as a literary masterpiece, an American classic, and uniquely, an epic exposition of the black experience in America.

Morrison draws upon her race, her sex, and the group experiences of which she is an heir for the stuff of her novels. All writers do this, and when they are exceptional writers, they are able to communicate their particularities to reveal universal themes. White Americans have never been able to comprehend, however, the fact that the experience of African Americans is different from all others' because of the uniqueness of chattel slavery.

Particularly in the mythic *Beloved*, Morrison achieves a new level of insight into and celebration of American blackness. Her strength, her anger, her sensitivity, her radicalness, her immersion in the African-American folk tradition, and, finally, her own sheer creative ability as a writer, all add up to form an illumination of black life, and thus of American life, we simply have not had before.

If you want to know more:

Toni Morrison. *Beloved*. New York: Alfred A. Knopf, 1987.

"We die. That may be the meaning of life. But we do have language. That may be the measure of our lives."
—Toni Morrison Nobel Prize acceptance speech

"And she had nothing to fall back on: not maleness, not whiteness, not ladyhood, not anything. And out of the profound desolation of her reality she may very well have invented herself."
—Toni Morrison, *Beloved*

"I simply wanted to write literature that was irrevocably, indisputably black, not because its characters were, or because I was, but because it took as its creative task and sought as its credentials those recognized and verifiable principles of black art."

—Toni Morrison

Index

Liebowitz, Samuel, 228
Lincoln, Abraham, 79, 87, 89, 90, 100–105, 107, 109, 111, 112, 118
Little, Earl, 275
Litwack, Leon, 158
Livingston, David, 7
Lloyd, Edward, 90–91
Locke, Alain, 139, 174, 184, 185
Locke, Dixie, 256
Logan, Rayford, 158
London, Jack, 128
Lott, Eric, 77
Louisiana Native Guards, 104
L'ouverture, Toussaint, 279
Love, Earl, 202
Lucy, Autherine, 261
Lyles, Aubrey, 179–80
Lynching, 132–35, 155, 227–29, 245

McCullers, Carson, 234
McDaniel, Hattie, 232, 238, 239–40
McDaniels, Mildred, 274
McDonald, Carrie, 187
McDonnell, Calvin, 133
McDowell, Frederick, 231
McFeely, William S., 94
McGuire, George Alexander, 86
McHenry, Senator James, 55, 56
McKay, Claude, 172, 182, 212
McKay, Nellie, 183
McNair, Denise, 263
McQueen, Butterfly, 238
Maffly-Kipp, Laurie, 31
Mahara, W. A., 76
Malcolm X, 160, 275–78
Malone, Dumas, 57
Mamba's Daughters, 234
Mammy Lou, 140
Manucy, Holstead "Hoss," 270
"Maple Leaf Rag," 140, 151–52, 154
Marable, Fate, 198
Ma Rainey's Black Bottom (Wilson), 163
Maroons, 211

Marquis, Donald M., 137
Marrakesh, Pasha of, 189
Marsalis, Wynton, 200
Marsh, J. B., 122
Marshall, Thurgood, 290–92
Martha and the Vandellas, 286
Martin, Arthur, 297
Martin, Roberta, 236
Martin, Sallie, 236
Mason, Charles H., 149–50
Massachusetts Anti-Slavery Society, 91
Massachusetts 33rd Regiment, 99
Massachusetts 54th Regiment, 82–83, 93, 105, 107
Matthews, Robert, 78
Matthias, Prophet, 78
Mayer, Al, 188
Mayor of Dixie, 180
Mays, Benjamin E., 244–47
Mays, Private William J., 108–109
Mays, Willie, 193
"Mean Old Frisco," 257
Meier, August, 115
Melody Hounds, 239
Member of the Wedding (McCullers), 234
Mennonites, 20
Meredith, James, 261
Merritt, Theresa, 163
Merry Whirl, The, 153
Methodists, 51–52, 67, 77, 160
Michaux, Elder Solomon Lightfoot, 240
Middle Passage, 7–9
Migration of the Negro, The, 278–79
Miller, Flornoy, 179–80
Miller, Kelly, 159
Mills, Florence, 174–78, 179, 188, 232–33
Minstrel shows, 74–77, 139, 239
Mississippi Freedom Democratic Party (MFDP), 264
Missouri Compromise of 1820, 61–62, 73, 89
Mitchell, Margaret, 238

Rabbit Foot Minstrels, 162
Raboteau, Albert J., 27, 31, 32
"Race records," 201–202, 286
Racial segregation, 74–75, 113, 158, 245, 251–55, 258–66, 280
Racism, 13–15, 16, 75, 102–103, 114, 146, 156, 158, 187, 189, 190–94, 227–29, 231, 245–46, 267, 286, 289
Radcliffe, Ted "Double-Duty," 192
Radical Republicans, 112, 113, 164
Ragtime, 138–42, 151–54
Ragime Dance, The, 152
Rainey, Gertrude Pridgett "Ma," 161–63, 201, 233, 236
Rainey, William, 162
Rampersad, Arnold, 216, 280
Razaf, Andy, 180
Reagon, Bernice Johnson, 266
Reconstruction, 110–15, 132, 138, 163–67, 228, 237–39, 245
Redmon, Don, 202
Reeves, Martha, 287
Republican Party, 73, 93, 94, 100, 113, 114, 264
Reynolds, Mary, 16
Rhapsody in Black, 233
"Rhythm and Blues," 286–87, 292–95
Rice, Thomas "Daddy," 74
Rickey, Branch, 193
Riedel, Johannes, 154
Rifkin, Joshua, 153
Righteous Government Platform, 242
Ritching, Edna Rose, 243
Roach, Mary Jane, 128
Roberson, Ida Mae, 195
Robertson, Carole, 263
Robeson, Paul, 179
Robichaux, John, 137
Robinson, John Roosevelt "Jackie," 193
Robinson, Smokey, 286, 287
Robinson, William H., 38

Rock and roll, 210, 255–58
Rockwell, John, 294
Roland, Oliver, 6
Roosevelt, Eleanor, 95, 282
Roosevelt, Franklin Delano, 228, 252
Roosevelt, Theodore, 156
Rose, Al, 143
Ross, Araminta, 81
Ross, Benjamin, 81
Ross, Diana, 286, 287
Rourke, Constance, 76
Rudolph, Ed and Blanch, 273–74
Rudolph, Wilma, 273–74
Rudwick, Elliott M., 115
Running a Thousand Miles for Freedom (Craft and Craft), 64
Runnin' Wild, 173
Russo, C. J., 254

Sadler's Wells Ballet, 176
"St. Louis Blues," 130, 202–203
St. Louis Woman (Bontemps), 195
Sally Hemings (Chase-Riboud), 60, 61
Samuels, Charles, 234
San Domingo revolt, 66, 67
Sankey, Ira, 121
Saunders, Gertrude, 176, 179, 202
Savage, Augusta, 173
Schafer, William J., 154
Schomburg, Arthur Alfonso, 9–11, 158, 219–21
Schomburg Center for Research in Black Culture, 220, 278
School of Ragtime (Joplin), 152
Schuyler, George, 184
Schwartzman, Myron, 273
Scott, Dred, 88–90
Scottsboro Boys, 226–29
Scott v. Sandford, 88–90
Sea Wolf, The (London), 128
Selznick, David O., 237, 240
Seward, T. F., 121
Seward, William, 83
Seymour, William J., 150
Shabazz, Betty, 276